Employment Tribur

Tactics and precedents

Naomi Cunningham was called to the Bar in 1994 and worked at a number of London law centres before joining the Free Representation Unit (FRU) as employment caseworker in 2000. While at FRU she appeared regularly for claimants in the employment tribunals and the Employment Appeal Tribunal (EAT), and also had responsibility for training and supervising the employment tribunal and EAT work of a large number of volunteers. She has written for the *Industrial Law Journal* (OUP) and *Adviser* (Citizens Advice), and contributed to Supperstone and O'Dempsey's *Immigration and Asylum* (FT Law and Tax, 1997). In October 2004 she joined Farrar's Building, where she practises as a member of the employment team.

Employment Tribunal Claims

Tactics and precedents

by Naomi Cunningham

Legal Action Group
2005

This edition published in Great Britain 2005
by LAG Education and Service Trust Limited
242 Pentonville Road, London N1 9UN
www.lag.org.uk

© Naomi Cunningham

While every effort has been made to ensure that the details in this text
are correct, readers must be aware that the law changes and that the
accuracy of the material cannot be guaranteed and the author and the
publisher accept no responsibility for any losses or damage sustained.

The rights of the authors to be identified as authors of this work has
been asserted by them in accordance with the Copyright, Designs and
Patents Act 1988.

British Library Cataloguing in Publication Data
a CIP catalogue record for this book is available from the British Library.

Crown copyright material is produced with the permission of the
Controller of HMSO and the Queen's Printer for Scotland.

ISBN-10 1 903307 33 3
ISBN-13 978 1 903307 33 3

Typeset and printed by Hobbs the Printers,
Totton, Hampshire SO40 3WX

Foreword

by The Hon Mrs Justice Laura Cox DBE

When, as a law student, I first developed an interest in the law governing employment relationships, that law was to be found secreted away in the standard contract textbooks under the quaint heading: 'The Law relating to Master and Servant'. The right not to be unfairly dismissed had yet to enter the statute books; and the process of revolutionising what had hitherto been an entirely contractual relationship was just about to begin.

Now, some 35 years later, employment law is threatening to drown us all in the sea of case law and legislation, both domestic and European, that it has become. Employment tribunals too have moved well away from their original concept as a straightforward, cost-free system for the speedy resolution of employment disputes, to the modern, sophisticated arena they have become for determining what are often cases involving inordinate factual and legal complexity. There are now new and complex procedural regulations governing the conduct of the increasing number of cases which come before them.

Yet, as we struggle to keep up with all this, we can lose sight of the fact that the art of running a claim in the tribunal, and knowing how best, tactically, to prepare for and conduct a hearing, involve skills which are just as important as a sound knowledge of the substantive law and procedure. Given our adversarial process, they are skills which can make all the difference to winning or losing a case. Intimate knowledge of how tribunals work, the art of writing good letters, where to look for the relevant law, how and when to press for disclosure, effective use of the questionnaire procedure, deciding which witnesses to call or, sometimes more importantly, not to call, knowing how to present good arguments in closing a case, negotiating a beneficial settlement, settling grounds of appeal from an adverse decision – the list is endless; and each of them is a vital component in the weaponry of an employment adviser.

How useful therefore, to be able to reach for a book like this and find, all in one place, sensible and realistic guidance on every conceivable aspect of employment litigation. This text, as its title suggests, marks a change from the Legal Action Group practitioner texts now so familiar to those who work in the various LAG specialist areas. It concentrates on the practical and the tactical and, in my view, neatly fills a gap in the employment adviser's library, where information and advice of this kind, on this scale and in this format has not previously been accessible.

The author observes that this book is aimed primarily at those unqualified or part-qualified employment advisers; but it will in my view be extremely attractive to a far wider audience, including the busy, the newly qualified and indeed the not so newly qualified employment practitioner, when advising or appearing for either employees or employers.

The real value of this text lies in the straightforward and comprehensive advice it provides; and in its success in demystifying the legal process and lawyers' jargon. We lawyers, so familiar with the terminology of our discipline, tend to forget how perplexing it can be to those outside our sheltered world. A tribunal Chairman, once giving directions to unrepresented litigants on how to prepare for a hearing and referring to the need for 'skeleton arguments' was met, predictably, by the question from one of them, 'do you mean thin?'

Most useful of all perhaps is the comprehensive collection of precedents, those important documents which have already stood someone in good stead and can therefore confidently be used by the novice, the busy or the less experienced adviser, to whom they will become real friends.

The author is to be congratulated for producing what will undoubtedly become a most helpful, informative and well-used resource for those working in one of the most dynamic and fascinating areas of the law.

Laura Cox
Royal Courts of Justice
February 2005

Introduction

This book grew out of a file of precedents created for volunteers at the Free Representation Unit (FRU) in London where from August 2000 to April 2004 I was caseworker with responsibility for training and supervising volunteer employment tribunal representatives. FRU volunteers are typically postgraduate law students, pupil barristers or trainee solicitors who come to the organisation with little or no prior knowledge of employment law and practice. They found a broad collection of precedents reassuring when taking their first steps in employment tribunal litigation, and that suggested that a similar collection might be of use as well to other non-specialist, unqualified or part-qualified advisers and to lay people representing themselves in the employment tribunals.

The book was originally conceived as a collection of precedents, supported by footnotes and short sections of explanatory text. The explanatory text has expanded greatly in the writing. Much of this, too, reflects my experience at FRU. Volunteers grappling with a difficult legal problem would have a wealth of specialist law reports, text books and articles to rely on. Guidance on softer questions – questions about the 'feel' of the process, how a tribunal is likely to react to a particular application, how to go about structuring a cross-examination, where to pitch the next offer in a negotiation, etc – is much harder to find in written form. One of the main aims of this book is to fill that gap. The book does not set out the substantive or procedural law except to the minimum extent necessary to place the precedents and tactical guidance in their context.[1]

Although the book is primarily written with unqualified or part-qualified advisers in mind, I hope that it will also prove useful to lawyers who only occasionally practise employment law, and to

---

1 For accessible guides to employment law and employment tribunal procedure, see Lewis, *Employment Law an Adviser's Handbook* (ELAH 5) (5th edn, Legal Action Group, 2003) and McMullen, Tuck and Criddle, *Employment Tribunal Procedure* (ETP 3) (3rd edn, Legal Action Group, December 2004); for a much more detailed and technical treatment, see *Harvey on Industrial Relations and Employment Law*, (Butterworths, Looseleaf). *Butterworths Employment Law Handbook* (12th edn, Butterworths, 2004) edited by Peter Wallington is a comprehensive collection of employment legislation.

specialist employment lawyers early in their careers. The focus of the book, true to its origins, is on the conduct of proceedings by or on behalf of employees. Most of the text is applicable to both sides, however, and many of the precedents could be used with minor adaptations by employers and their advisers.

The collection of precedents deliberately makes no attempt at comprehensiveness. Its aim is to demonstrate techniques and tactics through examples rather than to provide a precedent for every occasion. For this reason it is both broader and shallower than its closest comparators. It is shallower in that it offers a relatively small range of examples of formal employment tribunal pleadings, and makes no attempt to illustrate all the kinds of complaint[2] that can be brought to an employment tribunal.[3] It is broader in that it does offer a greater range of kinds of documents – correspondence with the respondent and the tribunal, written submissions, cross-examination notes, chronologies, draft directions, etc, as well as formal employment tribunal pleadings – than is usual. The intention in this is not to persuade users that they should depend on a precedent for every need: on the contrary, the intention is to provide varied enough examples to give users the confidence to draft their own documents flexibly and responsively. Precedents – like water-wings – cannot be said to have finished their job until their users discard them.

Many of the precedents in this book are loosely based on documents drafted for real disputes, so they are not simplified textbook cases: some of them raise problematic legal arguments or tactical decisions. They are offered as demonstrations of the kinds of documents that claimants or their advisers may need to draft at various stages of the dispute rather than as templates to be followed closely.

The book is divided into chapters that broadly follow the sequence of employment tribunal proceedings. Each chapter aims to give clear practical guidance on the stage of proceedings discussed, to alert users to unwritten rules, conventional practice and pit-falls, and to give them insights into the likely thought processes of the tribunal and the other parties. Sample pleadings, letters and other documents appear throughout each chapter to illustrate the points made. These are given numbers that correspond to the chapter in which they fall: for example, the third precedent in chapter 3 will be P3.3. Occasionally where it seems useful to show the structure of the document before giving a

---

2 See ETP 3 pp22–30.

3 For a wide range of sample claims and defences, for example, see *Harvey on Industrial Relations and Employment Law* (Butterworths) division U.

sample, there will be what I have called a 'document outline.' These are numbered similarly: the first document outline in chapter 6 will be DO 6.1.

Employment tribunals and the lawyers who appear in them often have their own habits and expectations. They sometimes act as if these were self-explanatory when in fact, to an outsider or a beginner, they are not. One particular source of difficulty for the non-lawyer operating in employment tribunals comes – ironically – directly from efforts to make the process informal and non-legalistic. The tribunal system is supposed to provide a quick, cheap and informal process; procedure rules are expressed in non-technical language, and everything is supposed to be plain and straightforward.

The difficulty with this is that the whole structure is still dominated by lawyers. Employment tribunal chairmen[4] are trained lawyers, as are very many of those who represent claimants and respondents before them. The employment tribunal rules are in many ways a simplified version of the rules that apply in the ordinary courts, many of which have literally centuries of development and case law behind them. The result is that the employment tribunal procedure rules look very different from the perspective of a non-lawyer who simply reads the words and tries to work out what they mean, than from the perspective of a lawyer who instinctively compares them to the rules he or she is familiar with in other legal contexts. Tribunal chairmen may throw their hands up in horror at what they see as a basic failure of good practice or tribunal etiquette, and claimants acting in person or inexperienced advisers can sometimes be made to feel that the process – for all its supposed informality – is in fact a minefield of obscure unwritten rules and embarrassing unexpected howlers.[5]

A key aim of this book is to alert users to the unwritten rules and guide them in the art of staying on the right side of the decision-making body. A subsidiary aim is to encourage inexperienced advisers not to let the occasional 'telling off' from the tribunal rattle them unduly: although the adviser who is constantly in hot water with the tribunal is undoubtedly doing something wrong, the adviser who never

---

4   'Chairman' is the term used in the legislation and is not gender specific.
5   For example: in one hearing, the chairman was heard to bark at an unrepresented employer, repeatedly and with rising irritation, 'Don't lead the witness!' The employer clearly had no idea what this meant, but was too rattled to ask – and so carried on asking leading questions until the claimant's representative intervened to suggest that it might be better if the chairman explained what he meant by 'leading' and why it was unhelpful. (For an explanation of this, see para 5.2 below, and glossary at pxxxi.)

makes him or herself unpopular with the tribunal is probably not serving his or her clients well either. Beginners in the field should also take courage from the thought that all practitioners learn by their mistakes. Where I warn against specific errors, there is a good chance that I have road-tested them myself.

The form 'he or she' is used where practicable, but the feminine should be taken to include the masculine or the masculine the feminine as appropriate. All names are fictional, and where documents are adapted from real cases, other details have been changed to preserve anonymity. Letters are written in the name of Natalie Cummings, a fictional alter-ego of the author, who practises employment law from the imaginary North London Law Centre. Curiously, all the respondents with whom Ms Cummings deals are represented by the same George Bean of Carrot & Marrow Solicitors in Islington; even more curiously, a series of computer glitches in the tribunal service has assigned all her cases the same number, 123456/2004.

Acknowledgements

I am indebted to countless FRU volunteers whose constant stream of questions and problems taught me so much – and whose courage and enthusiasm inspired me – between 2000 and 2004; specifically to Michael Reed who has been appointed to my old post at FRU, Michael Gleeson, a FRU volunteer, and Nigel Duncan (Principal Lecturer at the Inns of Court School of Law, City University), all of whom read and commented usefully on substantial parts of the manuscript; to Juliette Nash of Palmer Wade Solicitors and Jane Vernon, legal officer at the RNIB who between them know all there is to know about running Disability Discrimination Act 1995 cases; to colleagues in the employment team at Farrar's Building and Darren Lewis, a pupil there, for various useful conversations, to Cherry Lavell for invaluable end expert help with proof-reading; to Michael Pitt-Payne for the photograph on p23 and most of all to my husband, Tim Pitt-Payne, who first suggested the book and whose experience and insights have informed it throughout. Any remaining errors are my own.

In memory of Giles Cunningham 1965 – 1989
and for FRU, of course

Contents

Table of cases

Table of statutes

Table of statutory instruments

Table of European legislation

Abbreviations

BPBU	Bar Pro Bono Unit
CAB(x)	Citizens Advice Bureau(x)
CFA	Conditional fee agreement
CMD	Case management discussion
CPR	Civil Procedure Rules
CRE	Commission for Racial Equality
DCA	Department of Constitutional Affairs
DDA 1995	Disability Discrimination Act 1995
DDP	Dismissal and disciplinary procedure
DPA 1998	Data Protection Act 1998
DRC	Disability Rights Commission
EA 2002	Employment Act 2002
EA(DR)R 2004	Employment Act 2002 (Dispute Resolution) Regulations 2004 SI No 752
EAT	Employment Appeal Tribunal
EDT	Effective date of termination
ELAAS	Employment Lawyers Appeals Advice Scheme
ELAH 5	Lewis *Employment Law: an adviser's handbook* (5th edn, Legal Action Group, 2003)
EOC	Equal Opportunities Commission
EqPA 1970	Equal Pay Act 1970
ERA 1996	Employment Rights Act 1996
ETP 3	McMullen, Tuck and Criddle *Employment Tribunal Procedure* (3rd edn, Legal Action Group, December 2004)
FOIA 2000	Freedom of Information Act 2000
FRU	Free Representation Unit
GP	Grievance procedure
HR	Human resources
ICR	Industrial Case Reports
IRLR	Industrial Relations Law Reports
NCIS	National Criminal Intelligence Service
PHR	Pre-hearing review
POCA 2002	Proceeds of Crime Act 2002
REC	Racial Equality Council
RNIB	Royal National Institute for the Blind
RNID	Royal National Institute for the Deaf

Glossary

Glossary
The purpose of this glossary is to provide non-technical working definitions for the terms in common use in the employment tribunals that are most likely to give non-lawyers difficulty. Many of these terms are explained at greater length in the main text of this book; some are defined by statute, and this glossary is no substitute for considering the language of the statutory definition.

ACAS
Advisory, Conciliation and Arbitration Service: the statutory body that has a duty to attempt to bring about the settlement of employment tribunal disputes; see *conciliation*.

actual dismissal
Dismissal where the employer has terminated the contract of employment: contrasted with *constructive dismissal*, where the employee has resigned in response to the employer's fundamental breach of the contract of employment.

additional information
Further details of the *claim* or *response* provided at the request of the opposing party.

adjournment
A hearing is said to be adjourned if after it has begun it is put off to another day, or to later in the same day.

affidavit
A formal sworn statement used in legal proceedings. An affidavit has to be sworn in front of a solicitor or barrister.

affirm
1. An employee is said to affirm her contract of employment if, after the employer has committed a fundamental breach of contract, she acts in a way that implies that she intends to keep the contract alive. This deprives her of the right to resign and complain of *constructive dismissal*.

2. Before giving evidence a witness must either swear an oath to tell the truth (on a holy book of his or her choice), or affirm, that is, make a solemn non-religious promise to tell the truth.

appellant
The party – whether the employer or the employee – who appeals against a decision.

attendance note
A file note recording what was said at a meeting or in the course of a telephone conversation.

authorities
Previously decided cases relied on by a party in support of its arguments.

bundle
The papers prepared for use at a hearing – for example, a bundle of documents, a bundle of authorities, etc – usually paginated, indexed, and held together securely (for example, in a lever arch file).

burden of proof
The party that has the job of persuading the tribunal that its assertions on any issue are correct is said to bear the *burden of proof* on that issue. For example: a claimant who says that she was dismissed for raising health and safety issues must show that this was the reason for her dismissal if she is to succeed in her unfair dismissal claim, and so if the tribunal cannot decide what was the reason for her dismissal she fails. If her employer says that she has failed to take reasonable steps to *mitigate* her loss, however, it is for the employer to show that that is true: it is not for her to show that she has done everything she reasonably could.

case management discussion
A hearing before a chairman at which procedural arrangements for the hearing are made.

case law
Previously decided cases that establish points of principle; law derived from that source as opposed to *legislation*.

cast list
A list of the individuals involved in the events on which the claim is based.

chairman
The lawyer who presides over an employment tribunal hearing; see also *wing member.*

chronology
A list of key events, with dates, in date order.

claim
1. The document by which the claimant starts employment tribunal proceedings. 2. The subject-matter of the claimant's case.

claimant
The individual who brings the claim to the employment tribunal.

comparator
In a discrimination case, the claimant may say that the employer treated someone else more favourably than him or her in comparable circumstances. This other person is referred to as the *comparator.* Comparators may be actual or hypothetical: often the allegation is not that a real other person was better treated, but that another person with the same characteristics as the claimant except for his or her race (or sex, or religious belief, etc) *would have been* better treated.

conciliation
The attempt (usually by ACAS) to bring about a negotiated settlement of the claim.

consolidate
To link two (or more) related cases so that they are heard together.

constructive dismissal
Resignation in response to a fundamental breach of contract by the employer, which is treated as dismissal for the purposes of unfair dismissal protection. Compare *actual dismissal.*

contributory fault
Culpable conduct by an employee that has contributed to his or her dismissal, relied on by the employer as a reason to reduce compensation.

costs order
An order that one party should pay the other a sum of money representing some or all of the legal fees that the second party has incurred in the case (expenses order in Scotland). See also *preparation time order.*

COT3
The form on which an ACAS officer records a settlement.

cross-examination
Questioning of a witness in order to undermine the case of the party who called the witness, or to discredit the witness's evidence.

culpable
Deserving blame.

declaration
A *remedy* that may be given by a court or tribunal. A declaration is a formal, binding statement about the legal rights of a party.

direct discrimination
Treating a person unfavourably on a prohibited ground, for example, because of his or her race, sex etc. See also *indirect discrimination.*

directions hearing
The old term for a *case management discussion.*

directions
Orders issued by the tribunal as to the procedural aspects of the case – for example, as to disclosure of documents, exchange of witness statements, bundles of documents, etc.

disclosure
The process by which one party tells the other party what relevant documents it has, and/or provides copies of them.

discovery
The old term for *disclosure.*

discretion
A decision-maker is said to have a discretion if it has a choice between different courses of action that is not governed by a fixed rule but instead requires consideration of all the circumstances. For example, a tribunal that has found that an employer has made unauthorised deductions from the claimant's wages must order the employer to pay the sum deducted – it has no discretion as to whether or not to do so. By contrast, a tribunal that considers that a claimant's case was *misconceived* has the power to order him or her to pay some or all of the respondent's costs: but it has a wide discretion whether to make a costs order, and if so how much to order the claimant to pay.

discrimination by way of victimisation
Treating an employee unfavourably because he or she has made a complaint of discrimination (or helped another person to do so). For example, it is *discrimination by way of victimisation* to dismiss a woman because she has complained of sex discrimination. To an employment lawyer, 'victimisation' is a technical term meaning this kind of discrimination. Hence a claim that uses the word in its non-technical sense of bullying or harassment is likely to prompt a request for additional information seeking confirmation that no form of discrimination is alleged.

distinguish
An argument that the tribunal need not follow a previously decided case because it is different in some material respect from the case before them is referred to as *distinguishing* the earlier case: see paragraph 1.22.

effective date of termination
The day on which the employment terminated, often important for calculating time limits for presenting a claim.

Employment Appeal Tribunal
The body that hears appeals from the employment tribunals.

ET1

The form (otherwise referred to as the *claim*) by which the claimant starts tribunal proceedings.

ET3

The form (otherwise referred to as the *response*) on which the respondent responds to the claim.

evidence in chief

The main body of evidence given by a witness – usually by way of a witness statement – before cross-examination by or on behalf of the opposing party.

examination in chief

Asking questions of one's own witness.

expeditious

prompt

extempore

Reasons or a judgment are said to have been given extempore if given straight away at the end of the hearing; compare *reserved*.

floating

Sometimes, on arrival at tribunal on the hearing day, the parties are told that the starting time for their hearing has not been fixed but that their case will be heard once a tribunal or chairman becomes free. In this situation the case is said to be *floating*.

further particulars

The old term for *additional information*.

hearsay evidence

Evidence given by a witness of a statement made by another person, given for the purpose of establishing the truth of the statement.

indirect discrimination
In general, applying a rule or practice that is on its face neutral as between different groups, but that imposes a disproportionate and unjustified disadvantage on members of one race, sex, etc. Applying the same minimum height requirement to male and female job applicants, for example, would usually be unlawful on grounds of indirect discrimination, unless justified by the requirements of the job.

inference
A conclusion drawn from established facts.

interlocutory
Preliminary and/or procedural

issues
The questions on which the parties disagree, and which the tribunal will have to adjudicate on.

judgment
The tribunal's final determination of an issue or the issues in the case.

leading question
A question that indicates the answer expected. Leading questions are generally allowed in *cross-examination* but not – except on uncontroversial matters – in *examination in chief*. Hence, representatives may be told by the tribunal not to 'lead' their own witnesses.

Legal Services Commission
The body that administers public funding for legal advice and representation.

legalese
Unnecessarily obscure or pompous language used by lawyers to enhance their importance/mystery/fees.

legislation
Law that is set out in Acts of Parliament or regulations (or comparable European documents) as opposed to being derived from previously decided cases.

liability
What courts or tribunals have to decide is often divided into questions about liability – that is, whether a legal wrong has been done to the claimant – and questions about *remedy* – that is what is to be done about it.

limitation period
The period within which a claim must be brought.

liquidated damages
A sum agreed between the parties to a contract to be payable in the event of breach (or a certain defined breach) by one party, provided that the sum represents a genuine attempt to value the loss or damage that would be caused to the innocent party by the breach. If it is simply an arbitrary sum intended to coerce full compliance with the terms of the contract, then it is a *penalty clause* and unenforceable.

listing
The process of fixing a date for a hearing.

misconceived
Having no foundation, or no reasonable prospect of success.

mitigation
The process by which a claimant reduces the amount she has lost (by reason of dismissal, discrimination, etc) by her own efforts – for example, by getting another job.

notice of appearance
The old term for the *response* or *ET3*.

open
Correspondence or a meeting is said to be open if it is not 'without prejudice' (see below).

order
An instruction by the tribunal that requires a person or party to do something.

organogram
A chart showing an organisation's structure.

originating application
The old term for the *claim* or *ET1*.

party
A claimant or respondent: the persons whose rights and obligations are to be decided in the proceedings.

penalty clause
A clause in a contract that imposes a disproportionate financial penalty on one party for breach of the contract in order to coerce that party into strict compliance: for example, a clause in a contract of employment that provided that an hour's pay would be docked for every five minutes by which the employee arrived late. Penalty clauses are unenforceable, but see liquidated damages.

plain English
A good idea in theory.

pleadings
The old term for *statements of case*.

postponement
Putting off a hearing to another date.

precedent
1. A decided case that establishes a point of principle to be followed in other cases in the future. 2. A document intended as an example of how to draft documents of the particular kind demonstrated.

pre-hearing review
A hearing that takes place before the main or substantive hearing, usually before a chairman alone, in order to decide preliminary matters.

preparation time order
An order that one party pay the other a sum of money representing the time they have spent preparing the case, available in place of a costs order if the receiving party has not been legally represented.

privilege
A document is said to be privileged if it does not have to be disclosed to the other party despite being relevant. The rule that the content of *without prejudice* negotiations must not be disclosed to the tribunal is also a variety of privilege.

pro bono
Legalese (Latin) for 'for free.' Where a lawyer is acting *pro bono* he or she is acting without charging the client a fee.

promulgate
Legalese for 'send out'.

quantum
Latin for 'how much,' used as legal shorthand for the amount that the claim is worth. See also *liability, remedy.*

questionnaire
A list of questions that a claimant or potential claimant in a discrimination case can serve on the other party.

re-engagement
A remedy for unfair dismissal: the claimant must be re-employed in a job comparable to his or her old job.

reinstatement
A remedy for unfair dismissal: the claimant must be given his or her old job back.

remedy
What the claimant gets from the respondent if she is successful in her claim. By far the most common remedy awarded by employment tribunals is compensation, but other remedies are available in some cases: for example, a declaration, reinstatement or re-engagement.

repudiation
Fundamental breach of contract: an employer or employee who has acted in fundamental breach of the contract of employment is said to have *repudiated* it.

reserved decision
A decision that is not given on the day of the hearing but at a later date.

respondent
1. The party against whom a claim is made. 2. In an appeal, the party resisting the appeal.

response
The respondent's answer to the *claim*.

review
The process by which the tribunal may revisit its own decision and, if it thinks fit, revoke or vary it.

skeleton argument
A written summary of the arguments that a party will put forward at a hearing.

statement of truth
An assertion, contained in a witness statement, that the contents of it are true.

statements of case
In the employment tribunals, the *claim* and *response* (often still referred to as pleadings).

statute
Another term for an Act of Parliament.

submissions
The points made by a party or his or her representative to persuade the tribunal to find in his or her favour.

substantive
Relating to the substance of the claim, rather than to procedural or interlocutory matters.

'Tomlin' order
An order staying proceedings while the terms of a settlement are put into effect.

whistleblowing
The familiar name for making a protected disclosure.

wing member
An employment tribunal is made up of a *chairman*, who is legally qualified, and two *wing members*. The wing members need not be, and are usually not, legally qualified, but they will have relevant experience, for example, as trade unionists or personnel managers.

without prejudice
The phrase used to indicate that a letter or conversation is directed to achieving a settlement and is therefore not to be disclosed to the tribunal.

witness statement
The written account of the evidence given by a witness. In England and Wales it forms the basis of that witness's *evidence in chief* and may be read aloud by the witness or taken as read. In Scotland, witness statements are not used: *evidence in chief* is given orally.

CHAPTER 1

Understanding the process and preliminary matters

Sources of employment law advice and representation

1.1 This book is partly aimed at individuals representing themselves in employment tribunal claims. The employment tribunal process is intended to be accessible to people without specialist knowledge, and many individuals do represent themselves. Nevertheless, most individual claimants[1] will prefer to have representation if they can find it, and in most cases representation will improve their chances of a successful outcome.

1.2 It is suggested that claimants who cannot afford to pay substantial sums of money for representation should consider the possibilities of free or affordable representation in this order:

- their trade union, if they belong to one;
- their household insurance;
- a voluntary sector advice centre or one of the statutory Commissions;
- high street solicitors;
- employment consultants.

Trade unions

1.3 A claimant who is a member of a trade union should normally expect to be represented by the union in a dispute with his or her employer. Unions have different rules about which cases they will support, and some will withdraw support (sometimes shortly before the hearing) if the claimant refuses to accept what the union's lawyers advise is a good offer of settlement. Claimants considering relying on union assistance should make sure that they have been given clear information about the circumstances in which the union will withdraw its assistance.

Household insurance

1.4 Household insurance policies include legal expenses insurance surprisingly often. This tends to be a neglected source of assistance

---

1 The claimant is the individual complaining to an employment tribunal of a breach of his or her employment rights. Until October 2004 the correct term was 'applicant' and this term is likely still to be used occasionally. The other party – usually the employer – is called the respondent.

for claimants for the simple reason that many do not realise that they have the cover. It can be extraordinarily good value: the insurance may cover all legal expenses, including specialist representation at the hearing, with no claw-back even if the claimant recovers a large award. It is important to investigate this at an early stage in the dispute, however, because a claimant who has already taken steps in employment tribunal proceedings without the advice of an insurer-approved lawyer may find that she has invalidated her insurance.

Voluntary sector advice agencies

1.5   There are various kinds of voluntary sector advice agencies that may be able to offer free advice and/or representation. Almost all of them are badly overstretched, and sadly many claimants will spend fruitless hours telephoning advice agencies only to be told that no-one can help. However, some of them will deliver an exceptional service that rivals the best that private practice solicitors can offer, so (within limits) it is worth persevering. The process may well be frustrating, but anyone seeking free representation should try not to let the frustration show. Mostly 'we cannot help' means just that – the organisation simply has no spare capacity, or does not do this sort of work. If there is any flexibility, human nature is as it is, charm almost always gets further than aggression.[2]

1.6   Most voluntary sector advice agencies belong to an umbrella organisation, and that organisation's website will often be the best starting point for finding local services. The main umbrella organisations are the Law Centres Federation,[3] Citizens Advice (formerly the National Association of Citizens Advice Bureaux)[4] and AdviceUK (formerly the Federation of Independent Advice Agencies).[5]

---

2   There is a practical insight of wide application here. Even where aggression may be effective, charm should always be tried *first*. The reason is that if charm does not work, aggression is still available as a last resort. Starting with aggression and then trying to backtrack to charm is futile.

3   www.lawcentres.org.uk.

4   www.citizensadvice.org.uk.

5   www.adviceuk.org.uk.

Law centres

1.7 Law centres are, in effect, not-for-profit solicitors' practices that specialise in what is broadly defined as 'social welfare law' – typically housing, immigration, employment and welfare rights. Most, if not all, law centres operate a catchment area policy and will only advise those who live (or sometimes work or worked) in their area. Many will only accept clients who are financially eligible for public funding, and the rest are likely to impose some kind of means test on access to their services. Most employ an employment lawyer or specialist adviser. The website of the umbrella body, the Law Centres Federation, lists 60 law centres, roughly half of them in Greater London and most of the rest in substantial town or city centres.

Citizens Advice Bureaux

1.8 Citizens Advice Bureaux (CABx) tend to offer a generalist service, and only some employ a specialist employment adviser. CABx do not generally have a catchment area policy and will advise anyone who approaches, subject to availability of advisers. CABx do not generally means-test their clients except for Legal Services Commission[6] funded work. There are around 3,200 CABx in the UK: any sizeable town centre is likely to have one.

Racial Equality Councils

1.9 Racial Equality Councils (RECs) are specialist advice agencies that serve their local area but will deal only with claims that involve an element of race discrimination. They are funded in part by the Commission for Racial Equality, which publishes a list of 93 RECs and similar organisations on its website.[7]

---

6 The body – formerly the Legal Aid Board – that administers state funding for litigation.

7 www.cre.gov.uk.

The Commissions

1.10   The Equal Opportunities Commission (EOC),[8] Commission for Racial Equality (CRE)[9] and Disability Rights Commission (DRC)[10] are national bodies. All three bodies offer helpline advice for individuals and employ specialist discrimination lawyers, but they will only rarely be able to take on the conduct of a case. They will normally only do this if they consider that the case is exceptionally serious, or if the result could have an impact on a large number of other individuals. The Equal Opportunities Commission website provides extensive resources for claimants in sex discrimination claims, although at the time of writing this had not been updated to reflect the changes that came into force on 1 October 2004.

The Free Representation Unit and the Bar Pro Bono Unit

1.11   In London, the Free Representation Unit (FRU) can sometimes provide representation at employment tribunals, but it does not deal direct with members of the public. Cases must be referred, after a hearing date has been fixed, by a solicitor, law centre, CAB or other advice agency. Claimants in London who are receiving advice and assistance for case preparation, but whose adviser is not able to represent them at a hearing should make sure their cases are referred to FRU as soon as a hearing date is set to have the best chance of representation. Most FRU volunteers are student or trainee lawyers who work under the supervision of a specialist employment lawyer. They choose their own cases, rather than having cases assigned to them, so FRU can never guarantee representation in any given case until a particular volunteer has offered to take the case on.

1.12   The Bar Pro Bono Unit (BPBU) is a charity funded by the Bar Council and others that matches clients in need of free representation with barristers willing to give their time. Because the kind of work barristers are permitted to do is restricted, BPBU is best able to assist clients who are represented by a solicitor's firm or advice agency that is willing to retain conduct of the case and instruct the barrister to do defined pieces of work – to draft a document, for example, or appear at the hearing. Unlike FRU, BPBU will, at the time of writing, accept referrals from any organisation or from the applicant him or herself (but see paras 11.10 below). BPBU puts applications for assistance

---

8   www.eoc.org.uk.
9   www.cre.gov.uk.
10   www.drc.org.uk.

through a careful sift to decide whether or not to offer help, so an application to BPBU should always be made as early as possible. BPBU itself is located in London, but its services are potentially available throughout England and Wales. As with FRU, the fact that BPBU has accepted a referral is no guarantee that it will be able to assist. The Unit's website is www.barprobono.org.uk.

Specialist charities

1.13   Some of the larger disability charities, including RNIB (Royal National Institute for the Blind),[10a] RNID (Royal National Institute for the Deaf),[11] and the Disability Law Service,[11a] employ specialist advisers who can advise and sometimes represent in disability discrimination cases. Public Concern at Work[12] provides a helpline on whistleblowing issues but does not undertake casework. The Terence Higgins Trust[12a] provides helpline advice on HIV-status employment issues, and may be able to refer on to other agencies for casework.

1.14   This is not a comprehensive list, and policies and personnel can change rapidly, so it is always worth investigating carefully whether there is a specialist charity that may be able to help.

Private practice solicitors

1.15   Claimants who are eligible for Legal Services Commission[13] funding (those who are dependent on means-tested benefits, or are on very low incomes) may be able to find a solicitor who can advise and assist with preparation of the case. There is no public funding (in any but the most exceptional cases) for representation at the tribunal hearing so claimants who take advantage of this scheme are likely to find that they either have to represent themselves at tribunal or pay privately for a solicitor or a barrister to represent them. In London, some solicitors will be able to refer the case to the Free Representation Unit at this stage, so before choosing a solicitor it may be worth finding out whether they subscribe to FRU's service.[14]

10a www.rnib.org.uk.
11 www.rnid.org.uk.
11a www.dls.org.uk.
12 www.pcaw.co.uk.
12a www.tht.org.uk.
13 See glossary.
14 FRU only accepts referrals from solicitors and advice agencies that are signed up with the organisation and pay an annual subscription.

1.16   The decision to pay privately for employment law advice should be approached with caution. Lawyers' fees can mount up frighteningly fast, and the total value of an employment tribunal claim is often too small to justify them. Some solicitors offer 'no win no fee' agreements, but the drawback to these is that, because the solicitor is taking a risk of not being paid at all, the fee if the case is successful will be higher than it would otherwise have been. There can also be sums that the client has to pay anyway, such as fees for medical or other experts' reports or Counsel's fees. Occasionally this will be the best, or the only practical, way of funding an employment tribunal claim, but a claimant considering taking this course should make sure she or he has had a very clear explanation of the 'worst case' outcome before making a decision.

Employment consultants

1.17   There are no restrictions on who may appear as a representative in the employment tribunals, and a number of firms of employment consultants offer their services in this area. Some of these market their services aggressively to claimants and respondents in employment tribunal cases. They vary in quality and although some can provide a good and relatively cheap service, others are worse than useless. Unlike barristers and solicitors, they are not regulated by a professional body. It is suggested that claimants should do their research carefully before using the services of these organisations. One question to ask is how many costs orders have been made against clients of the organisation in the past year, compared to the total number of clients represented. Costs orders are still rare in the employment tribunal, and they tend – though not invariably – to suggest bad advice or poor conduct of the case by the representative. Costs orders running at significantly more than about 3% of cases would give serious cause for concern.

Outline of the employment tribunal process

1.18   Strictly speaking an employment tribunal case begins with a formal claim on form ET1 (see 3.1 below), but since the introduction of the statutory dispute resolution procedures, an internal grievance procedure is now a necessary first step in many cases. Broadly, there is a distinction between complaints of dismissal (other than constructive dismissal)[15] and other complaints (including constructive dismissal). An employee whose complaint is about dismissal (other than constructive dismissal) is not required to bring a statutory grievance,[16] but may proceed direct to a complaint to the employment tribunal.

1.19   In very broad outline, the process falls into four stages: (1) the statements of case[17] – in other words, the employee's formal claim and the employer's response which are presented on forms ET1 and ET3 respectively; (2) requests by each side for information and documents, and requests to the tribunal for orders if these requests are not voluntarily complied with; (3) preparation by each side of all the documents that will be required for the hearing: the witness statements, an agreed bundle of all relevant documentary evidence, any written representations, chronologies, lists of issues, etc; and (4) the hearing itself. There may be negotiations at any of these stages. The parties are normally referred to as the claimant (the employee who brings the claim) and the respondent (the employer, who responds to it).

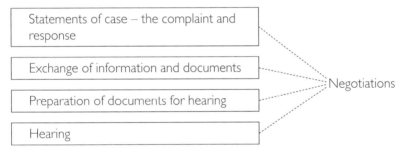

1.20   In the more detailed outline that follows, the players are referred to as C (for claimant) and R (for respondent), and T (the employment tribunal). A constructive dismissal is taken as an example, and it is assumed that the case goes all the way to a decision by the employment tribunal. There could be different outcomes at many points: this example should be seen as one of the possible paths through a fairly complicated flow-chart rather than a recipe for what must happen in every case.

15 For an explanation of this term see ELAH 5 paras 6.37–6.46 and glossary at pxx.
16 Although it is strongly advisable to pursue any internal appeal that is offered.
17 This term is borrowed from the Civil Procedure Rules applicable in the ordinary courts; the old term 'pleadings' is also still in common use.

R tells C that his application for promotion has been unsuccessful.

C presents a grievance.

R invites C to a hearing to consider the grievance.

R gives a decision on the grievance.

C is dissatisfied with R's decision and appeals.

R invites C to an appeal hearing

R gives C a decision on the appeal

C is dissatisfied and completes and presents formal claim to tribunal on form ET1

T accepts the ET1 [18]

T sends ET1 to R

R responds by completing form ET3

T accepts the ET3 and forwards it to C [19]

T lists the case for a directions hearing or T issues directions without a hearing

C sends request for additional information and disclosure of documents to R

R sends request for additional information and disclosure of documents to C

18 If T considers that the claim does not include all the required information, the statutory grievance procedure has not been followed, or it does not have jurisdiction to consider the claim – or, from 6 April 2005 (but see paras 1.63–1.64 below), if it has not been presented on the required form – it will reject the claim. In that case it may be necessary either to redraft the claim and try again, or to appeal the decision to reject the claim or seek a review. See paras 3.9–3.11 below.

19 Again, there are grounds on which it may not be accepted.

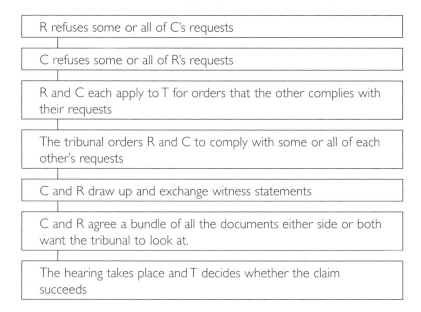

Sources of employment law

1.21   Much of employment law is contained in legislation,[20] but it must also be remembered that at the heart of the employment relationship is the contract of employment. Contract law is what is called a *common law* subject: that is, its main principles are to be found in previously decided cases rather than in statutes. Employment tribunals must apply common law principles where appropriate as well as the relevant statutory rules.[21] To complicate matters further, there is a substantial body of European employment law; and the European Convention on

---

20 The *Butterworths Employment Law Handbook* by Peter Wallington is a comprehensive (and annually updated) collection of employment statutes which most lawyers will take with them to the tribunal, and the tribunal will always have available for its own use at the hearing. The HMSO website (www.hmso.gov.uk) is a useful source for recent material, but for older material – eg, the much-amended Employment Rights Act 1996 – it should be used with caution because statutes are provided in their original form and not updated to reflect amending legislation.

21 The standard practitioners' textbook is *Chitty on Contracts* (Sweet & Maxwell, 29th edn, 2004). *Chitty* is very comprehensive, but is likely to be forbiddingly technical for anyone without a legal training. The important point, for non-lawyers, is simply to be aware that there are two different kinds of law operating in this field.

Human Rights, applied in the UK by way of the Human Rights Act 1998, also has many applications in this area.

1.22   Whether the tribunal is considering a statutory or a common law rule, cases that have been decided in the past by the Employment Appeal Tribunal (EAT) or higher courts set precedents that must be followed by the employment tribunals. Courts and tribunals are generally bound to follow the decisions of higher courts: so, for example, the employment tribunals must decide cases in a way consistent with the previous decisions of the EAT, the EAT must follow the rulings of the Court of Appeal,[22] and the Court of Appeal must follow its own previous rulings and the rulings of the House of Lords.[23] Sometimes the argument between the parties will focus on whether or not the facts of the case are similar in the relevant way to the facts of a previously decided case, so that the result in the earlier case is binding on the tribunal that decides the later. The party seeking to apply the result in a previous case will say that the two cases are alike in all relevant respects; the other party will argue that there is a material difference between the cases[24] that means that the earlier case need not be followed.

1.23   The only way to gain a proper understanding of this process of reasoning is to read reports of cases. Employment cases are reported in two monthly series, the *Industrial Case Reports* (ICR) and the *Industrial Relations Law Reports* (IRLR), both of which should be available in any law library.[25] The standard method of referring to a case reported in one of these, or similar, series follows the pattern: *Party v Other Party* [2004] IRLR 382. This indicates that the report of the case will be found at page 382 of the volume of the Industrial Relations Law Reports for the year 2004. In addition, more recent decisions of the Employment Appeal Tribunal, the Court of Appeal and the House of Lords are all available online.[26] Two volumes, M Rubenstein *Unfair dismissal: a guide to*

---

22 The EAT is not bound by its own previous rulings, but will normally be reluctant to depart from them.

23 See paras 4.40–4.45 below.

24 The latter kind of argument is often referred to as 'distinguishing' the earlier case.

25 In London, the Hammersmith, Holborn and Westminster Public Libraries maintain a specialist law collection, and the Supreme Court Library at the Royal Courts of Justice on the Strand is open to the public. Any university law school will have a law library and some will allow members of the public to use reference facilities in some circumstances: inquiries should be made of the local law school.

26 Key websites are BAILII (British and Irish Legal Information Institute) at www.bailii.org, the EAT website at www.employmentappeals.gov.uk and the Court Service website at www.courtservice.gov.uk.

relevant case law[27] and M Rubenstein and Y Frost *Discrimination: a guide to the relevant case law on sex, race and disability discrimination and equal pay*[28] provide helpful quick reference to the case law in those two areas.

Books

1.24   A great many books are published on employment law, and the following represent a tiny sample of what is available. Lewis, *Employment Law: an adviser's handbook* (ELAH 5)[29] is an excellent and accessible short guide to the substantive law,[30] and McMullen et al *Employment Tribunal Procedure* (ETP 3)[31] gives a clear and detailed explanation of tribunal procedure. *Harvey on Industrial Relations and Employment Law*, published by Butterworths, is a large loose-leaf publication in several volumes that explains the law in great detail and is updated regularly throughout the year.[32] It is likely to be dauntingly technical for anyone without a legal training, but if a difficult question arises to which the answer cannot be found in one of the shorter books it will be worth consulting. Any law library should have a copy.

Key employment cases

1.25   There are certain decided cases that determine points of such fundamental importance to employment law that all those advising in the area need to be aware of them, and preferably to have read them. No two employment lawyers would compile the same list, and the decision whether to list 10, 50 or 100 cases is arbitrary. With those reservations, the following is offered as a list of some of the fundamental cases – divided into broad subject areas – that advisers should be familiar with. A few less well-known cases of particular practical usefulness to claimants are also listed, these are marked *.

27 LexisNexis Butterworths, 22nd edn, 2004.
28 LexisNexis Butterworths, 17th edn, 2004.
29 Legal Action Group, 5th edn, 2003.
30 The sixth edition, taking account of the major changes in employment law from 1 October 2004, is due in the Autumn of 2005.
31 Legal Action Group, 3rd edn, December 2004.
32 It is also available as an online subscription service.

Unfair dismissal

Iceland Frozen Foods v Jones [1983] ICR 17, EAT
Post Office v Foley [2000] ICR 1283, CA

Conduct dismissal

Burchell v British Home Stores [1980] ICR 303, EAT
Linfood Cash & Carry Ltd v Thomson [1989] IRLR 235, EAT

Procedural fairness

Polkey v AE Dayton Services [1987] IRLR 503, HL[33]

Redundancy dismissal

Williams v Compair Maxam [1982] ICR 156, EAT
Murray v Foyle Meats [1999] ICR 827, HL
*Elkouil v Coney Island Ltd [2002] IRLR 174, EAT
W Devis & Sons Ltd v Atkins [1977] IRLR 314, HL

Constructive dismissal

Western Excavating v Sharp [1978] ICR 221, CA

Trust and confidence term

Eastwood v Magnox Electric plc [2004] ICR 1064, HL

Who is an employee

Ready Mixed Concrete v Minister of Pensions [1968] 2QB 497, CA
Carmichael v National Power [1999] ICR 1226, HL

Discrimination

Shamoon v Chief Constable of the Royal Ulster Constabulary [2003] ICR 337, HL
King v Great Britain-China Centre [1992] ICR 516, CA

---

33   The effect of this decision has been altered since 1 October 2004 by the new Employment Rights Act 1996 s98A, but it has been such an important part of the landscape for employment lawyers for so long that it is still helpful to be familiar with it.

Nagarajan v London Regional Transport [1999] IRLR 572, HL
Chief Constable of West Yorkshire Police v Khan [2000] ICR 1169, HL
Glasgow City Council v Zafar [1998] ICR 120, HL
Vento v Chief Constable of West Yorkshire [2001] IRLR 124, EAT

Transfer of Undertakings (Protection of Employees) Regulations

Litster v Forth Dry Dock & Engineering Co Ltd [1989] ICR 341, HL
Suzen v Zehnacker Gebaudereinigung GmbH Krankenhausservice [1997] ICR 662, ECJ

Postponements

Yearwood v Royal Mail EAT/747/97, unreported[34]

Mitigation of loss

Wilding v British Telecom [2002] IRLR 524, CA

Appeals

Anya v University of Oxford [2001] ICR 847, CA
Meek v City of Birmingham District Council [1987] IRLR 250, CA
Kumchyk v Derby City Council [1978] ICR 1116, EAT
Yeboah v Crofton [2002] IRLR 634, CA

The tribunal's powers

1.26   The tribunals operate under the Employment Tribunals (Constitution and Rules of Procedure) Regulations 2004,[35] and in particular under Schedule 1 to these Regulations, the Employment Tribunal Rules of Procedure. These are referred to throughout this book simply as the 'procedure rules.'

1.27   It is worthwhile for any claimant or adviser with limited experience in this area to read through the regulations and the procedure rules at an early stage in proceedings so as to be broadly familiar with the scope of the tribunal's powers. Particular provisions to note are the

34 See appendix A at p376 below for the transcript.
35 SI No 1861.

interpretation provisions at regulation 2, the overriding objective at regulation 3 and the guidance on calculation of time limits at regulation 15. Rules 1 to 48 of the procedure rules are the main rules that govern most types of proceedings, and rules 10 (case management), 11 (applications), and 37 to 48 (costs and preparation time orders) are also of great practical significance.

1.28   The President of the employment tribunals has power to issue practice directions[36] giving detailed guidance about how cases should be conducted. At the time of writing no employment tribunal practice direction has been issued under the new rules, and there is no proposal to issue any in the near future.

1.29   As stated above, the procedure rules will not be the only material informing the tribunal in its procedural decisions. Tribunals are very often guided – sometimes consciously, sometimes not – by principles and procedures that operate in the ordinary courts, often drawn from the Civil Procedure Rules (CPR) which apply there. If the tribunal criticises a claimant for some failure to observe 'obvious common sense' or 'basic good practice' in some aspect of the conduct of proceedings on which neither the claimant's own common sense nor the procedure rules provide any guidance, the chances are that this is what is going on. The chairman has absorbed principles from the CPR or rules of conduct or etiquette in the ordinary courts, and is now treating them as self-evident.

1.30   For this reason, some familiarity with the CPR is, although not essential, certainly helpful for employment advisers – partly so that they are not taken by surprise when the tribunal borrows from the CPR, and partly so that they are in a position either to warn the tribunal against automatic adherence to rules devised for a more formal (and unequivocally adversarial)[37] setting, or sometimes to propose that the manner of dealing with particular practical problems set out in the

---

36 Compare the EAT Practice Direction of 2004.
37 Legal systems are often divided into 'adversarial' systems where the judge's only task is to listen to the case put by each side and to make a decision based on what the parties have put before him or her; and 'inquisitorial' systems where the decision-maker has a duty to investigate. Employment tribunal hearings are broadly adversarial, but because parties are not necessarily expected to be represented, the tribunal also has an inquisitorial role expressed in the duty at rule 14(3) of the procedure rules to make such enquiries of persons appearing before them and of witnesses as they consider appropriate. Once again, because tribunals are dominated by lawyers who are used to a wholly adversarial system, this duty often gets overlooked.

CPR should be adapted for the employment tribunal. The CPR can sometimes provide helpful insights into the thinking behind the tribunal procedure rules. In many instances, the latter is a simplified version of the former; sometimes, on the other hand, it is clear that a deliberate distinction has been made[38] between the tribunal rules and the CPR.

1.31   The up-to-date CPR can be found on the Department for Constitutional Affairs website.[39] This should be regarded as a recommendation only for advisers who will run a substantial number of cases for clients, however: grappling with the fairly forbidding CPR will rarely, if ever, be the best use of time for a claimant representing him or herself in a single case.

General note on correspondence

1.32   Much of a party's correspondence with the tribunal or the other side will have a secondary tactical motive as well as the purpose it has on its face. It should be remembered that any correspondence[40] may in some circumstances be read by the tribunal, so it is advisable always to maintain a calm and co-operative style. This will not invariably be reflected by the respondent or its advisers[41] but it will almost always be in the client's interests to resist any temptation to be abrasive or sarcastic. This can be particularly important if there is a costs application by either side. If there is unavoidable delay, or if there has been a misunderstanding, apology costs nothing and can help avoid unnecessary conflict with the other party. A well placed and graceful apology may even help tip the tribunal away from making a costs award if otherwise there are grounds for one.

1.33   There are good reasons in any event to keep relations with the respondent as calm as possible. Many aspects of the preparation of the case will go more smoothly if there is co-operation between the

---

38 See for instance *Kopel v Safeway Stores plc* [2003] IRLR 753, EAT.

39 http://www.dca.gov.uk/civil/procrules_fin/menus/rules.htm.

40 See below para 6.10 for the distinction between 'open' and 'without prejudice' correspondence.

41 Correspondence from the other side may well reflect the adviser's wish to demonstrate to their own client that they are conducting the litigation vigorously.

parties.[42] Both sides are likely to encounter certain difficulties along the way, and will sometimes need the other side's indulgence when they are unable to meet deadlines, etc. If the tone of the proceedings has been quarrelsome from the start, each side may waste a great deal of time (and in some cases their client's money too) scoring every possible point off the other. It is far better to be pragmatic and flexible about things that do not matter, and to conserve energy for the few battles that will win or lose the case.

1.34   Letters should make their point in plain language and as few words as possible. Fancy type-faces should be avoided. Inexperienced advisers sometimes feel that they ought to act the part and write legalese. This is never a good idea. Opening and closing gambits like 'I write further to our conversation [/my letter] of [date]' or 'I write in relation to the above-mentioned matter and refer to your letter of [date]' or 'I look forward to hearing from you at your earliest convenience and thank you for your attention' are redundant. The heading indicates the subject-matter of the letter, and 'thank you for your letter of [date]' is ample to provide the link to the letter being answered. If there is a particular need for an urgent answer, it is sensible to spell that out, but otherwise there is not normally any need to ask for a reply.

1.35   Many solicitors still routinely duplicate faxed or e-mailed correspondence by post. This is unnecessary[43] and causes the tribunal and the other party additional work. If the other party finds it at all difficult to deal with correspondence (by reason of a visual impairment, for example, or dyslexia) it is particularly unhelpful and time-wasting. The tribunals positively request that parties should not do it. If it is essential to ensure that a document arrives by a certain date, the sensible thing is to fax it and then follow the fax with a telephone call

---

42 Litigation is very like a formal game with a serious outcome. To win any game, it is necessary to co-operate sufficiently with the other player to complete it. A game of chess can only be won by a player who is prepared to agree a venue and duration, use the same chessboard, complete his or her moves within a reasonable time or within agreed time limits, stick to the decision who is playing black and who is playing white, and so on. Angry squabbling about when exactly witness statements should be exchanged, who prepares the bundle for the hearing, whether the hearing is likely to last for 3 days or 4 or similar is as futile and as little likely to affect the outcome as a dispute between two chess players about whether the 12 inch or the 18 inch chessboard should be used.

43 Not to say superstitious – it seems to reflect a belief that only a hard copy really 'counts.'

to confirm arrival. An attendance note[44] of that conversation, identifying the person spoken to, should be ample proof of delivery if the point arises subsequently.

1.36   E-mail is a fast and efficient method of communicating with the other party or the tribunal, and is perfectly acceptable. If a plain text e-mail does not seem to give the right degree of formality, a letter can be attached as a separate document. The main danger of using e-mail for this purpose is that the speed of e-mail exchanges can escalate a difference of views into a quarrel very quickly, and e-mails leave a permanent record that may later be shown to the tribunal. E-mails need to be drafted with the same care as any other correspondence, and should always be calm and reasonable. It is sensible to get into the habit of removing personal information (information about previous drafts, etc) from any e-mailed attachment. This can be done, in a Word document, by choosing 'options' from the 'tools' menu and then, on the 'security' tab, ticking the box marked 'remove personal information from this file on save.' Sending a witness statement to the respondent with recoverable information about previous drafts could be very damaging.

1.37   All letters to the tribunal (apart from requests for witness orders, see para 5.27) should be copied to the respondent. Many advisers will routinely copy all correspondence with the respondent other than 'without prejudice' correspondence to the tribunal, but this is unnecessary. It is preferable to copy correspondence to the tribunal only if it is relevant to something that the tribunal is being asked to do. So, for example, it is not necessary to copy a request for additional information to the tribunal when it is first made; but if the respondent refuses to comply with the request, then it should be copied to the tribunal with the request for an order. If there has been an extended wrangle between the parties over some aspect of case preparation, the tribunal will only need to see the relevant correspondence if and when it is asked to arbitrate on the wrangle, or if one party seeks costs on grounds of the other party's unreasonable conduct. At that point the whole correspondence can be copied to the tribunal, or collated into a bundle to support a costs application at the hearing.

1.38   Thought should be given at all stages to the convenience of both the other party and the tribunal. A history of conspicuously considerate letters will be one of the best defences against a costs order if there is an application for costs at any stage. So, for example, if the claimant is

44 See P1.1 below.

unable to meet a deadline that has been set by the tribunal or agreed between the parties, the tribunal and/or the other side should be informed of the difficulty as soon as the claimant is aware of it, and a realistic revised timetable should be proposed. If the claimant seeks to amend his or her claim, then it is likely that the respondent will need time to amend their response to deal with the new points: the letter requesting permission to amend should recognise this and propose suitable arrangements.

1.39   It is conventional to address letters sent to the tribunal to 'the Regional Secretary,' with a request, where appropriate, to refer the letter or the application to a chairman for his or her attention. The regional secretaries are the administrative heads of the employment tribunals; the regional chairmen are the judicial heads. Similarly, correspondence with the Employment Appeal Tribunal is addressed to the Registrar, who is the administrative head of the EAT. At the time of writing a majority of the regional secretaries were women and the Registrar at the EAT was also a woman. The examples in this book use the salutation 'Dear Madam' throughout.

1.40   Letters are drafted in the first person in this book because this gives the writer personal responsibility for the content. 'We' is too often an excuse for pomposity. The form of address 'Dear Sirs' is still in common use but can cause annoyance, so letters are either addressed to the individual with conduct of the case ('Dear Mr Bean', 'Dear Ms Marrow', 'Dear Madam') or else solicitors' firms and other organisations are addressed by name – as for example 'Dear Carrot & Marrow', 'Dear Marks & Spencer,' 'Dear Camden Council.'

1.41   Documents other than letters are given formal headings showing the parties' names, the tribunal, the case number and the title of the document laid out in a conventional way.[45] These headings are not compulsory and are far from universal in employment tribunal litigation; it is largely a matter of personal taste whether or not to use them though they may, marginally, help to convey a sense of competence and professionalism to the tribunal and the other party.

Telephone calls

1.42   The choice between writing a letter and making a telephone call to the tribunal or the respondent will often be obvious. Self-evidently a formal request for disclosure of documents or an application for

45 See for example P3.1 below.

permission to amend the claim or postpone the hearing must be made in writing. If the respondent has faxed a letter part of which is illegible, then equally clearly the only sensible thing is to pick up the telephone to them straight away and ask them to re-send it.

1.43   Between these extremes there will be many communications for which either a letter or a telephone call will do. To a large extent the choice will be a matter of personal preference, although those who are not used to conducting litigation probably tend to make their task harder than necessary by dealing with almost everything by letter. For this reason it is worth suggesting that as a rule claimants should keep letters to a reasonable minimum and use the telephone instead where possible.[46] This will save time and energy, and will also tend to encourage practical co-operation between the parties.

1.44   It is also worth remembering that tribunal staff and lawyers acting for the respondent can both be a valuable source of background information about how things are usually done or what the tribunal's expectations will be, and this kind of information is much easier to tap into in a fairly informal telephone conversation than in an exchange of letters.[47]

File and diary management

1.45   Running an employment tribunal case requires habits that are second nature to solicitors, and to many others whose normal work requires them to handle correspondence files over months or years. For others they will be unfamiliar and will need to be learned.

1.46   The first and most obvious point to make is that the papers relating to the case should be kept together in a ring-binder, lever-arch file or cardboard wallet file. Probably a wallet file is the most convenient. Copies of all documents sent out should be filed, and all documents received should be filed. Handwritten originals should be retained on the file even if subsequently typed up. A brief attendance note should

---

46 Provided clear file notes are made promptly after all conversations and filed with the rest of the papers.

47 And note too that the forces that encourage professional representatives to write quarrelsome letters – see note 41 above – do not operate in the same way when they speak on the telephone. This explains the solicitor who writes consistently abrasive letters but is charming and co-operative on the telephone: it is not a fiendish plot to disorientate the claimant, just a consequence of the fact that he sends his client copies of his letters but not tapes of his telephone calls.

be made promptly of any telephone conversation or meeting. The question 'was that phone call worth recording?' does not arise. If the conversation was short and seemingly trivial, the time taken to decide whether or not there could be any circumstances in the future in which it might be important to have a record of it will be greater than the time taken to record it. If it was of any length, it is bound to need a record. In case of a subsequent application for a costs or preparation time order,[48] it is sensible to record the time spent.

P1.1 Attendance note

Attendance notes do not need to follow any particular format, and a hand-written note (provided it is legible) is perfectly adequate.

Attendance note

Client: Davis
Date: 30 September 2004

T/C[49] to client to discuss schedule of loss. The figure of £500 p/w is gross, but without overtime pay. She will look out payslips for last 6 months of employment and send them. Will also send all payslips for temp work since dismissal.

Explained need for evidence of mitigation.[50] Client will collect all rejection letters and copy applications that she has retained so far into a file, and will start to keep notes of any inquiries and copies of all applications.

10 minutes

1.47   Papers should be subdivided into logical categories. The following categories are suggested: (i) correspondence and attendance notes, held together with a treasury tag, with the most recent item on the top; (ii) statements of case and orders[51] – the claim, the response, any directions from the tribunal, the decision; (iii) documentary evidence; and (iv) statements. These sub-files can be enclosed in a folded sheet of paper to keep them separate from each other. A running list of the

48 See paras 10.4–10.23 below.
49 'Telephone call'.
50 See paras 1.70–1.74 below.
51 In other words, formal tribunal documents.

telephone and fax numbers of all the people who may need to be contacted in connection with the case on the outside cover of the file is a useful time-saving device. It is also a good idea to keep a prominent note of key dates on the outside of the file.

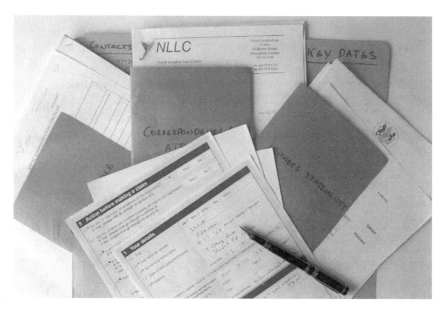

Time recording

1.48   Because from October 2004 the tribunals have power in certain circumstances to make 'preparation time orders' to compensate parties for the time they have spent preparing the case, it is prudent for claimants and their advisers[52] to get into the habit of recording the time they spend on the case in order to be able to show the tribunal how long they have spent. Preparation time can mount up to a surprising extent: it is much easier to demonstrate this convincingly by keeping a running log of time spent than by looking back at the work done weeks or months after the event and trying to estimate how long it would have taken. Claimants who are representing themselves should remember to record time that a lawyer might not have to spend – such as time travelling to a library or to a local print shop to fax a document. A note of any expenses, and itemised telephone bills, should also be kept.

---

52 Including advisers acting for free: there is a standard hourly rate of £25 applicable that does not depend on showing that any charge has been made.

1.49   Probably the simplest method of keeping a rough account of the time spent on a file is to keep a sheet or two laid out along the lines of the following precedent at the front of the file, and to try to remember to complete it at the end of each telephone call or session of work on the case.

P1.2 Time sheet

Date	Activity	Time spent	expenses
4/10/04	t/c to EOC helpline	20 mins	
4/10/04	Trip to library for research (incl travel)	4 hours	£1.40 fare £5.20 copying
5/10/04	t/c to EOC helpline	5 mins	
5/10/04	Drafting grievance letter	1 hour	
24/10/04	Considering E's response	20 mins	
8/11/04	Trip to library for research	3½ hours	£1.40 fare £2.00 copying
9/11/04	Drafting ET1	3 hours	
9/11/04	t/c to EOC helpline	20 mins	
9/11/04	Redrafting ET1 in light of advice	1½ hours	
9/11/04	Trip to print shop to fax ET1	40 mins	£2 fare £1.20 fax
13/11/04	Drafting questionnaire	2 hours	
13/11/04	t/c to ACAS	5 mins	
13/11/04	Reading letter from E's solicitor	20 mins	
13/11/04	t/c to CAB	5 mins	
14/11/04	Drafting letter to E's solicitor	30 mins	

Key dates and time limits

1.50   It is particularly important to establish a rigid habit of noting key dates in such a way that it is impossible to forget them. There are many ways of setting up automatic reminders, though an old-fashioned diary will still be the most effective for many people. Whatever method is chosen, there is a pit-fall to be avoided at each end of the process. The first is to forget to make the initial entry. An adviser who is busy when first consulted by a new client may be tempted to postpone the task of calculating and noting key dates until a calmer moment. This is always a mistake: a calm moment may not present itself for some time, and by the time it does the task may have been forgotten. An adviser who does not have time to calculate and record key dates at once *does not have time to take on a new case.*

1.51   The second pit-fall is to set up the reminder, but then to fail to register it. There is no point noting key dates in a diary that is rarely opened, or setting up a reminder on an e-mail account that is not accessed every day. It is far better to link reminders to existing habits than to try to establish completely new habits: someone who already checks an e-mail account daily will do better to set up an automatic reminder on the e-mail account than to resolve to buy a desk diary and look in it every day. Someone who already has and constantly uses a desk diary will be better served by an entry in that.

1.52   It is beyond the scope of this book to discuss time limits in detail,[53] but two calculations need to be second nature to employment advisers. The first is the end of the normal time limit for presentation of the claim, which for the great majority of claims over which the tribunal has jurisdiction is three months less one day from the date of dismissal (in complaints about dismissal) or from the act complained of (in the case of most other complaints).[54] Discrimination complaints can present difficulties as there will often be allegations of a number of discriminatory acts on different dates. Sometimes it will be possible to argue that these all form part of the same continuing act, but this argument can be complicated. The safest course is to present the claim within three months of the *earliest* of the acts complained of. Often this will be impossible because the client will have put up with mistreatment for weeks, months or sometimes even years before

---

53 See ETP 3 Chapter 3.
54 For details, see ETP 3 Chapter 3.

seeking advice; in that case the claim should be presented as soon as it can be drafted.

1.53   The second crucial calculation is the last day for presentation of an appeal to the Employment Appeal Tribunal, which is 42 days from the date when the employment tribunal's judgment or order is sent to the parties. This means that if the judgment is sent to the parties on Tuesday 1 March 2005, then the notice of appeal together with forms ET1 and ET3, a copy of the judgment appealed must be received by the Employment Appeal Tribunal before 4pm on Tuesday 12 April. In either case, it is essential – especially if the deadline is close – to make sure that the document has arrived, and was complete on arrival.

1.54   This last cannot be over-emphasised: there is no method of delivery[55] that is 100% fool-proof, and a missed deadline for presenting a claim or an appeal is the kind of error most likely to get an adviser sued for negligence. If a claim or appeal in the last few days is unavoidable, the best course is to fax the document, print and retain a transmission confirmation on the file, telephone the tribunal to check that each page has arrived and is complete, and to make and retain on the file a note of this conversation and the name of the individual spoken to. This is in fact good practice even where the expiry of a time limit is not imminent: if a new claim is posted four weeks before the deadline but lost in the post, the deadline may have passed by the time the claimant or adviser wonders why no acknowledgment has yet been received from the tribunal. A document lost in the post will not usually provide a sufficient excuse for a late claim or appeal, so advisers should either make a diary note to chase if no acknowledgment is received within a reasonable time (but still within the limitation period); or else – which is probably easier – simply fax the document and double-check safe arrival at once.

Time limits after the October 2004 changes

1.55   Since 1 October 2004, the whole subject of time limits in the employment tribunals has become immensely more complicated. Again, detailed consideration of the relevant provisions is beyond the scope of

---

55   Not even hand-delivery: for a cautionary tale see *Gdynia American Shipping Lines v Chelminski* [2004] IRLR 725, CA.

this book, but a practical guide to tribunal litigation would fail its users if it did not lay down a very clear warning that the rules about presentation of claims are now extremely treacherous for claimants and their advisers.

1.56   There are two main sources of difficulty. The first is the new dispute resolution procedures laid down by the Employment Act 2002 and regulations under it. The second is the tribunals' new duty to reject a complaint under rule 3 of the procedure rules if it does not provide all the 'relevant required information.'

The effects of the dispute resolution regime

1.57   For a fuller account of the regime implemented by the Employment Act (EA) 2002 and the Employment Act 2002 (Dispute Resolution) Regulations (EA(DR)R) 2004 see ETP 3 paras 3.3–3.15. In very broad outline, this legislation does three things:

- It requires employers to go through a statutory procedure (a dismissal and disciplinary procedure (DDP)) before dismissing any employee, and provides that a dismissal in the absence of those procedures is unfair.
- It requires employees to raise an internal grievance through a statutory grievance procedure (GP) *and then wait 28 days* before making a complaint to the tribunal about anything[56] other than a dismissal.
- It provides for adjustments up or down of awards to claimants in cases where DDP or GP (as the case may be) has not been completed: the award will be adjusted upwards if it is the employer's fault that the procedure was not completed, down if it was the employee's fault.

1.58   These provisions have the effect that employees cannot always present their claims immediately when they arise, and for that reason the time limits for presentation of claims is *sometimes but not always* extended by 3 months.

1.59   The rules governing these extensions of time are at EA(DR)R 2004 reg 15. Again a broad outline of the effect of them is necessary here.

---

56 Almost anything: see Employment Act 2002 s32 and Sch 4 for the list of claims affected.

For complaints about grievances,[59] the extension of time is gained by doing one of two things:

- raising a grievance; or
- presenting a claim to the tribunal that is premature either because no grievance has been raised, or because 28 days have not yet passed since the grievance was raised.

1.60   For complaints about dismissal, the additional three months is available in one situation only:

- if at the time the normal time limit for the complaint expired the claimant had reasonable grounds for believing that there was an ongoing disciplinary or dismissal procedure.

1.61   There are various troublesome consequences of all this. Because the rules are complicated, workplace myths are likely to grow up that are dangerous over-simplifications of the rules. It is *not* the case, for example, that a claimant must always wait for the outcome of an internal appeal against dismissal or against the outcome of his or her grievance before presenting a claim to the tribunal. Similarly it is not the case that time will always be extended to six months.

Multiple claims

1.62   Multiple claims[60] are very common: they are probably the rule rather than the exception. Most complaints about dismissal are accompanied by a wages claim, or a contract claim; many are accompanied by a discrimination claim as well.

    The dispute resolution regime means that careful thought has to be given to what the relevant limitation period is for each claim separately. Sometimes the periods will coincide or overlap, but that is not to be assumed.

---

59 That is – again – almost anything other than dismissal.
60 In the sense of a series of complaints by the same employee about a number of different matters.

Example

Tanya Waters is employed as a semi-skilled machinist in a factory. All the other machinists in her department are men. Her male colleagues are often offered overtime work at busy times. She is only rarely offered overtime. On 8 October 2005 the factory receives a large order with a tight deadline and several of her colleagues are given two hours overtime a night that day and for the whole of the following week, ending 15 October. Tanya complains to her department supervisor about this and says that she thinks she is being left out because she is a woman. He tells her she is a nuisance and always moaning about something, and tells her to get a life.

On 26 October Tanya is handed a letter inviting her to a disciplinary meeting on 28 October to discuss her persistent lateness. She went through a bad patch for time-keeping a few months earlier because of child-care difficulties and was given a written warning, but her time-keeping had been mostly good for the last couple of months: she has only been late on two or three occasions since the beginning of August, and nothing was said at the time. At the end of the meeting on 28 October she is dismissed with immediate effect, but with pay in lieu of notice. She appeals the dismissal the next day. The appeal is heard on 5 November and dismissed.

Towards the end of November Tanya gets an appointment with her local CAB. She is advised that she has potential claims of sex discrimination in the allocation of overtime, and also of unfair dismissal and sex discrimination by way of victimisation in relation to the dismissal. She is advised to raise a grievance about the overtime complaint, but because of money worries arising from the loss of her job she does not get around to it until 4 January 2006.

Tanya was dismissed on 28 October 2005, so the normal period for presentation of her unfair dismissal complaint and her complaint that her dismissal was discriminatory ends on 27 January 2006. The last unfair allocation of overtime ended on 15 October 2005, so the normal period for presenting that complaint ends on 14 January 2006. Because she raised a grievance about the overtime allocation on 5 January 2006 – inside the normal period for presentation of the claim – she has the benefit of a three month extension, so her sex discrimination claim in relation to that must now be presented to the tribunal by 14 April 2005. That claim cannot be presented until 2 February, because she must wait 28 days after raising her grievance. For her unfair dismissal claim and her complaint that the dismissal was an act of victimisation, on the other hand, she does not get a three month extension on the normal time limit. This is because her appeal was concluded back in November: she does not have reasonable grounds to believe that there is an ongoing DDP.

This means that Tanya has separate, non-overlapping windows of opportunity in which to present her claims. She must present her unfair dismissal and victimisation claims on or before 27 January 2005; she must present her sex discrimination claim on or before 14 April 2005, but she may not present it until 2 February.

The tribunal's duty to reject incomplete claims

1.63   The new rules insist that certain 'required information' must be included on all claims, and (from 6 April 2005 or 1 October 2005. See note 62 below) that claims must be presented on the prescribed form. Because the tribunals have a duty to reject claims that do not comply with these requirements, this is a further source of potential difficulty in presenting a valid claim within the relevant time limit. There is no automatic extension of time in a case where a claim is presented within the applicable time limit but rejected, although in some cases tribunals may be amenable to the argument either that it was not reasonably practicable to present the claim in time or that an extension should be granted on just and equitable grounds.[61]

1.64   If an employee presents a complaint near the end of the limitation period, and the tribunal rejects it as incomplete, or because[62] it is not presented on the prescribed form, the employee may by the time she knows her claim has been rejected either be too late to correct her claim and resubmit it, or have a very limited time indeed in which to do so. For this reason it is important to present the claim as soon as possible in order to have time to correct and present again in the event of rejection.

61   Depending which test applies: see ETP 3 paras 3.28–3.29.
62   From 6 April 2005 or, if proposed regulations before parliament at the time of writing are made, 1 October 2005.

Whether to present the claim or wait for the outcome of the statutory procedure

1.65 Complaints about grievances may not be presented until 28 days have elapsed since the grievance was raised, but it is important to be aware that aside from that there is no requirement for employees to wait a reasonable period, or any period, for their employers to complete statutory procedures before presenting a tribunal claim. Employment Act (EA) 2002 s31 provides for the reduction of awards where non-completion of the statutory procedure is attributable to a failure by the employee *either* to comply with a requirement of the procedure, *or* to exercise a right of appeal, but those are the only two circumstances in which the employee will be blamed for non-completion of the process. It follows that there will be no penalty[63] for presenting an appeal (against dismissal, or against an unsatisfactory outcome to a grievance) and immediately presenting a claim.

1.66 The risk of having the claim rejected as incomplete on the first attempt means that the safest course is:

- to present a complaint about dismissal as soon as possible after the effective date of termination;[64]
- to present a complaint about a grievance as soon as possible once 28 days have elapsed after the presentation of the initial grievance.

1.67 Employees who are very confident that they know exactly when the relevant limitation period expires and can present a valid claim on the first attempt may sometimes be able to get a tactical advantage by waiting for a period after presenting an internal appeal before presenting the claim. The reason for this is that giving the employer the opportunity to deal with the appeal before presenting the claim also gives the employer the opportunity to fail to deal with the appeal within a reasonable time, and that can give rise to an enhanced award of compensation.

1.68 If the employee presents a claim a day or two after appealing, the employee will not suffer a reduction of his award by reason of the non-completion of the procedure because EA 2002 s31(2)(c) gives only two situations in which non-completion of the procedure will be treated as the employee's fault[65] and this is not one of them. However, if

---

63 Apart from the loss of a possible tactical advantage – see para 1.67 below.
64 See glossary, and ELAH 5 paras 20.25–20.26.
65 Where the employee has failed to comply with a requirement of the procedure, or where he or she has failed to exercise a right of appeal.

non-completion of the statutory procedure is attributable to the employer's failure to deal with an appeal within a reasonable time, then any award made to the employee should be adjusted upwards.

1.69   It follows that in some cases a tactical pause (probably for 28 days or so, time limits permitting) after appealing the employer's internal decision and before presenting a claim to the tribunal may result in an enhanced award for the claimant. However, this tactic should be used, if at all, with great caution: the most important thing is to ensure the claim is presented in time.

Mitigating the loss

1.70   Considerations about maximising the award made by the employment tribunal might seem more suitable for the last chapter or so of a book of this nature, but there is a real sense in which this is very much a preliminary matter. This is that the most important things that a claimant can do to improve her chances of a significant award must be done at the same time as, or even before, the claim is presented.

The meaning of mitigation

1.71   In most cases before an employment tribunal there will, if the claimant succeeds in her complaint, be a claim for lost earnings – normally wages that the claimant would have earned if she had not been dismissed, or if she had not been refused a position or promotion because of unlawful discrimination. Where there is a claim for lost earnings, there is almost always also a duty to 'mitigate the loss' – that is, the employee who has been dismissed unfairly or as a result of unlawful discrimination may not retire at that point on the strength of her claim: she must do her best to get another job. The tribunal will only order the respondent to compensate the claimant for losses reasonably incurred; if the tribunal believes that the claimant has failed to take reasonable steps to mitigate her loss, she will not be compensated for whatever element of her loss she could reasonably have avoided.

Heading off criticism of efforts to mitigate

1.72   Claimants whose complaint is about the loss of their jobs should start to look for another job as soon as they reasonably can. If they are too ill, or too upset or depressed, to look for work straight away, they should see their doctor. They should document their job-search minutely. They should make a note of every telephone call, keep a copy of every letter and completed application form they have sent out, keep all rejection letters. They should make a note every time they look in the 'situations vacant' section of a newspaper, and keep a copy or clipping of each advertisement they have responded to. They should print out details of any websites they visit, and print out and keep all e-mails they send or receive. If they seek any career advice, they should keep notes of the advice received and any action taken on it. They should also keep records of any expenses incurred in the job search – retaining tickets if they have travelled to an interview, keeping receipts for meals if they have had to be away from home at a meal time, keeping receipts for any photocopying or printing and so on.

1.73   The best situation for a claimant to be in at the time of the hearing is to have a small claim for lost earnings because he or she has by the time of the hearing got a better-paid job than before. If that is not achievable, the second best outcome is to have a lower-paid job. This tends to be regarded by tribunals as convincing evidence that the claimant is serious about mitigating her loss, so it will tend to maximise his or her chances of securing compensation for a substantial period into the future.

1.74   The worst outcome is still to be looking for work at the time of the hearing. If the claimant is still unavoidably unemployed by the time of the hearing, he or she should come armed with a fat file of evidence of mitigation. Here, for once, sheer length and weight is a virtue: the aim is to deter the respondent from even attempting to argue that there has been insufficient effort to mitigate. Most respondents faced with a credible 300 page mitigation bundle will decide to concentrate on other approaches to damage limitation rather than take the claimant through the bundle in detail and cross-examine on every page.

Proceeds of Crime Act 2002*

Introduction

1.75   It is worth including a brief note on the Proceeds of Crime Act (POCA) 2002 because it puts both claimants and their advisers at risk of committing criminal offences by the most innocuous-seeming action to enforce employment rights. Although the likelihood of prosecution arising out of the kinds of circumstances that employment advisers and their clients deal with seems a remote risk, the Act presents those who advise claimants with difficult choices.

* **Important**: See note at end of this chapter.

The section 328 offence

1.76   POCA 2002 creates by section 328[66] an offence where a person 'enters into or becomes concerned in an arrangement which he knows or suspects facilitates (by whatever means) the acquisition, retention, use or control of criminal property. 'Criminal property' is broadly defined at section 340(3):

Property is criminal property if–

(a) it constitutes a person's benefit from criminal conduct or it repre- sents such a benefit (in whole or in part and whether directly or indirectly) ...

1.77   A defence can be established by making an 'authorised disclosure' to the National Criminal Intelligence Service under POCA 2002 s338 and then proceeding with the case only if no notice has been received within the period of seven working days after the disclosure was made[67] prohibiting further action.[68]

1.78   The effect of the provisions is draconian: advisers (including pro- fessional legal advisers) are required to inform the NCIS if in the course of advising their clients they become aware, or are given reason to suspect, that a claim includes a claim for 'criminal property' – because in assisting the client with the recovery of that money they become 'concerned in an arrangement' which they know or suspect facilitates the acquisition of criminal property.

1.79   Advisers who do not comply with the duty to make a report to the NCIS will be guilty of an offence. The Act is not restricted to major or large-scale crime, so for example money in an individual's possession that he or she should have, but has not, paid by way of tax on earnings counts as the 'proceeds of crime.' This kind of crime is very wide- spread, and is of course the kind of thing that claimants' advisers very often become aware of in the course of their work.

When the duty arises

1.80   Those advising employers will often have a duty to make reports where they become aware that their clients' resources are, or are partly, criminal property by reason of the employer's failure to make proper

---

66 Among other things.
67 'From a constable or customs officer': section 335(4)(a).
68 There is a procedure for requesting urgent consent to proceed if action needs to be taken before seven days after the notification has expired: see guidance at www.ncis.co.uk.

deductions, or a cost-saving breach of health and safety law, etc. Solicitors firms need to have a detailed awareness of the POCA 2002 provisions: guidance for solicitors is to be found at www.lawsociety.org.uk and for barristers at www.barcouncil.org.uk.

1.81   For claimants, the duty to report does arise where the adviser knows or suspects that the money that the claimant is claiming is itself the proceeds of crime. Because criminal property is defined as property that constitutes a person's benefit from criminal conduct 'in whole or in part,' this seems to mean that the duty to report arises whenever the adviser knows or suspects that the employer is benefiting financially *or has benefited in the past* from any criminal infringement. If some proportion of the employer's resources represents the proceeds of a crime, then any action for compensation or damages against that employer is an arrangement that facilitates the acquisition of criminal property by the employee.

1.82   It follows that there is at least arguably a duty to make a report to the NCIS whenever the adviser becomes aware that the claimant was not taxed properly on his or her full earnings because some proportion of the resources available to the employer – from which any award will be paid – represents the employer's benefit from that offence. The same will be true if the adviser is aware (or suspects) that the employer is in breach of health and safety regulations, or is or has been paying any other employee without proper deductions, or employs or has employed illegal immigrants, etc.

1.83   Claimants' advisers will less often be bound to make a report to the NCIS whose direct effect is to inform on their own client's criminal conduct. A claim for lost earnings in a case where, at the time the client was earning, she was not paying proper tax is not a claim for the proceeds of crime. This is because the actual money that the employee is claiming is not the proceeds of any crime. She would have been guilty of a crime if she had earned the money and pocketed without paying the tax that due on it, but her complaint is that she was never allowed to earn it in the first place. She did not in fact commit any offence in respect of that money, so the claim is not a claim for the proceeds of any crime. However, if the adviser suspects that the employer made its own savings by failing to make proper PAYE deductions (and it almost certainly will have done) then a duty to report will arise.

1.84   It seems that no obligation to report in respect of any criminal conduct on the part of the claimant will necessarily arise where the claimant's previous employment was legitimate but she is now working and either failing to pay tax on her earnings or claiming benefits to which she is not entitled, or both. This is because the claim for lost earnings is not a claim for 'criminal property': the claim for lost earnings is reduced by the amount of the actual net income, whether or not that represents the proceeds of a crime.[69]

1.85 That state of affairs can change suddenly, however. A claimant who is not declaring his current earnings may bring a claim in respect of his former legitimate employment without any duty to report falling on his adviser. If at the end of the hearing the respondent makes an application for costs, at this point the claimant's representative would seem, in resisting the costs application, to be concerned in an arrangement that is likely to facilitate the retention by his client of criminal property. Presumably the correct course is to ask for the costs application to be postponed pending a report and authorisation by the NCIS.

1.86 Advisers who comply scrupulously with the POCA 2002 will inevitably find the obligation burdensome. The reporting process is time-consuming, and the need to wait seven days before proceeding will often be extremely inconvenient. Advisers acting under the Legal Help scheme are presumably entitled to charge for the additional time spent, but that is of no comfort to those acting for free.

1.87 In *P v P*,[70] a Court of Appeal judgment on the effect of the Act, Butler-Sloss P said this:[71]

> Whatever may be the resource implications, the legal profession would appear to be bound by the provision of the Act in all cases, however big or small. If this approach is scrupulously followed by the legal advisers, the result is likely to have a considerable and potentially adverse impact upon the NCIS and would create serious consequential delays in listing and hearing family cases, including child cases.

1.88 It is difficult not to read this as an invitation to lawyers – and by implication to other advisers too – to use scrupulous compliance with the POCA 2002 as a campaigning tool to demonstrate the unworkability of the Act. If the campaign were taken up widely enough, it would have catastrophic consequences for the entire legal system. Unfortunately, it would also be extremely inconvenient for litigants.[72]

---

69 Obviously in these circumstances an adviser should always advise the client to comply with the law.

70 [2003] 3 WLR 1350, CA.

71 At paragraph 56.

72 And as Butler-Sloss P implies, the delays caused could in the most serious cases have consequences much worse than inconvenience.

1.89   The unattractive alternative is to commit, or risk committing, an offence capable in theory at least of leading to a sentence of imprisonment.[73]

Making a report to the NCIS

1.90   Disclosure should be made on the forms provided on the NCIS website.[74] The standard disclosure report form (which should be used in these cases) is divided into 6 modules. Modules 2,3,5 and 6 need to be completed in all cases. Module 1 only needs to be completed when an organisation makes a first report to NCIS, or when its contact details change. Module 4 will rarely if ever be applicable in the employment tribunal context.

1.91   The forms should be completed on a computer, in which case they may then be printed out and posted or faxed to the NCIS. If for any reason it is not possible to complete the form on a computer, it must not be printed and completed by hand: instead a special version of the form for completion by hand must be requested from the NCIS by telephoning 020 7238 8282.

1.92   Although the forms are daunting at first sight – and certainly fiddly and time-consuming to complete – they are not difficult. There is extensive guidance on how they should be completed on the NCIS website. Probably the easiest way to complete them is to print off all 6 forms, complete them in draft by hand and then copy the details back onto the forms on the computer before printing and faxing them. The NCIS, like the employment tribunals, positively requests faxed forms should not followed up by a hard copy in the post.

Important note

Paragraphs 1.75 to 1.92 above have since superseded by *Bowman v Fels* [2005] EWCA Civ 226, in which the Court of Appeal ruled that section 328 has no application to steps taken in the conduct or settlement of proceedings. The judgment speaks throughout of conduct of proceedings by lawyers, or by solicitors and barristers, but the main part of the reasoning is equally applicable to the conduct of proceedings by the parties themselves or by their lay advisers. This judgment was

---

73   The aim throughout this book is to offer practical solutions to the problems faced by claimants and their advisers. Unfortunately the only solutions to the problems posed by the POCA 2002 seem to lie in amendment or repeal.

74   www.ncis.co.uk/disclosure.asp.

handed down at the time of going to press allowing no time to make changes to the text of this section. For a fuller discussion online go to the author's profile at www.farrarsbuilding.co.uk and follow the appropriate link.

Before the claim

Introduction

2.1   As touched on in chapter 1, new statutory dispute resolution procedures are created with effect from 1 October 2004 by the Employment Act (EA) 2002 and the Employment Act 2002 (Dispute Resolution) Regulations (EA(DR)R 2004.[1] The dispute resolution regime makes it compulsory in many circumstances for employees to present their employers with a written grievance and give them 28 days to deal with it before they are allowed to make a complaint in relation to the same matter to an employment tribunal.

2.2   The new regime is misconceived at the policy level: it is far more likely to intensify and prolong disputes and increase reliance on lawyers than to lead to early and informal resolution. At the level of detail it is even worse: the rules are obscure, cumbersome and over-complicated, and raise many difficult practical problems for both employees and employers. This chapter aims to give some assistance with the most important difficulties, but until the tribunals have been operating the new procedures for some time there will be many questions to which it is impossible to give a definite answer.

2.3   One crumb of comfort for employees considering a grievance is that the grievance procedures themselves are straightforward. The complexities arise in working out when they are compulsory, whether or not they have been complied with (and if not, whose fault it is), and what the consequences are of any non-compliance. While those questions are important for claimants, they fall to be answered in the end by tribunals. Claimants should focus on raising a grievance where necessary and then following the process through to the end.

2.4   This chapter deals with grievances because they are a step that the employee must take in many cases before being allowed to present a claim to the employment tribunal. Where there has been an actual (as opposed to constructive)[2] dismissal, the employer is under duties to follow statutory disciplinary and dismissal procedures that are in many ways parallel to the employee's duty to raise a grievance. The statutory disciplinary procedures are not dealt with in this book since the duties under them fall primarily on the employer, and a failure to comply with them does not prevent an employee from presenting a claim to the employment tribunal.

---

1   SI No 752.
2   See glossary.

The two types of grievance procedure

2.5 The EA 2002 provides for 'standard' and 'modified' grievance procedures. Each procedure is, as mentioned above, straightforward in itself.

Standard grievance procedure

2.6 The standard procedure has the following six stages:

1. A written statement of the grievance, which the employee must give or send to the employer.
2. A meeting, which the employer must arrange and the employee must take all reasonable steps to attend, to discuss the grievance.
3. Notification to the employee of the employer's decision on its response to the grievance, in which the employee must also be notified of his or her right of appeal.
4. Notification by the employee[3] that he or she wishes to appeal.
5. An appeal meeting, which the employer must arrange and the employee must take all reasonable steps to attend.
6. The employer's decision on the appeal.

2.7 Employees should normally follow the entire process through to the end, even if they do not have any confidence in their employers dealing with the grievance in good faith. The requirement to comply with the grievance procedures before presenting a tribunal claim does not apply if, for example, it is not reasonably practicable to raise a grievance, or if there are reasonable grounds for thinking that raising a grievance will lead to a threat to a person or property or a continuation of harassment. However, these exemptions are strictly defined, and it will be difficult to predict in advance when the tribunals will be prepared to accept that they apply. On the rare occasions that an employee genuinely believes that raising a grievance will expose him or her to personal risk, that consideration must obviously outweigh the danger of damaging a subsequent tribunal claim. Otherwise, it is suggested that employees should make all possible efforts to comply with the procedures.

---

3 Which need not be in writing, although it is advisable for the sake of being able to prove later to the tribunal that notification was given.

The modified procedure

2.8 The modified procedure applies if the employment has ended and the employer and employee have agreed in writing that the modified procedure should apply.

2.9 The modified procedure leaves out the meetings and the appeal stage and consists of two steps:

1. A written statement of the grievance, which the employee must give or send to the employer.
2. The employer's written response to the grievance.

2.10 An employee whose employment has ended and who wishes to raise a grievance will need to decide whether to propose the modified procedure. It is suggested that this will often be preferable: grievance meetings are likely to be stressful for the employee, and the longer standard process presents the employee with more stages to complete and therefore more stages, potentially, to be blamed by the tribunal for failing to complete. However, the modified procedure can *only* be adopted with the employer's agreement, so if the employer declines to run the modified procedure and proposes a meeting, the employee should attend and then complete the full standard procedure.

The initial statement of grievance

2.11 Section 32 of the EA 2002 provides:

(2) An employee shall not present a complaint to an employment tribunal [*of one of the specified kinds*][5] if–
   (a) it concerns a matter in relation to which the requirement [*to follow a grievance procedure*] applies, and
   (b) the requirement has not been complied with.

2.12 Employees, therefore, are generally prohibited from presenting complaints to employment tribunals concerning 'matters' in relation to which they have not previously raised as grievances with their employers. However, it is far from clear how this will work in practice.

---

5 These include most complaints that can be made to a tribunal other than complaints about actual – as opposed to constructive – dismissal.

Example

Suppose Anwara Begum feels aggrieved about how much she is being paid by her employers and about their refusal to vary her working day to ease problems with her childcare arrangements. She presents a formal grievance that says:

> I do not think it is fair that I am paid less than John Kandle I have mentioned this on several occasions and you have promised to do something about it each time but you have never done anything, and now I have discovered that John got a 7% pay rise last April. I did not even get a pay rise to keep pace with inflation because you said the company was going through a difficult time.
>
> I also think it is unfair that you have refused my request to work at home for part of the week in order to ease the terrible difficulties I have been suffering with childcare.

Her employers fail to resolve her grievance to her satisfaction and, having taken advice, she presents complaints to the tribunal of sex and race discrimination, under the Equal Pay Act (EqPA) 1970 and under the flexible working provisions of the Employment Rights Act (ERA) 1996. Before it decides whether or not to accept the formal claim, the tribunal must decide whether these matters have been raised in Ms Begum's grievance.

2.13   It is clear from this that the drafting of the initial grievance will require some care. The procedures appear to be intended to be operated by the parties before the involvement of lawyers on either side, so it cannot be the deliberate intention that the employee should be required to name the legal basis on which he or she founds her grievance. At the same time, the employment tribunals are required to reject claims that concern complaints to which the statutory grievance procedure applies if a grievance has not been raised in relation to that matter.

2.14   It remains to be seen how rigid an approach the tribunals will take to whether or not a 'matter' has been raised in a grievance.[6] The prudent course must be to take care to ensure that the factual basis of *all* the complaints that the employee may subsequently wish a tribunal

---

6   It is possible that the case law relating to whether the formal claim contains sufficient details to raise a particular head of claim will be relevant: see *Employment Tribunal Procedure* (ETP 3) (McMullen, Tuck and Criddle, 3rd edn, Legal Action Group, 2004) para 7.5.

to consider are raised in the internal grievance. The approach taken here is to spell out the legal basis for the complaints in terms little, if at all, different from what would be included in the narrative sections of a formal claim. In effect this means that employees who are considering an internal grievance are likely to need legal advice at this stage. This runs contrary to the intention with which the rules appear to have been drafted, but it seems nevertheless to be the only safe course.[7]

2.15   It is sensible for the employee to spell out in the grievance letter any practical steps that she thinks the employer ought to take to resolve the grievance, but it is probably not appropriate to ask for a specified sum in compensation at this stage.

P2.1 Written grievance

Seamus McNally
McNally & Sons
26 Lower Street
London
N19 2PQ

21 October 2004

Dear Mr McNally

Statement of grievance

I would like to ask you to consider my grievance about two matters.

1. I do not think it is fair that I am paid less than John Kandler. We have the same job title and we do almost exactly the same work and cover for each other's absences, but he is paid nearly £4,000 per year more than me. I believe that this is a breach of my right to equal pay under the Equal Pay Act 1970 and/or not to suffer discrimination on racial grounds under the Race Relations Act 1976.

    I want you to agree to pay me the same as Mr Kandler from now on. I also want to discuss how much back pay you should pay me.

---

7 This is not to say that they will necessarily be able to get legal advice unless they can afford to pay solicitors, but see paras 1.1– 1.13 above for possible sources of free advice and assistance.

2. You have refused to consider the request that I made in my letter of [date] for a change in my working arrangements so that I can pick my daughter up from her kindergarten. I have a right under Part VIIIA of the Employment Rights Act 1996 to have this request properly considered at a meeting. I also believe that your refusal to let me work at home for part of the week constitutes indirect discrimination on grounds of sex.

I want you to hold a meeting to discuss the practicalities of my working at home for two days each week.

I hope to hear from you shortly with a proposed date for a grievance meeting about these matters.

Yours sincerely

Anwara Begum

Dispute resolution procedures and 'without prejudice' communications

2.16   A problem that is not directly addressed in the legislation is the question whether in any circumstances a statutory grievance procedure will take on the character of *without prejudice* negotiations.[8] For employers, there are two potential problems. The first is that if a grievance procedure gives way to negotiations that ultimately fail, difficult questions may arise about whether the statutory grievance procedure has been completed or not. The second is that employers may conduct what they *believe* to be without prejudice negotiations in the course of which they make damaging admissions that the tribunal subsequently holds are not privileged.[9] Each problem for the employer is an opportunity for the employee.

2.17   As a matter of principle the distinction between an open statutory grievance procedure and without prejudice negotiations depends on whether or not there is a live dispute between the parties which they are attempting to settle: see *BNP Paribas v Mezzotero*.[10] If compromise of

---

8 See para 6.10 below and glossary.
9 See glossary and para 6.10 below.
10 [2004] IRLR 508, EAT.

a live dispute is contemplated, then the process, whatever it is called and irrespective of whether the parties state that their letters and/or meetings are 'without prejudice,' is privileged. If that is so, it seems to follow that if negotiations fail, then unless it has conducted an open grievance procedure in parallel, the employer may be penalised by a tribunal for failing to operate the grievance procedure.

2.18   It will often be a difficult question whether the process does represent an attempt to settle a live dispute. In *BNP Paribas*[11] the EAT held that the fact that a grievance had been raised did not mean that there was a live dispute between the parties, and consequently the employee was allowed to give evidence about what had been said at a grievance meeting that the employer had sought to label 'without prejudice.' This approach to grievance meetings may not survive long: it is one of the ironies of the dispute resolution regime that it is likely to force employers to treat every grievance as a potential tribunal case, so it is possible that the next time this question comes before the EAT it will be decided differently.

2.19   Some employers no doubt will be advised to adopt a cautious approach to all this: they may conduct an open grievance procedure, in which their stance is defensive, and not initiate without prejudice negotiations until after a claim has been presented to the tribunal and it is beyond doubt that there is an extant dispute. Alternatively they may seek to open without prejudice negotiations straight away, but to minimise any risk of the negotiations not being treated as privileged by getting the employee's explicit confirmation that the grievance is the first stage of a proposed tribunal claim, and run an open grievance procedure in parallel in order not to be accused subsequently of having failed to complete the required grievance procedure.

2.20   Where employers are less cautious, employees can seek to exploit their difficulty in one of two ways. If supposedly 'without prejudice' negotiations contain material that will help the employee win in the employment tribunal, he or she should keep careful notes of what has been said (and of course retain any correspondence) and rely on *BNP Paribas* in inviting the tribunal to consider that material. If negotiations have not produced anything useful, the employee can take the opposite tack: maintain that the negotiations are privileged, and claim an enhanced award by reason of the employer's failure to complete the grievance procedure.

---

11 Above para 2.17.

Constructive dismissal and grievance procedures

2.21 An employee who has resigned in response to his or her employer's fundamental breach of contract is deemed by virtue of ERA 1996 s95(1)(c) to have been dismissed. This is widely referred to (although the term does not appear in the Act) as 'constructive dismissal'.[12]

2.22 Constructive dismissal has always been a tactical minefield for employees and those who advise them. Timing is important, because an employee who does not resign reasonably promptly after the employer's fundamental breach may be said to have 'affirmed'[13] the contract and lost the right to treat the breach as terminating the contract. At the same time, if the employer's conduct is not yet sufficiently definite, the employee may be said to have resigned prematurely – for example, where an employer has threatened but not yet committed a fundamental breach of the contract of employment. The compulsory grievance procedures complicate matters even further.

Resignation or grievance first?

2.23 An employee considering resignation and a constructive dismissal must begin with a tactical decision whether to resign first or to raise a formal grievance first. In some ways, constructive dismissal is the mirror image of dismissal for gross misconduct: one party to the employment contract has done something so bad that the other party cannot be expected to continue the relationship. A key difference, however, is that the employee, unlike the employer, has no obligation to act fairly, to conduct a fair investigation or to consider alternatives before resigning: if the employer has committed a fundamental breach of contract, the employee may simply walk out and complain of constructive dismissal.

2.24 The statutory dispute resolution procedures do not change this. This is important: the definition of constructive dismissal is not altered by the introduction of statutory grievance procedures. Some tribunals may need to be specifically warned against the error of assuming the contrary, however: even before the introduction of the dispute resolution procedures some tended to proceed as if there was an obligation on

---

12 See glossary; for a fuller explanation, see generally *Employment Law: an adviser's handbook* (ELAH 5) (Lewis, 5th edn, Legal Action Group, 2003) paras 6.37–6.46 or *Harvey on Industrial Relations and Employment Law (Harvey)* (Butterworths, Looseleaf) paras 401–600.
13 See glossary.

employees to give their employers a warning and an opportunity to improve before resigning.

2.25   An employee who considers that they have been constructively dismissed must now raise a statutory grievance and wait 28 days for the outcome before they may present a claim to an employment tribunal, but they may resign before, after, or at the same time as they raise their grievance. Employees who wish to attempt to resolve the problem by way of the grievance procedure before resigning should expressly reserve the right to resign in reliance on the employer's breach.[14]

2.26   There is a possible argument that under the EA(DR)R 2004 and the EA 2002, an employee who raises a grievance and then resigns when the grievance is not satisfactorily resolved must present a further grievance about the constructive dismissal itself before presenting a complaint of constructive dismissal to the tribunal. It seems likely that it will be established in due course by the EAT or the Court of Appeal that this is not necessary. Meanwhile, an employee wishing to be absolutely sure of being able to bring a claim should raise a further grievance after resigning.

P2.2 Written grievance[15] – Unauthorised deductions from wages complaint[16] and possible future constructive dismissal

Ms P Denny
Supaclean Ltd
14 Hartwell Way
Croydon
Surrey CR0 1AB

9 December 2004

Dear Ms Denny

Enhanced wages for weekend work

I have worked for Supaclean for 12 years now, first as a cleaner and since March 1999 as a cleaning supervisor. I have always been paid time and a half for hours worked between 6 pm on Friday and 8 am on Monday.

---

14   See ELAH 5 para 6.43.
15   In this case the standard procedure must apply because the employment is on-going.
16   Employment Rights Act 1996 s13.

On 15 October 2004 I received a letter from Andy Parsons, the cleaning manager at the Celtic Bank where I work, telling me that from the following week I would not get extra pay for weekend work any more, and I have received reduced pay for all seven weeks since the week beginning 18 October.

I think this is unfair. Please treat this letter as starting a grievance under the statutory grievance procedure.[17]

I think this is a fundamental breach of my contract of employment, and I reserve the right to resign in response if you do not resolve my grievance satisfactorily.

Yours sincerely

Sufiya Halai

Resignation before outcome of grievance

2.27 An employee who is convinced that the outcome of the grievance procedure will not make it tolerable for him or her to remain employed should probably resign at once. The first tactical question at this point is whether to resign with or without notice. Resigning on notice will not be taken as an affirmation of the contract of employment,[18] although it may partially undermine an employee who is asserting that his or her working conditions had simply become intolerable. Quite often an employee contemplating resignation in response to a fundamental breach of contract will be signed off sick with stress at the relevant time: in that event, there may be very little to lose – and a few weeks' sick pay to gain – by resigning on notice. It should be remembered, however, that the final outcome of the dispute may well involve an agreed reference, and for that reason the employee may be better advised not to end his or her employment with a substantial period of sick leave.

2.28 A new tactical advantage in resigning on notice introduced by the dispute resolution regime is that provided the resignation is accompanied by a grievance, the 28 days after presentation of the grievance (during which the employee cannot validly present a claim to the

---

17 It is not essential, but is probably prudent, to refer directly to the statutory procedure.
18 See ELAH 5 para 6.43.

employment tribunal) can start to run *before* the resignation takes
effect – and therefore before the standard limitation period of three
months for presenting the claim starts to run.

2.29   If the claimant has resigned with immediate effect, the modified
grievance procedure[19] will normally be appropriate. In this case the
grievance should be started *after* the employment has ended, but
preferably immediately after. The reason for this is that provided a
grievance has been presented within the normal time limit for presenting a complaint to the tribunal (in most cases three months), that
time limit will be extended for a further three months. Probably an
employee who resigns and presents the grievance in the same letter has
the benefit of that extension, but the Regulations are not completely
clear on the point and an employer might argue that the grievance
was presented before the employment ended and therefore not inside
the normal time limit.

2.30   In many cases this will not matter, but it is suggested that the safest
course is to write two letters, one a day or two after the other. The first
should be the resignation, and the second should start the grievance.
Both resignation and grievance should be unambiguous about the
reason for the resignation.

P2.3 Constructive dismissal – resignation

Philip Badger
Bubbles Packaging Ltd
Handley Lane Industrial Estate
Ashford
Kent AS12 3AB

21 October 2004

Dear Mr Badger

Resignation

On Monday 18 October at around 4pm I was in the middle of a conversation with Tina, about this month's sales report when you stormed
into my office holding a copy of my draft strategy report to the Board.

---

19 See Employment Act 2002 Sch 2, Pt 2.

In the hearing of Tina and three other managers in my department you shouted, "Can't you get anything right, you useless fuckwit?" I asked Tina to leave and closed the door of my office, and then asked you if you had anything more constructive to say. You dropped the report in the wastepaper basket and said, "It's hopeless. I'll just have to do it myself." You then returned to your office.

Your behaviour towards me over the last several months has been increasingly abrupt and undermining. This Monday's incident is beyond what I am prepared or can be expected to tolerate, and I resign with immediate effect.

Yours sincerely

Amanda Kulpa

P2.4 Constructive dismissal – grievance

Philip Badger
Bubbles Packaging Ltd
Handley Lane Industrial Estate
Ashford
Kent AS12 3AB

25 October 2004

Dear Mr Badger

Grievance

You will by now have received my letter resigning with immediate effect on Thursday 21 October.

On Monday 18 October at around 4pm I was in the middle of a conversation with Tina, my PA, about this month's sales report when you stormed into my office holding a copy of my draft strategy report to the Board. In the hearing of Tina and three other managers in my department you shouted, "Can't you get anything right, you useless fuckwit?" I asked

Tina to leave and closed the door of my office, and then asked you if you had anything more constructive to say. You dropped the report in the wastepaper basket and said, "It's hopeless. I'll just have to do it myself." You then returned to your office.

You have treated me with increasing contempt over the last 3 or 4 months. You have had an increasing tendency throughout that period to sigh loudly, raise your eyes heavenwards or mutter 'Really!' when I have addressed you, you have used curt e-mails copied to my subordinates to communicate with me on many occasions when it would have been more convenient and more courteous to speak to me direct, and in the last couple of weeks you have avoided any eye contact with me and ignored me when I have greeted you. I consider that your brusque and undermining conduct towards me over recent months, culminating in your outburst on Monday last week, constituted a fundamental breach of the implied term of trust and confidence that is part of my contract of employment. I have therefore been constructively dismissed, and I believe that my dismissal was unfair. I wish to raise a formal grievance about these matters.[20]

Because my employment has come to an end, there is a choice to be made between the standard and the modified grievance procedures as set out at Chapters 1 and 2 of Part 2 of Schedule 2 to the Employment Act 2002. My view is that the modified procedure is appropriate. Please confirm in writing, by return, your agreement that the modified procedure should apply.

Yours sincerely

Amanda Kulpa

---

20 It is advisable to make it clear that the grievance is about both the manager's conduct, *and* about the constructive dismissal itself.

Borderline cases of constructive or actual dismissal

2.31   A further complication will arise in cases falling on the borderline between constructive and actual dismissal.

> **Example**
> Suppose Mike works as a florist, making up bouquets. He likes this work and is good at it, but his time-keeping is hit-or-miss. His employer, Rob, gets impatient with this, and says 'If you don't buck your ideas up I'll put you on deliveries and we'll see how you like that.' The next Monday morning, Mike is 20 minutes late again, and his employer says, 'Right. I warned you. You're on deliveries this week. If your timekeeping improves over the next few weeks we'll think about putting you back in the shop. Here's your list of drops – the van's already loaded and you know where it is.' Mike objects that he is not employed as a driver, but Rob says, 'Here's the list – it's your choice, you can either do the deliveries or you can bugger off and not come back.' Mike leaves.

2.32   Mike has either resigned in response to his employer's breach of contract, or he has been summarily dismissed – without any disciplinary process – for refusing to obey an order; but it is not entirely clear which it is. He would probably prefer to argue that he has been actually dismissed, but he had better commence a grievance in case a tribunal subsequently takes the other view. At the same time, he should make it clear from the outset that he takes the view that there has been an actual dismissal so that his grievance letter is not able to be treated as evidence that he has resigned.

P2.5 Conditional grievance in a borderline constructive/ actual dismissal case

Rob Selassie
Flower Power
44 Broadway Lane
Camden
London WC1X 1AB

19 November 2004

Dear Rob

Last Monday you ordered me to carry out delivery work instead of my usual floristry work, and you said that I could either do that or 'bugger off and not come back.' I was employed as a florist and I do not believe you were entitled to make me work as a delivery driver instead. In the circumstances, I believe that you have dismissed me from my job as a florist, and I intend to complain to an employment tribunal of unfair dismissal.

Without prejudice to my contention that your conduct last Monday amounted to actual dismissal, I invite you to treat this letter as starting a formal grievance under the statutory grievance procedure. Because my employment has already come to an end, if the grievance procedures apply at all, there is a choice to be made between the standard and the modified grievance procedures as set out at Chapters 1 and 2 of Part 2 of Schedule 2 to the Employment Act 2002. My view is that if any grievance procedure is needed, it is the modified procedure that is appropriate. Please confirm in writing your agreement that the modified procedure should apply.

Yours sincerely

Mike O'Donnell

P2.6 Written grievance relating to sex discrimination

Jane Slough
Personnel Department
Fencemarket plc
212-220 Station Approach
Manchester M1 2BA

17 July 2004

Dear Ms Slough

Grievance: sex discrimination

I have worked in the Manchester branch of Fencemarket for the last six years. I work four hours a day, from 8am to 12 noon. I became pregnant early this year and announced my pregnancy to my line manager on 7 April. I am due to start my maternity leave on 4 October.

When I told my line manager that I was pregnant, she said, 'You'll have to stay on the tills from now on, then.' I asked her why, and she said, 'We can't have you waddling about the shop in your condition. The aisles are too narrow. I wouldn't answer for the consequences.' She has taken me off all duties apart from checkout duties since 7 April. I get very tired and bored sitting on the tills all day and my head aches. I used to like the variety of doing different duties.

I think the way I am being treated is sex discrimination. I am only being treated this way because I am pregnant. I want my manager to be told that I must be allowed to return to the full range of duties until I start my maternity leave.

[If the employee might wish to resign over this issue, a paragraph here asserting that the treatment amounts to a fundamental breach of contract and reserving the right to resign in response should be included.]

Yours sincerely

Elaine Brown

P2.7 Appeal against unsatisfactory outcome of grievance[21]

Mrs Alison Parker
Supaclean Ltd
14 Hartwell Way
Croydon
Surrey CR0 1AB

11 January 2005

Dear Ms Parker

Grievance: enhanced wages for weekend work

I enclose copies of my previous correspondence with Ms Denny, and minutes of the grievance meeting that was held last week. I wish to appeal Ms Denny's decision on my grievance.

I do not accept that Supaclean is entitled to change my terms and conditions of employment by giving me a month's notice. I have never been given a written contract to sign, and it has never previously been suggested to me that Supaclean has this right.

Please let me know when you can hear my appeal. I still reserve the right to resign in response to this fundamental breach of my contract of employment if you do not satisfactorily resolve my grievance.

Yours sincerely

Sufiya Halai

---

21   Cross-refer to the previous letter in this series at P2.2; Ms Denny has responded to the grievance by making up four weeks' enhanced pay but asserting that after four weeks the company has the right to impose the change.

Questionnaires

2.33   Since the point of questionnaires is to get information out of the employer, this subject is dealt with more fully at chapter 4 below. However, it is important to note in the context of what can or should be done before a claim starts that in discrimination cases, a potential claimant may wish to serve a questionnaire on the employer before taking the final decision whether to make a claim to the employment tribunal. Employees or unsuccessful job applicants who are considering a discrimination claim should read ETP 3 paras 4.17–4.22 at an early stage and think about whether they wish to serve a questionnaire before presenting a claim to the employment tribunal.

The claim and the employer's response

The formal claim

3.1   A complaint to the employment tribunal is made on form ET1 which was available for use from 1 October 2004 and will be compulsory for all claims made on or after 6 April 2005 (or more likely, 1 October 2005. See paras 1.63–1.64 above). The main narrative part of the complaint will be the content of boxes 5.1, 6.2, 7.1, 8.3 and 9: this is the claimant's opportunity to set out, briefly, the story of what her employer did that she considers unlawful. If the complaint is straightforward, this can simply be written or typed in the box provided, but it is also acceptable – and common practice – to write 'see attached' in the relevant box and provide a separate document headed 'details of complaint.'

3.2   The purpose of the formal claim[1] is to explain to the tribunal, and the other party, what it is that the employee complains of and why she says that it was unlawful. There is no need to set out the evidence in great detail at this stage, or to argue the law, but it is necessary to give the employer enough information that it knows what factual allegations it has to meet and what the legal nature of the complaint is. It is important to make explicit *all* the complaints that the employee wishes to raise at the initial stage: employment tribunal time limits are strict, and an amendment raising a new complaint will often be treated, for the purposes of the time limits, as a separate claim.[2]

3.3   How much detail is enough for the formal claim is a question of judgement in each case. It is always possible to tell a story in more detail: the length of a story can increase infinitely, like the length of a coastline, depending on the degree of magnification through which it is observed. 'I was dismissed and it was unfair and discriminatory' is clearly inadequate: the employer will need to know whether actual or constructive dismissal is alleged, whether the claimant complains that the reason for dismissal was inadmissible, or of the procedure adopted in dismissing or the substantive decision to dismiss or both, what kind of discrimination – sex, race, disability, sexual orientation, religion – is complained of and whether direct or indirect, and so on. On the

---

1   This used to be called the 'originating application'; it is now simply called 'the claim'. This attempt at plain English confusing as it blurs the distinction between the subject or subjects of complaint and the formal document that sets it out. In this book the expression 'the formal claim' is used to signify the document that starts employment tribunal proceedings and to distinguish the document from the subject-matter of the case.

2   See McMullen, Tuck and Criddle *Employment Tribunal Procedure* (ETP 3) (3rd edn, Legal Action Group, December 2004) paras 7.3–7.8.

other hand, a claim that gives verbatim accounts of conversations and quotes at length from the company handbook or minutes of meetings is probably going into a great deal of detail that could safely be left to the witness statement. A comparison between precedents P3.2 and P5.2 below illustrates the difference between the formal claim and the claimant's witness statement.

3.4   A good way of testing whether a draft claim has included all the essentials is to ask the question: if we prove everything we have asserted here, will we win the case? Or will the tribunal have to make other assumptions or find facts that we have not asserted in order to give the claimant an award? If the tribunal cannot make an award to the claimant without finding facts that the claimant has not asserted in the formal claim, then the claim has not included everything it should have. So for example to make an award for unauthorised deductions from wages, the tribunal will need to be satisfied: (i) that the employee was entitled under her contract of employment be paid certain amounts; (ii) that the employer paid her less than the amount to which she was entitled on one or more occasions; (iii) that she had not authorised the deduction(s) in writing; (iv) that there was no statutory or contractual authority for the deductions. All of these elements must be present as assertions in the formal claim.

The employment tribunal form

3.5   The new form, replacing the two-page IT1, is in use from 1 October 2004 and will be compulsory from 6 April 2005 (or more likely, 1 October 2005. See paras 1.63–1.64 above). It is called ET1, and it is nine pages long.

3.6   Most of the information asked for on the form should simply be written (or, if and when an online version of the form is made available, typed) on the form itself, and in simpler cases it will be possible to write all the necessary information on the form. However, where there is a story to tell that is at all complicated, it is still more convenient to attach separate sheets to the form. Any attached sheets should show clearly which sections of the form they relate to. It is suggested that claimants should write a note at box 10 ('Other information') indicating how many additional sheets are attached to the form.

3.7   The claim is likely to be rejected for any failure to provide compulsory information. Questions marked * on the form must be answered in all cases. Questions marked ● must be answered if relevant. If separate sheets are attached dealing with certain sections of the form, care should still be taken to ensure that any necessary tick-boxes or specific questions at those sections have been dealt with.

3.8   The first precedent opposite shows the entire form completed for a disability discrimination claim. The subsequent precedents only show the additional pages that would be attached to the form, but not the form itself.

P3.1 ET1 – disability discrimination

1 Your details

1.1	Title:	Mr ☐ Mrs ☐ Miss ☐ Ms ✓ Other
1.2*	First name (or names):	Pauline Cecilia
1.3*	Surname or family name:	Phelps
1.4	Date of birth (date/month/year):	27 / 9 /53 Are you: male? ☐ female? ✓
1.5*	Address:	14 Strawberry Field, Gotherington, Cheltenham, Gloucestershire Postcode GL52 1AB

You do not need to answer 1.6 and 1.7 if you have appointed a representative (see section 11).

1.6	Phone number **(where we can contact you during normal working hours)**:	
1.7	How would you prefer us to communicate with you?	Post ☐ Fax ☐ E-mail ☐ Fax: E-mail address:

2 Respondent's details

2.1*	Give the name of your employer or the organisation or person you are complaining about (the respondent).	Gentleman, Sharpe & Co Solicitors
2.2*	Address:	2 Abbey Close, Tewkesbury, Gloucestershire Postcode GL20 5AB
2.3	If you worked at an address different from the one you have given at 2.2, please give the full address.	 Postcode

2.4● If your complaint is against more than one respondent please give the names, addresses and postcodes of additional respondents.

3   Action before making a claim

3.1* Are you, or were you, an employee of the respondent?   Yes ☑   No ☐
If 'Yes', please now go straight to section 3.3.

3.2 Are you, or were you, a worker providing services to the respondent?   Yes ☐   No ☐
If 'Yes', please now go straight to section 4.
If 'No', please now go straight to section 6.

3.3● Is your claim, or part of it, about a dismissal by the respondent?   Yes ☐   No ☑
If 'No', please now go straight to section 3.5.

3.4● Is your claim about anything else, in addition to the dismissal?   Yes ☑   No ☐
If 'No', please now go straight to section 4.
If 'Yes', please answer questions 3.5 to 3.7 about the
non-dismissal aspects of your claim.

3.5● Have you put your complaint in writing to the respondent?

| Yes ☑ Please give the date you put it to them in writing. | 9 / 5 /2005 |
| No ☐ | |

If 'No', please now go straight to section 3.7.

3.6● Did you allow at least 28 days between the date you put your   Yes ☑   No ☐
complaint to the respondent and the date you sent us this claim?
If 'Yes', please now go straight to section 4.

3.7● Please explain why you did not put your complaint in writing to the respondent or,
if you did, why you did not allow at least 28 days before sending us your claim.
(In most cases, it is a legal requirement to take these procedural steps. Your claim
will not be accepted unless you give a valid reason why you did not have to meet
the requirement in your case. If you are not sure, you may want to get legal advice.)

See question 3.3 above. Confusingly, constructive dismissal does not count as
'dismissal' for the purposes of this question.

4 Employment details

4.1 Please give the following information if possible.

When did your employment start? 17 / 6 / 82

When did or will it end? / /

Is your employment continuing? Yes ✓ No ☐

4.2 Please say what job you do or did. **Secretary**

4.3 How many hours do or did you work each week? ..35...hours each week

4.4 How much are or were you paid?

Pay before tax £18,750 each **year**

Normal take-home pay (including overtime, commission, bonuses and so on) £15,688 each **year**

4.5 If your employment has ended, did you work (or were you paid for) a period of notice? Yes ☐ No ☐

If 'Yes', how many weeks or months did you work or were you paid for? ....weeks ....months

5 Unfair dismissal or constructive dismissal

Please fill in this section only if you believe you have been unfairly or constructively dismissed.

5.1 ● If you were dismissed by your employer, you should explain why you think your dismissal was unfair. If you resigned because of something your employer did or failed to do which made you feel you could no longer continue to work for them (constructive dismissal) you should explain what happened.

please see attached sheet

5   Unfair dismissal or constructive dismissal continued

5.1 continued

5.2   Were you in your employer's pension scheme?   Yes ✓   No ☐

5.3   If you received any other benefits from your employer, please give details.

5.4   Since leaving your employment have you got another job?   Yes ☐   No ✓
      If 'No', please now go straight to section 5.7.

5.5   Please say when you started (or will start) work.

n/a

5.6   Please say how much you are now earning (or will earn).   £   each

5.7   Please tick the box to say what you want if your case is successful:
      a   To get your old job back and compensation (reinstatement)   ☐
      b   To get another job with the same employer and compensation (re-engagement)   ☐
      c   Compensation only   ☐

6   Discrimination

Please fill in this section only if you believe you have been discriminated against.

6.1 Please tick the box or boxes to indicate what discrimination (including victimisation) you are complaining about:

Sex (including equal pay)	☐	Race	☐
Disability	✓	Religion or belief	☐
Sexual orientation	☐		

6.2 Please describe the incidents which you believe amounted to discrimination, the dates of these incidents and the people involved.

please see attached sheet

7   Redundancy payments

Please fill in this section only if you believe you are owed a redundancy payment.

7.1● Please explain why you believe you are entitled to this payment and set out the steps you have taken to get it.

8   Other payments you are owed

Please fill in this section only if you believe you are owed other payments.

8.1● Please tick the box or boxes to indicate that money is owed to you for:

unpaid wages?	☐
holiday pay?	☐
notice pay?	☐
other unpaid amounts?	☐

8.2   How much are you claiming?

Is this: before tax? ☐   after tax? ☐

8.3● Please explain why you believe you are entitled to this payment. If you have specified an amount, please set out how you have worked this out.

9 Other complaints

Please fill in this section only if you believe you have a complaint that is not covered elsewhere.

9.1 • Please explain what you are complaining about and why.
Please include any relevant dates.

10 Other information

10.1 Please do not send a covering letter with this form.
You should add any extra information you want us to know here.

[please insert the correct number] additional sheets are attached to this form

11 Your representative

Please fill in this section only if you have appointed a representative. If you do fill this section in, we will in future only send correspondence to your representative and not to you.

11.1 Representative's name:	Natalie Cummings
11.2 Name of the representative's organisation:	North London Law Centre
11.3 Address:	14 Border Street, Shoreditch, London
	Postcode EC2A 1AB
11.4 Phone number:	020 7123 4567
11.5 Reference:	NC/PP/0123
11.6 How would they prefer us to communicate with them?	Post ☐ Fax ☐ E-mail ☑ Fax: E-mail address: ncummings@northlondonlaw.org.uk

Please sign and date here

Signature: *Natalie Cummings*   Date: 20 / 6 / 2005

Data Protection Act 1998. We will send a copy of this form to the respondent(s) and Acas. We will put some of the information you give us on this form onto a computer. This helps us to monitor progress and produce statistics.

IN THE EMPLOYMENT TRIBUNAL   Case No_____ [3]
BRISTOL

BETWEEN

PAULINE PHELPS

Claimant

and

SHARPE, GENTLEMAN & CO SOLICITORS

Respondent

DETAILS OF CLAIM
ET1 SECTION 5.1

---

1. The claimant suffers from depression and agoraphobia and has a facial disfigurement. She has suffered from these conditions for all of her life. She has a disability within the meaning section 1 of the Disability Discrimination Act 1995.

2. The claimant was first employed by Sharpe, Gentleman & Co as a secretary in June 1982. It was a fundamental term of her contract of employment that the respondent would not act in a manner calculated to destroy the trust and confidence that should exist between employer and employee.[4]

3. The claimant was interviewed for the post by Alistair Gentleman and his then secretary, Margaret Church. At the interview she explained that because of her facial disfigurement she was shy with new people and would prefer to work somewhere quiet where she would not have to deal with the public. Mr Gentleman assured her that that would not be a problem. Before she started work she filled in a form for the Respondent about her general health. On the form she indicated that she had suffered from severe depression in the past, but that she was not at that time receiving any treatment.[5]

---

3 The case number is assigned by the tribunal once the claim is received, so the number cannot be given here because it is not known yet.

4 This is an implied term of every contract of employment. Where it is to be relied on it should preferably be spelled out like this.

5 This is included because it is important to establish that the respondent was aware of the claimant's disability.

4. The claimant worked for Mr Gentleman until his retirement in July 2004. She was happy in the role and Mr Gentleman made it clear that he was very satisfied with her work. She sat in an inner office adjoining Mr Gentleman's room on the third floor of the building where she never encountered clients. During the 22 years she worked for Mr Gentleman the claimant never took a day's sick leave. Her depression recurred from time to time and she took anti-depressants for three periods of a year or two each during this time, but she was able to continue working on each occasion. Mr Gentleman was aware of her condition and was understanding if she was depressed or tearful at work.

5. At the time of Mr Gentleman's retirement there were four part-ners in the firm, 10 further fee-earners, nine secretaries and two part-time receptionists. The claimant and another three secretaries each worked full-time for the four partners, and the other six formed a pool that shared the work generated by the 10 assistant solicitors. The appointment of one of the assistant solicitors, Madeleine Grey, as a new partner had been announced to take effect from September 2004.

6. Mr Sharpe told the claimant that he wanted her to join the pool of secretaries. Members of the pool worked in a large open-plan office on the ground floor of the building and they had to pass through the public waiting room to enter or leave the building or to get to the kitchenette or the toilet. The claimant told Mr Sharpe that she would find this difficult and stressful, but he refused to consider her suggestion that she should work full-time for Miss Grey.

7. The claimant started work in the pool on 16 August 2004. She found it very stressful from the first day. All of the other members of the pool were in their twenties, so at 50 the claimant was the eldest by more than 20 years. The working environment was noisy and the claimant found the other secretaries' conversations distracting. She also became convinced that they disliked her. During the week beginning 16 August, four different temporary secretaries worked in the pool for a day or two each.

8. On 20 August the claimant went to see Mr Sharpe to ask him to move her to a different room. She was distressed and in tears at several points during his meeting. She explained that the environment in the room used by the pool was very difficult for her and was affecting her ability to concentrate on her work, that she had recently started to have difficulty sleeping and that she was worried about the effect on her health. She said that she was afraid she would get depressed again. Mr Sharpe told her that he knew it

was a big change for her but that she had shown herself to be a survivor in the past and he was sure she would get used to it in time.

9. The claimant continued to work for the next few weeks, but became increasingly depressed and anxious. Finally on 20 October 2004 she had a panic attack on the way to work and was picked up by the police shaking and crying at the wheel of her car. She was admitted to hospital for two nights and was then signed off work for 12 weeks by her GP, who also prescribed anti-depressants.

10. When the claimant returned to work on 5 January 2005, the other members of the secretarial pool welcomed her warmly. They had arranged between them to place her desk in a corner partly screened from the rest of the room by pot plants, and she became aware that they were making a real effort to keep noise levels in the room down. The claimant felt better able to cope, but she continued to find the working environment stressful. She was often tearful by the end of the day, and she had difficulty sleeping. She started to work additional hours in the evenings to catch up on work that she felt she should have been able to do during the day.

11. On 17 February 2005 the claimant's GP wrote to Mr Sharpe explaining that the claimant's mental health was suffering from the conditions in which she was working and asking him to consider moving her to a different room. He explained that the claimant was taking anti-depressants and that he did not think it was likely that she would be able to stop taking them unless her work situation improved considerably. Mr Sharpe did not reply to this letter.

12. At the end of February 2005 one of the respondent's receptionists started a period of maternity leave and it was announced that her position would be covered during her absence by the pool secretaries on a rota. When the first rota was circulated on 1 March 2005, the claimant was horrified to see her name on it. She went to see Mr Sharpe in tears and told him that she could not possibly sit at the front desk dealing with members of the public. He told her that it would not be fair on the other secretaries if he took her off the rota and said that it would probably be good for her. He said that as she was obviously upset she should go home straight away that day and get a good night's sleep. He said he hoped she would feel calmer in the morning.

13. The claimant went to see her GP the next day and was signed off sick for 8 weeks.

14. The claimant sent the respondent a written statement of grievance on 9 May 2005 and a letter of resignation on 10 May 2005.

15. The respondent was in breach of the trust and confidence term of the claimant's contract of employment in the following ways:

   (i) in refusing to consider her suggestion that she might work full-time for Miss Grey, despite being aware of the reasons why she was bound to find the secretarial pool a difficult working environment;

   (ii) in refusing on 20 August 2004 to consider moving the claimant to work in a different room despite her evident distress;

   (iii) in failing to reply to the letter of 17 February 2005 from her GP;

   (iv) in imposing on her on 1 March 2005 the requirement that she provide reception cover on a rota despite knowing that this was bound to cause her extreme distress and was likely to be injurious to her health.

16. In presenting her resignation on 10 May 2005 the claimant has accepted the respondent's repudiation of her contract of employment and is therefore constructively dismissed.

17. The respondent's dismissal of the claimant was unfair, and the claimant seeks a basic award and compensation for unfair dismissal.

DETAILS OF CLAIM
ET1 SECTION 6.2

18. The following provisions, criteria or practices adopted by the respondent placed the claimant at a substantial disadvantage in comparison with persons who were not disabled:

  (i) the requirement from August 2004 that the claimant work as a 'pool' secretary instead of assigning her to a specific fee-earner or fee-earners;

  (ii) the requirement from August 2004 that the claimant work in the open-plan office shared by members of the pool;

  (iii) the requirement that she provide reception cover on a rota from March 2005.

19. It was the duty of the respondent to take such steps as it was reasonable in all the circumstances for it to have to take in order to prevent these matters from placing the claimant at a disadvantage. The respondent did not take any such steps and has accordingly discriminated against the claimant contrary to the Disability Discrimination Act 1995.

20. The claimant claims compensation for disability discrimination including damages for injury to feelings and interest.

Natalie Cummings
North London Law Centre
20 June 2005

P3.2 Whistleblowing dismissal

IN THE EMPLOYMENT TRIBUNAL   Case No_____
LONDON CENTRAL

BETWEEN

SAIFUR RAHMAN

Claimant

and

SAINT JULIAN'S HOSPITAL NHS TRUST

Respondent

PARTICULARS OF CLAIM
ET I SECTION 5.1

1. The claimant started working for the Hospital as a porter in December 2000. His job was to transport patients and equipment from one part of the hospital to another, as instructed by medical staff.
2. The claimant was employed on an initial probationary period of six months. In about May 2001 he attended a probationary review meeting at which his line manager, Mark Bowland, congratulated him on his performance and told him that his employment would be confirmed. He was given a letter confirming this the next day.
3. There were no further formal appraisals, but the claimant was never given any reason to believe that there were any concerns about his performance, and in November 2001 he was promoted to the position of supervising porter.
4. On 7 May 2005, the claimant was sent to Coventry Ward, a geriatric ward, to collect a patient for physiotherapy. As he reached the ward he heard the Ward Sister, Lorraine Winston, say to a junior nurse 'Give him some Somnex, it's the only way we'll get any peace round here. Don't put it on his chart or the doctor will create.' When the Sister saw that he had heard her she looked embarrassed and said 'Only joking.'
5. The claimant was concerned about this. He knew that Somnex was a powerful prescription sedative, and he thought it sounded as if a patient was being given it without a prescription to keep him quiet. He reported his concerns to Mr Bowland, but Mr Bowland refused to take any action.

6. On 12 May the claimant wrote to the Chief Executive of the Hospital about what he had overheard. This was a protected disclosure within the meaning of section 43A of the Employment Rights Act 1996.

7. On 17 May the Chief Executive replied promising that his allegation would be looked into, and on 24 May the claimant received a letter from Martin Ogunfowora, a human resources manager at the hospital, saying that his allegation had been thoroughly investigated and no evidence of unauthorised medication had been found.

8. On the same day, when the claimant visited the Coventry Ward to collect Mrs Goody for another physiotherapy session, Sister Winston said to him, 'You're toast.' He said 'What do you mean?' but she just said, 'You're toast. Just you wait.'

9. On 27 May 2005 the claimant received a letter dated 26 May from Maisie Lee, another human resources manager. The letter said that he had been accused of swearing at a Sister in the presence of patients and junior nurses and he was suspended with immediate effect and invited to a disciplinary hearing at 10.30 on 3 June 2005. It enclosed copies of statements from Sister Winston and two other nurses from the Coventry Ward. All the statements said that when Sister Winston had asked him why he was late to collect a patient on 24 May he had shouted, 'I've had enough of your fucking nagging. Why don't you take the fucking patient yourself if you're in such a hurry?' The statements said he had then wheeled the patient's pushchair out of the ward so fast that the patient had cried out in alarm, and slammed the door behind him.

10. At the disciplinary hearing on 3 June 2005 the panel refused to believe the claimant when he said that this allegation was completely untrue. When he tried to tell them about the concern he had raised about medication of a patient in the Coventry Ward the chairman of the panel insisted that that was a completely separate matter that had been investigated already and had no relevance to the disciplinary proceedings. When he asked them if they had spoken to Mrs Goody, one member of the panel said that that would have been completely inappropriate.

11. The chairman of the panel asked the claimant if he would apologise to Sister Winston if they decided not to dismiss him. The claimant said that he would not, because the allegation was a complete fabrication.

12. At the end of the disciplinary hearing the claimant was dismissed for gross misconduct. When he asked about an appeal, the chairman told him that the only way an appeal could succeed was if he offered to apologise to Sister Winston. The claimant was not prepared to admit untrue allegations, so when he received the dismissal letter he did not appeal.

13. When the claimant told Penny Short, a student nurse he was friendly with, about his dismissal, she told him that she had seen him collect a patient on 24 May and could have confirmed that he had collected Mrs Goody quietly and without incident. She said that no-one had asked her what she had seen or heard.

14. On 10 June 2005 the claimant started to look for advice on a potential unfair dismissal claim against the Hospital. Between 10 and 15 June he telephoned eight different advice agencies, most of which could not offer him an appointment at all. Finally the Care Workers' Advice Project (CWAP) offered him an appointment on 8 July 2005. He attended that appointment, but on arrival he was told that the adviser he was due to see was off work that day. He was not able to get another appointment until 22 July 2005. On 22 July, the adviser at the CWAP told him that he would have to appeal the decision to dismiss him and wait 28 days before he could present a claim. He was also told that he had until 2 December to present his claim to the tribunal.[6] The adviser also told him that public interest disclosure cases were very complicated and he ought to see a solicitor. She made an appointment for the claimant to see a solicitor at the North London Law Centre at 4pm on 9 September 2005.

15. Accordingly the claim is eight days' out of time. The claimant asserts that it was not reasonably practicable for him to present his claim by 2 September and that he has presented it promptly as soon as he was aware that it was late.

16. The reason or principal reason for the claimant's dismissal was that he had made a protected disclosure and his dismissal was therefore unfair.

17. Further or alternatively the claimant's dismissal was unfair because:

   (i) the respondent did not adequately investigate the allegations against the claimant, and in particular failed to make inquiries of either Mrs Goody or Penny Short;

   (ii) the disciplinary panel was not provided with full information about the reason why Sister Winston might have a grudge against him;

   (iii) he was denied an effective right of appeal.

18. The claimant seeks compensation for unfair dismissal.[7]

North London Law Centre
10 September 2004

6 This adviser has clearly heard something about the Employment Act 2002 (Dispute Resolution) Regulations 2004, but has misunderstood them very badly.

7 As Mr Rahman has been dismissed without notice for something that he has not done, he also has a claim for dismissal in breach of his contractual right to notice. This should be included at section 8 of the ET1 form.

P3.3 ET1 – race and sex discrimination

IN THE EMPLOYMENT TRIBUNAL   Case No_____
LONDON CENTRAL

BETWEEN

ABOSEDE OJO

Claimant

and

EAST LONDON RIGHTS SHOP

Respondent

PARTICULARS OF CLAIM
ET1 SECTION 6.2

1.   The claimant is a UK citizen of Nigerian national and ethnic origin. She is a qualified solicitor, admitted in January 2003, and she has worked both before and after qualifying as an immigration adviser. Since March 2002 she has worked full time as an immigration caseworker for the Haringey Refugee Centre, where she earns £21,800 per year.

2.   The respondent is a charity that provides free legal advice in immigration, housing, welfare rights, and employment.

3.   On 6 July 2005 the respondent's advertisement for an immigration solicitor appeared in the *Guardian*. The advertisement stated that the minimum requirements for the post were (i) qualification as a solicitor; (ii) at least three years' experience of immigration advice and casework. The advertised salary was £29,200. The closing date for applications was 5 August and interviews were to be held on 12 August.

4.   The claimant felt that the job was ideally suited to her, and it was within walking distance of her home. She also felt that in terms of her career development it was time for her to move on to a job that required a qualified solicitor. She requested an application pack, and on 22 July 2005 she hand-delivered her application to the respondent.

5.   By 12 August, the claimant had heard nothing further from the respondent, so she concluded that she had been unsuccessful in her application. She was very disappointed not to have been

short-listed. On 18 August, she telephoned the respondent to ask for feedback on her application. The man she spoke to was abrupt, but told her that her application was badly written and the panel had not found her account of her experience convincing. When she asked him to specify what they had not believed, he said that he was not prepared to continue the conversation. The claimant found this conversation extremely humiliating.

6. Towards the end of September 2005, the claimant met David Burn by chance. The claimant had known Mr Burn when he had worked for her as a volunteer at the Haringey Refugee Centre between April 2003 and May 2004. She discovered in conversation that he had been the successful candidate for the post for which she had applied with the respondent.

7. Mr Burn was only admitted as a solicitor in January 2004 and has not previously worked full-time, paid or unpaid, as an immigration adviser or caseworker.

8. The claimant has substantially more experience of immigration advice and casework than Mr Burn. The claimant believes in failing to short-list and/or appoint her to the post the respondent has discriminated against her on grounds of race or national or ethnic origin and/or on grounds of sex.

9. The claimant seeks compensation for race and/or sex discrimination, including damages for injury to feelings.

Natalie Cummings
North London Law Centre
21 October 2005

P3.4 ET1 – minimum wage

IN THE EMPLOYMENT TRIBUNAL   Case No_____
LONDON CENTRAL

BETWEEN

MICHAEL CHART

Claimant

and

JACK-IN-A-BOX OPERA LIMITED

Respondent

PARTICULARS OF CLAIM
ET1 SECTION 8.3

1. The claimant is a singer. On 11 October 2004 he auditioned for a production of *The Pirates of Penzance* put on by the respondent. At the end of the audition, the respondent's artistic director, Peter Jake, offered the claimant a part in the chorus for an initial six week run with the possibility of extension. The claimant accepted this offer.
2. Mr Jake explained that as a chorus member the claimant would be required for six evening performances and two matinees a week. Each performance would last for two hours, and the claimant would be paid £6 per hour.
3. The claimant was told to come to the theatre each afternoon of the week beginning 25 October 2004 for rehearsals. Performances would start on Monday 1 November. The claimant inquired about payment for rehearsals and Mr Jake said that there were separate arrangements for rehearsals which the theatre manager, Martin Joseph would explain.
4. The claimant attended rehearsals during the week beginning 25 October from 2pm until 5pm on Monday to Wednesday. On Thursday and Friday he was required to attend at 12.30 for make-up and costume because these were dress rehearsals.
5. Mr Joseph was not present for the rehearsals until Friday. On Friday the claimant asked him what he would be paid for rehearsal time. Mr Joseph told the him that it was not company policy to pay for rehearsals.

6. At the end of the week all members of the cast were told that they were required at the theatre from 6pm for a 7.30pm call and on Thursdays and Saturdays from 1pm for a 2.30pm call. The performance would last for two hours plus a twenty minute interval. They would be paid £12 per call.

7. The claimant sang in the production throughout the six week run, which was not extended. He usually left the theatre after an evening performance at about 10.05 or 10.10pm, and never earlier than 10pm. He was not free after the matinees until at least 5pm so he worked at least 32 hours each week of the run. He was paid £96 for each week, so he was paid £3 per hour. During the rehearsal week he was required to work 18 hours for no pay.

8. The claimant was entitled to be paid a minimum of £4.85 per hour throughout his working hours in accordance with the National Minimum Wage Act 1999 and Regulations under it. He did not at any time give the respondent written permission to make deductions from his wages, and he has accordingly suffered unauthorised deductions from his wages contrary to section 13 of the Employment Rights Act 1996.

9. The claimant seeks an order that the respondent repay the sums deducted, namely:

$18 \times £4.85 = £87.30$

$32 \times (£4.85 - £3) = 32 \times £1.85 = £59.20$

Total: £146.50

North London Law Centre
12 January 2005

P3.5 ET I – sex discrimination

IN THE EMPLOYMENT TRIBUNAL   Case No_____
LONDON CENTRAL

BETWEEN

YASMIN CREASEY

Claimant

and

BRISTOL ADVOCACY PROJECT

Respondent

PARTICULARS OF CLAIM
ET I SECTION 6.2

1. The claimant was employed by the Bristol Advocacy Project (the respondent) as a receptionist and filing clerk. She was told on starting work that she was on a nine month probationary period from 19 April 2004, but no arrangements were made for appraisal or review.
2. On 15 June 2004, the claimant told her line manager, Mary Smiling, that she was four months pregnant.
3. As far as the claimant was aware, her work was satisfactory. All her colleagues seemed friendly towards her and no-one made any complaints.
4. The claimant started her maternity leave on 1 November 2004. On Friday 29 October, her last day at work, her colleagues gave her a card and a bunch of flowers. Mrs Smiling wished her good luck and said 'See you next year.'
5. On 7 January 2005, the claimant received a letter dated 5 January from Reuben Fitzwell, Director of the respondent, informing her that as her performance during her probationary period had been unsatisfactory, her employment would not be confirmed and would accordingly come to an end on 14 January.
6. The respondent discriminated against the claimant on grounds of her sex in that the reason or the principal reason for her dismissal was that she was absent on maternity leave.
7. Alternatively the respondent discriminated against the claimant on grounds of her sex in that, by reason of her absence on maternity

leave, it assessed her probationary performance over the first 6½ months of her employment[8] instead of over the full 9 months.

8. The claimant seeks compensation for sex discrimination including damages for injury to feelings and interest.

ET1 SECTION 5.1

9. The claimant's dismissal was automatically unfair in that the reason or the principal reason for her dismissal was her absence on maternity leave.

10. The claimant seeks compensation for unfair dismissal.

North London Law Centre
23 March 2005

---

8 Ms Creasey has no need to lodge an internal grievance in relation to her complaint that the dismissal itself was discriminatory, because the grievance procedures do not apply to dismissals. This alternative complaint is that an act *other than* dismissal was also discriminatory, so she will have had to present a grievance in relation to that and wait 28 days before presenting her claim to the employment tribunal.

P3.6 ET I – equal pay

IN THE EMPLOYMENT TRIBUNAL   Case No_____
LONDON SOUTH

BETWEEN

ANNE COOPER

Claimant

and

THE BIG OFFICE SUPPLIERS LIMITED

Respondent

DETAILS OF CLAIM
ET I SECTION 6.2

1. The respondent is a supplier of stationery and general office equipment by mail order.
2. The claimant has been employed by the respondent as Manager of their Office Furniture Department since January 1996.
3. The claimant is employed on like work with Andrew Blight, her predecessor.
4. Alternatively the claimant is employed on work of equal or greater value to that performed by:

   (a) Marcus Plange, Manager of the respondent's Stationery Department;
   (b) Andrew Sharpe, Marketing Department; and
   (c) Timothy Carter, a member of her staff employed part-time in the Office Furniture Department and part-time in the Stationery Department.

5. Andrew Blight, Marcus Plange, Andrew Sharpe and Timothy Carter are referred to collectively as 'the comparators' in this document.
6. The claimant's contract of employment must be deemed to include an equality clause having the effect that if any term of her contract of employment is less favourable than the corresponding term of any of the comparators' contracts, her contract is deemed to be modified so as not to be less favourable.
7. The claimant complains of contraventions of the equality term in relation to each of the four comparators.

Particulars

(a) The claimant was at the time of her appointment as Manager offered £16,800 per annum;

(b) the claimant believes that OP, AS and JB were all paid in the region of £23,000 per annum around the time of her appointment;

(c) the claimant believes that TC, a member of her staff, has been paid more than her since his appointment to her department in about May or June 1997;

(d) Mr S had a company car when he worked for the respondent, but the claimant has at no time been offered a car;

(e) From 1997 until 1999, the respondent refused to pay the claimant's mobile telephone bills although it paid bills in comparable circumstances for all four comparators.

8. The claimant will provide further particulars of these comparisons after disclosure of documents.

Sex discrimination[9]

9. The claimant believes that the respondent has discriminated against her on grounds of her sex in paying her less than it would have paid a man in the same employment.

10. The claimant has been distressed and upset by the respondent's treatment of her. Her confidence in applying for other jobs in the sector has been undermined by the fact that she has been ashamed to admit to another prospective employer how little she has been paid.

11. The claimant claims compensation for financial loss caused by the respondent's discrimination that is not compensated by her claim under the equality clause.

North London Law Centre
17 January 2005

---

9 The Equal Pay Act (EqPA) 1970 and the Sex Discrimination Act (SDA) 1975 are carefully drafted so that any claim that can be made under the EqPA 1970 is excluded from the SDA 1975. However, the EqPA 1970 only provides a mechanism by which a claimant can claim to be paid what her comparator is or was paid. This creates difficulties for a claimant whose comparator is her predecessor: the EqPA 1970 will not compensate her fully for the difference between what she has been paid and what her predecessor would have been paid (including pay rises) had he remained. Hence a separate SDA 1975 claim.

Rejection of the claim

3.9 Under the Procedure Rules[9a] in force from 1 October 2004, the tribunal will reject a claim in four circumstances:

- in all claims presented on or after 6 April 2005 (or more likely, 1 October 2005. See paras 1.63–1.64 above), where the claim is not presented on the prescribed form (ET 1);
- where any of the required information has not been included (that is, where any question marked * on the form has not been answered, and where any relevant question marked ● has not been answered);
- where the tribunal does not have power to consider the claim; or
- if a grievance procedure is required to be followed before the claim is presented, where either no grievance has been sent to the employer or the claim is made before 28 days have elapsed since the grievance was presented.

3.10 The potential rejection of a claim means that it is now very important indeed to present claims as early as possible,[10] subject to the need in some cases to wait 28 days after sending the employer a written statement of grievance. If a claim is rejected as premature because the claimant has not presented a grievance or has not waited 28 days after doing so, rejection will not be disastrous: the claimant will simply have to lodge a grievance and then present the claim again in due course, and the premature presentation of the claim will have had the result of extending time for a further three months from the normal time limit for the claim.[11]

3.11 Rejection on the grounds that the tribunal does not have power to consider the claim need not be fatal either: if the tribunal's entitlement to consider the claim[12] is in doubt, then that question will have to be considered at some point, so there is no particular disadvantage to the claimant in having it made the subject of a decision at a preliminary stage. If the claimant believes that the claim has been wrongly rejected on this ground, he or she should apply for review of the decision under rule 34 of the Procedure Rules, and if necessary appeal to the Employment Appeal Tribunal.[13]

9a Employment Tribunals (Constitution and Rules of Procedure) Regulations 2004 SI 1861 Sch 1.
10 See paras 1.63–1.64 above.
11 See para 1.59 above.
12 Often called 'jurisdiction'.
13 See generally chapters 11 and 12 below.

P3.7 Application for review of the decision to reject a claim

In Mr Rahman's unfair dismissal case,[14] the tribunal has rejected his claim as being presented late. He applies for a review of that decision because although he admits that the claim is late, he says that it was not reasonably practicable for him to present it in time.

The Regional Secretary
London Central Employment Tribunal
19–29 Woburn Place
London WC1X 0LU
My ref NC/ir123
Your ref 123456/04

FAX ONLY 020 7273 8686

27 September 2005

Dear Madam

Saifur Rahman v St Julian's Hospital NHS Trust

Thank you for your letter of 26 September 2005.[15]

I wish to apply for a review of the decision to reject the claim on the grounds that it was wrongly made as a result of an administrative error and/or that the interests of justice require a review.

Administrative error
The narrative section at box 5.2 of the form ET1 explains that Mr Rahman was unable to present his claim in time because of difficulty, despite his strenuous efforts, in getting prompt and accurate advice. He asserts that in the circumstances it was not reasonably practicable for him to present his claim in time. It seems likely that the explanation given by Mr Rahman for the lateness of his claim on his ET1 form was simply overlooked when the decision was made to reject the claim on the ground that the tribunal lacked jurisdiction to hear it.

---

14 See P3.2 above.
15 The notification that the claim was rejected.

The interests of justice

The account given by Mr Rahman of the reasons why his claim was presented late is credible and convincing. The question whether it was reasonably practicable for him to present his claim is one that cannot fairly be resolved against him without hearing his oral evidence on the subject. In the circumstances it is suggested that the interests of justice require a review in order for this question to be properly explored.

Yours faithfully

Natalie Cummings

Rejection for lack of relevant required information

3.12   The potential for rejection on the ground that the form does not contain all the relevant required information is the most troubling ground of rejection for claimants. A failure by simple oversight to include one piece of required information can have the result that the claim is rejected. If the claim has been presented close to the deadline, it may be too late to correct an error of this nature by the time the tribunal has communicated its decision to reject.

3.13   This means that the form has to be completed with very great care, with particularly close attention paid to each question marked * or ●. Where the claimant is in any doubt whether a particular question marked ● is relevant, she should answer it to the best of her ability in case the tribunal takes the view that it is. If at all possible, claim forms should be presented to the tribunal several weeks before the expiry of the relevant deadline so as to allow time for presentation of a corrected claim within time if the original claim is rejected.

3.14   If a claim is rejected on this ground close to the deadline with the result that the corrected claim is inevitably late, it may sometimes be possible to persuade the tribunal that in all the circumstances (especially if the claimant was not receiving any advice at the time of the first attempt) it was not reasonably practicable to present the claim, or that it is just and equitable to extend time.[16] This possibility should certainly not be relied on, however.

16 For some claims (for example, unfair dismissal) it is necessary to persuade the tribunal that it was not reasonably practicable to present the claim in time if time is to be extended; in other cases (for example, discrimination claims) it is only necessary to persuade the tribunal that in all the circumstances it is 'just and equitable' to extend time.

Amendment of the claim

3.15   Sometimes it becomes clear, after a claim has been started, that the original claim form does not adequately explain the basis of the claim, or that additional claims need to be added. The tribunal has power under rule 10(q) of the Procedure Rules to permit amendment of a claim or response. There is a significant amount of case law on the question of whether and in what circumstances the tribunal should permit a claimant to amend his or her claim. The detail of that is beyond the scope of this book,[17] but some tactical points are worth making here.

3.16   Broadly, amendments close to the hearing will be harder to secure than amendments made soon after the claim was started, and more substantial amendments will be harder to secure than minor ones. If a claim has to be presented in a hurry because the time limit is close, it is legitimate to draft the bare bones of the claim in order to present it in time, but if this is done, an amendment fleshing out the claim should be forwarded to the tribunal as soon as possible. In these circumstances a covering letter with the original claim explaining that further details will follow shortly, and possibly suggesting that the respondent should not be required to present its response until after that step has been taken, is a good idea.

3.17   This tactic should only be used if there is genuine urgency. Where it is used, the claim, however brief, must make it clear what is the nature of the complaint. Some employee advisers believe that if a client presents with a complaint about discrimination, a claim merely alleging 'race discrimination' or 'sex discrimination', etc, should always be faxed to the tribunal the same day, with a promise of 'full details to follow,' to guard against the possibility that the time limit in respect of any particular act may be about to expire. This is probably futile, and certainly dangerous. A claim that gives no clue as to what is the nature of the discrimination alleged is at risk of being rejected outright as invalid, and will do nothing to preserve the claimant's position.

3.18   If the claim really has to be presented in a great hurry (for example, where the claimant comes to a law centre for advice on the last day of the limitation period), it may be very short, but it should not lack content altogether. The following words in boxes 5.1 and 6.2 of the claim form should be sufficient to start Mrs Creasy's claim.[17a]

---

17   See ETP 3 chapter 7.
17a See P3.5 above.

> **5.1**
> I was dismissed on 14 January 2005, during my maternity leave.
> I believe that the reason for my dismissal was that I was on
> maternity leave, so my dismissal was automatically unfair.
>
> **6.2**
> I believe that the reasons for my dismissal was that I was on
> maternity leave, so my employer's conduct in dismissing me
> amounted to sex discrimination.

This, on the other hand, is inadequate.

> **5.1**
> Unfair dismissal: full details to follow.
>
> **6.2**
> Sex discrimination: full details to follow

Late amendments

3.19   The main danger with a late application for amendment is that it will
be refused on the basis that there is insufficient time before the hearing
for the respondent to deal with the changes. The other danger is that
it will be granted, but that the case will be postponed or adjourned[18] in
order to allow the respondent to deal with the changes. In the circumstances a costs or preparation time order may be made in favour
of the respondent.

3.20   Under rule 40 of the Procedure Rules, the tribunal has power to
order one party to pay to the other side the costs incurred by reason of
a postponement or adjournment, and in contrast to the general power
to award costs, there is no requirement that the tribunal should be
satisfied that the paying party has behaved unreasonably or improperly
before making such an order. Tribunals will no doubt be slow to make
costs orders except against parties they consider to have been at fault
in some way, but this is a reason for particular caution when applying
for permission to amend.

18 A hearing is usually said to have been 'postponed' if it has been put off to a later
date before it started; if the parties attend on the hearing date and it is then
decided either before the hearing starts or part-way through it that it needs to
be put off to another day, it is said to have been 'adjourned.'

3.21   An amendment to add a completely new claim is likely to run into time limit difficulties[19] and may well require a postponement of the hearing in order to permit the respondent to deal with the new allegations. The claimant should be realistic about this: the best chance of heading off a cost application in these circumstances will lie in a co-operative approach.[20]

3.22   A worse complication that could now be caused by an amendment to add a new claim is the possibility that it will give rise to the need to raise a fresh grievance and wait 28 days before seeking the amendment. It is to be hoped that faced with this kind of situation tribunals will be prepared to take a broad view of the question whether a particular 'matter' has been raised by way of a grievance and will not insist on proceedings being held up while a fresh grievance procedure runs its course, but this cannot be guaranteed. Claimants will have to make a tactical decision whether to raise this possibility and ask for a case management discussion[21] on the question, or to keep quiet about it and hope that it is overlooked by the tribunal and the respondent. If the amendment constitutes a large proportion of the total claim, it may be better to raise the difficulty and invite the tribunal to deal with it at an early stage than to run the risk that the respondent thinks of it just before the hearing – or even during it – and this causes delay and inconvenience on all sides.

3.23   An application to amend that changes the way the claimant puts her case without starting a fresh complaint should address if possible both the reasons why the amendment could not have been made sooner, and the impact it will have on the respondent's preparation.

---

19 See ETP 3 paras 7.4–7.7.
20 See 3.2 below.
21 See glossary and paras 7.4–7.9 below.

DO3.1 Application for permission to amend to change the basis of the claim

Identification of the nature of the application – that is, application for permission to amend under rule 10(q) of the Procedure Rules

Terms of amendment sought

Explanation why the claim could not have been/was not pleaded in this way originally and/or why the amendment could not have been sought earlier

Reason(s) why the application should be granted including explanation of how this will enable the tribunal to deal with the case efficiently and fairly

Any consequential matters – for example, request for consequential postponement, or suggestion if appropriate that the respondent should have extra time for some step it needs to take

Instructions for the respondent on when and how to oppose the application

P3.8 Application for permission to amend the basis of the claim

The claimant here has applied unsuccessfully for a job with the respondent. She believes that she is better qualified than the successful male candidate, and she has already presented a claim form complaining of direct sex discrimination. She has now discovered that the respondent has a policy that gives internal candidates preferential treatment over external candidates. The Department employs far more men than women in positions from which they could realistically apply for a post of the relevant kind, so she now seeks to amend her claim to include a complaint of indirect discrimination.

The Regional Secretary
London Central Employment Tribunal
19-29 Woburn Place
London WC1X 0LU

My ref: NC/ir 123
Your ref: 123456/04

FAX ONLY 020 7273 8686

21 January 2005

Dear Madam

Annabel Firsk v Department for Administrative Affairs

1. Request for permission to amend the claim

I should be grateful if you would put before a Chairman my request for permission under rule 10(q) of the Employment Tribunal Rules of Procedure to amend this claim to insert at the end of the narrative at box 6.2 the following:[22]

'The minimum requirements for the post of Senior Operational Officer were (a) at least two years' relevant experience and (b) a postgraduate qualification in Administrative Policy.

---

22   Or the text of the amendment could be attached as a separate sheet or sheets.

The respondent's *Recruitment and Retention Policy* states, at paragraph 6.1:

> All posts will be advertised internally and externally. Internal candidates will be considered first. Any internal candidate will be considered on the basis of his written application together with the comments of his line manager and one other internal referee at the candidate's option. Interviews may be held.
>
> If the Recruiting Manager is satisfied that the needs of the Department will be met by the appointment of an internal candidate, he will appoint an internal candidate without considering external candidates. In this event external candidates will be informed that their application has been unsuccessful.
>
> If no appointment is made from among internal candidates, the Recruiting Manager will proceed to consider external candidates. External candidates will be considered on the basis of their written application and their performance at interview. References will be taken up only after a provisional decision to appoint has been made.

Of those already in the respondent's employment capable of meeting the minimum requirements for the post, 100% were men at the material time. It follows[23] that the respondent's policy of preferring internal over external candidates was a provision, criterion or practice which was such that it was to the detriment of a considerably larger proportion of women than of men, and it was to the detriment of the claimant because it meant that she was not permitted to compete on equal terms with internal candidates, and the respondent's policy was therefore indirectly discriminatory against the claimant on grounds of sex.'

It was not possible for the claimant to plead her complaint in this way when she presented her original claim because she was not aware of the respondent's preferential treatment of internal candidates until [12 January 2005] when the respondent provided a copy of its recruitment procedure.

This amendment will assist the tribunal in dealing with the case efficiently and fairly because (i) it clarifies the issues between the parties; and (ii) the prejudice to the claimant from a refusal of the application and

---

23 It is not completely clear that it does, but it is arguable.

depriving her of a significant part of her claim would be less than any prejudice to the respondent flowing from permitting the amendment.[24]

2. Request for consequential postponement

If this amendment is permitted, it is clear that the respondent will need time to make consequential amendments to its response, and both parties will have to reconsider what evidence they should call. In the circumstances I suggest that the hearing listed for 10-15 January 2005 should be postponed. It might be helpful to list the case for a directions hearing instead on the first day of that appointment.

3. Objection by the respondent[24a]

This letter is copied to the respondent. The respondent should note that if it objects to the application, it must write to the tribunal within seven days of receiving this letter, or before the date of the hearing (whichever date is the earlier) explaining the reasons for its objection,[25] and should copy that letter to me.[26] Rule 11 of the Procedure Rules has been complied with in relation to this application.

Yours faithfully

Natalie Cummings

---

24 Rule 11(3) of the Procedure Rules requires a statement of 'how the application will assist the chairman or tribunal in dealing with the case efficiently and fairly' to be included in every interlocutory application. The provision is ill-judged, and inevitably invites bland and formulaic treatment. This statement or something very like it will be adequate for most if not all amendment applications.

24a This paragraph, or something to the same effect, is required by rule 11 if the claimant is legally represented, and desirable in any event.

25 This quotes rule 11(4)(b). The rule is unsatisfactory, because it is not clear whether the alternative date to 'within seven days of receiving' the letter is merely 'before the hearing' or 'seven days before the hearing'. However, the party applying for an order cannot be faulted for giving the respondent ambiguous instructions if the ambiguity is the ambiguity of the rules themselves.

26 Or, where there are more than two parties, to all of them.

P3.9 Application for amendment to add an alternative basis for the claim

The Regional Secretary
London Central Employment Tribunal
19–29 Woburn Place
London WC1X 0LU

My ref: NC/ir 123
Your ref: 123456/04

FAX ONLY 020 7273 8686

15 March 2005

Dear Madam

Michael O'Donnell v Robert Selassiee t/a Flower Power

I should be grateful if you would put before a Chairman my request for permission to amend the claim in this case to delete the contents of box 5.1[27] and substitute the following:

'1. The claimant started work as a florist at the respondent's shop on 7 October 2003.
2. There was no written contract, but it was a fundamental term of the oral contract, alternatively an implied term, that the claimant was employed to work as a florist in the shop. His duties were making up bouquets and wreaths, selling flowers, advising customers on their purchases, unpacking and displaying new deliveries and ordering flowers from wholesalers. He enjoyed the work and was good at it.
3. It was an implied term of the claimant's contract of employment that the respondent would not conduct himself in a way calculated to destroy the mutual trust and confidence that should exist between employer and employee.
4. The claimant travels to work by Tube on the Northern Line, which is often subject to delays. The respondent was mostly understanding about this, but during the week beginning 15 November 2004 the claimant was delayed on four out of five

---

27 It will often be possible simply to add a paragraph or two to the existing text, but sometimes the end result will be clearer if the whole claim is rewritten.

days. When the claimant arrived 10 minutes late for work on Thursday 18 November, the respondent complained about his time-keeping and threatened to put him on deliveries if he did not improve.

5. On Monday 22 November the claimant left home half an hour earlier than usual in order to be sure to be at work on time, but his train was held up in a tunnel for 45 minutes because of a bomb alert. When he arrived at work 20 minutes late, the respondent told him that he was on deliveries this week. The claimant objected, and the respondent said 'You can either do the deliveries or you can bugger off and not come back.' The claimant was not prepared to be employed as a delivery driver, so he collected his coat and went home.

6. In the circumstances the respondent summarily dismissed the claimant from his job as a florist without any prior formal warnings and without following any disciplinary procedure. The dismissal was accordingly unfair.

7. Alternatively, in ordering the claimant to work for as a delivery driver, the respondent was in breach of the terms of the claimant's contract of employment referred to at paragraphs 2 and 3 above. In leaving the premises on 22 November and not returning, the claimant resigned in response to the respondent's fundamental breach of his contract of employment and was accordingly constructively dismissed. The dismissal was not preceded by any formal warnings or any disciplinary procedure and was accordingly unfair.

8. The claimant seeks basic and compensatory awards for unfair dismissal.

It was not possible to make this amendment earlier because the claimant presented his claim without the benefit of legal advice. His belief was that he had been constructively dismissed. It was not until he instructed me, at our first appointment on 11 March 2005 that I was in a position to advise him that his case is probably better characterised as actual dismissal.

The facts alleged by Mr O'Donnell are simple. Clearly these facts, if proved, are close to the borderline between actual and constructive dismissal. The factual allegations appeared in full in the original claim. The respondent has denied that Mr Selassiee issued an ultimatum and claims that he simply asked Mr O'Donnell, as a favour, to cover the deliveries that day but made no attempt to insist that he should do so. According to the respondent, Mr O'Donnell lost his temper for no obvious reason and stormed out.

The amendment, if permitted, will make little or no difference to the manner in which the respondent puts its case or the witnesses it needs to call. In the circumstances I suggest that although the hearing is only 3 weeks away, there can be no need for a postponement or for any consequential amendment of the respondent's response.

This amendment will assist the tribunal in dealing with the case efficiently and fairly because it would be unfair to the claimant if the claim were defeated by reason of a technical failure to characterise the dismissal correctly at the outset.

This letter is copied to the respondent. The respondent should note that if it objects to the application, it must write to the tribunal within seven days of receiving this letter, or before the date of the hearing (whichever date is the earlier)[28] explaining the reasons for its objection, and should copy that letter to me.[29] Rule 11 of the Procedure Rules has been complied with in relation to this application.

Yours faithfully

Natalie Cummings

The schedule of loss

3.24 It is advisable for the claimant to quantify his or her loss as early as possible in proceedings. There are two main reasons for this. First, the earlier the respondent knows the size of the claim, the greater the chances of realistic negotiations: the respondent will be more inclined to settle before it has spent substantial sums of money on legal fees than after. Secondly, if the respondent knows at an early stage what its maximum risk is, it is better equipped to judge how much it should spend on defending the claim. If the claimant wishes to argue subsequently, in opposing a costs application, that the respondent's legal costs were disproportionate to the size of the claim, she will be far better placed if she quantified the claim at an early stage.

---

28 See note 23 above.
29 See note 24 above.

3.25   General guidance on how to quantify claims can be found at chapters 18 and 19 of *Employment Law: an adviser's handbook.*[30] A schedule of loss should show clearly how the sum of money claimed is calculated, and should explain any assumptions made.

P3.10 Schedule of loss – unfair dismissal

IN THE EMPLOYMENT TRIBUNAL   Case No 123456/2004
LONDON CENTRAL

BETWEEN

JOSEPH CLARKSON

Claimant

and

NEW PIN CLEANING SERVICES LIMITED

Respondent

SCHEDULE OF LOSS

1. Compensation for unfair dismissal

(a) *Basic award*[31]
   a week's pay: £193.60
   2 years' continuous employment
   age at EDT:[32] 64
   multiplier:[33] 3

   3 × £193.60   £580.80

---

30   (ELAH 5); Lewis (5th edn, Legal Action Group, 2003).
31   See generally ELAH 5 paras 18.15–18.19.
32   Effective date of termination.
33   The multiplier is a figure derived from the claimant's age and lenght of service: ELAH 5 para 18.16.

(b) *Compensatory award*[34]
    take home pay: £170 p/w
    11 May 2004 to 1 October 2005
    20 weeks   £3,400.00

    less
    2 weeks' painting and decorating
    work @ £250 per week
    £500.00

    loss of statutory rights[35]   £300.00

2. TUPE Regulation 11 award[36]

    13 weeks' pay @ £193.60   £2,516.80

3. Section 13 unauthorised deductions[37]

    2 weeks' @ £170   £340.00

    TOTAL   £6,637.60

---

34 See generally ELAH 5 paras 18.24–18.27, but note that the House of Lords has now ruled that in an ordinary unfair dismissal case there can be no compensation for injury to feelings: *Dunnachie v Kingston upon Hull City Council* [2004] IRLR 727.

35 See ELAH 5 para 18.38.

36 An award to employees where the undertaking in which they are employed is transferred and the employer has not complied with the duty under the Transfer of Undertakings (Protection of Employees) Regulations 1981 to inform and consult employee representatives.

37 That is, unauthorised deductions from wages contrary to Employment Rights Act 1996 s13. See generally ELAH 5 paras 4.5–4.24.

P3.11 Schedule of loss – race discrimination

IN THE EMPLOYMENT TRIBUNAL   Case No 123456/2004
LONDON CENTRAL

BETWEEN
                        ABOSEDE OJO
                                                Claimant

                            and

                EAST LONDON RIGHTS SHOP
                                                Respondent

                    _____
                    SCHEDULE OF LOSS
                    _____

Lost earnings

net pay in current job: £16,394.18 p/a = £315.28 p/w
net pay in job applied for: £21,352.18 p/a = £410.61 p/w
net weekly loss = £95.34

net loss from 12 September 2004[†]
to hearing date on 6 February 2006: 21 weeks

21 × £95.34   £2,002.14

travel expenses: £20.20 per week
21 × 20.20   £424.20

Subtotal   £2428.34

interest @ 7% since mid-point date
10 November 2005[38]
47p per day
0.47 × 89   £41.83

[†] The claimant's current employment is terminable on 4 weeks' notice.

---

38 See ETP 3 para 20.9.

Injury to feelings

say £5,000.00[39]

interest since 12 August 2005 @ 7%[40]
178 days @ 96p per day   £170.88

Total   £7,641.05

---

39 The award for injury to feelings is assessed by the tribunal and is not capable of
    being calculated, but it is sensible to put in the figure for which the claimant
    proposes to argue into the schedule of loss. See ELAH 5 paras 19.13–19.25 for
    guidance on how to assess a realistic figure.
40 See ETP 3 paras 20.8 and 20.9.

CHAPTER 4

Getting information and responding to requests

Introduction

4.1 There are essentially five ways of getting information from the other side in the context of employment tribunal proceedings. Three come from the employment tribunals' general power to manage proceedings. The fourth, available in discrimination cases only, is the service of a questionnaire. The fifth is a subject access request under the Data Protection Act 1998.[1]

4.2 This chapter starts with general guidance about the first three of these taken together before considering disclosure of documents at paras 4.15–4.22, requests for additional information at para 4.36 and requests for written answers at para 4.37 separately. Requests for orders for all three categories of information are then taken together at paras 4.38–4.39. The last two sections of the chapter deal with questionnaires and the Data Protection Act (DPA) 1998 and then providing information to the respondent.

The tribunal's powers

4.3 The relevant powers of the tribunal are contained in Employment Tribunals (Constitution and Rules of Procedure) Regulations 2004 Sch 1, r10(2)(b),(d) and (f)[2] which give the tribunals specific powers to order a party to provide additional information, to disclose documents or information to another party, or to provide written answers to questions put by the tribunal.

4.4 The term 'additional information' at rule 10(2)(b) replaces the expression 'further particulars' in the old rules. This is presumably an attempt at 'plain English',[3] but it is an unfortunate one because it

---

1 A sixth, of which claimants may occasionally be able to take advantage is a request under the Freedom of Information Act (FOIA) 2000, in force from 1 January 2005. A claimant cannot demand personal information about him or herself under the FOIA 2000, but it is possible to imagine circumstances in which an FOIA 2000 request could assist with, for example, a claim under the public interest disclosure ('whistleblowing') provisions of the Employment Rights Act (ERA) 1996. See *Guide to the Freedom of Information Act* 2000 by Michael Supperstone and Timothy Pitt-Payne (Butterworths, 2001); *The Law of Freedom of Information* by John Macdonald QC and Clive Jones (OUP, 2003); *Information Rights* by Philip Coppel (Sweet & Maxwell, 2004).

2 SI No 1861. Schedule 1 contains the Employment Tribunals Rules of Procedure and will hereafter be referred to as the Procedure Rules.

3 One of the stated aims of the redrafted rules – see Government Response to Consultation on the new rules, 20 July 2004, paragraph 1; www.dti.gov.uk.

blurs a distinction that was useful. The distinction is between what used to be called 'further particulars' on the one hand, and written answers to questions put by the tribunal on the other.[4] A request for further particulars of a formal claim or the respondent's response was a request that the other party clarify some assertion that they have made in their document. A request for written answers was a free-standing request that they provide relevant information. In other words, the former was a question whose gist was 'When you say XYZ, what do you mean?' The latter was a question that did not refer to or seek clarification of something the other party had already said.

4.5 The power to order written answers to questions remains at rule 10(2)(f) of the Procedure Rules, so it seems likely – because there is nothing to indicate otherwise, and because tribunals and practitioners are familiar with it – that this distinction will persist. Tribunals are likely to treat a request for 'additional information' as being the same thing as would have been called a request for 'further particulars' under the old rules. For the sake of clarity, it is suggested that applicants and their advisers should continue to make the distinction. There will of course be cases on the borderline where it does not matter whether the question, provided it is put clearly, is put as a request for additional information or for a written answer.

Requests generally

4.6 Requests for documents, additional information and written answers should be kept to what is demonstrably relevant to a question that is a subject of dispute between the parties. Long requests of questionable relevance will be liable to be refused by the respondent, and the tribunal is unlikely to grant an order. The temptation to cross-examine by correspondence should be resisted,[5] as should the temptation to seek an unnecessary level of detail. Requests drafted by solicitors are often sprinkled with expressions like 'with full particularity,' 'giving the precise time of each meeting', 'giving the exact words used' and so on, but this is often futile. It is rare that witnesses will remember the exact words of an oral exchange or the precise time of anything, but rarer still that this level of detail will matter.

---

4 The rule refers to questions put *by the tribunal*, but this power is most often used at the request of one party or the other: the tribunal puts questions to one party at the request of the other.
5 See paras 4.11–4.13 below.

4.7   Questions and requests should be asked one at a time and numbered, so that if the respondent gives adequate answers to some but not others it is easy to identify, in asking the tribunal to order the respondent to answer, which questions have yet to be dealt with. Questions should be put one at a time, and should be short, clear and concrete. Often the aim will be to force a respondent whose ET 3 is drafted in vague generalisations ('an incident occurred', 'steps were taken', 'the claimant was abusive' and so on) to be specific about who did what, when, and what the consequence was. It is helpful to keep the different kinds of request separate: then the application for an order can refer to the correct sub-paragraph of rule 10 of the Procedure Rules in relation to each request or group of requests.

4.8   The letter should specify a date by which responses must be provided, and should warn that an order will be sought from the tribunal if that deadline is not met. If there is no particular reason for a longer or shorter period, 14 days should normally be a sufficient time to allow. If the request is made close to the hearing date, a shorter period may be inevitable. If the request is for information or documents which is likely to cause the respondent and/or their advisers substantial work, it is sensible to allow a longer period if possible. The closer before the hearing, and the more extensive the requests, the less likely the tribunal is to grant an order, so these requests should always be made as soon as possible after the response is received and should be carefully limited to what is genuinely relevant.[6]

4.9   Sometimes a late request is unavoidable. If the claimant's adviser realises four weeks before the hearing that a substantial request is called for, there may be a conflict between giving the respondent a realistic amount of time to comply, and still being in a position to ask the tribunal for an order if they refuse. The best solution to this problem is probably to ask the respondent for an indication by return if they are unwilling in principle to answer any of the requests. Then if they do so, the claimant's adviser can seek an order straight away; if they do not, but their answer when it comes is incomplete, the claimant's adviser may be able to persuade the tribunal to make a last minute order on the grounds that it is the respondent's fault that the application is made late.

---

6   The author once asked the Royal Mail for a year's sickness records for 'all employees,' forgetting to limit the request to comparable employees at the depot at which the claimant was employed. The response was an amused 'How many articulated lorry-loads do you think that will be?'

Deciding what to ask for

4.10   The best starting point for a request for disclosure, additional information and/or written answers is the response: it is a useful exercise to go through the ET3, line by line, checking for ambiguous or incomplete statements and documents that may or must exist. The following precedent is an employer's response to a claim annotated with thoughts about the requests that it suggests: see P4.3 below for the resulting request. A similar exercise can be done with the formal claim and any other relevant documents the claimant already has.[7]

P4.1 Employer's response to claim annotated for disclosure requests

IN THE EMPLOYMENT TRIBUNAL   Case No 123456/04
LONDON SOUTH

BETWEEN
                    CLAUDIA CHAMPION
                                                            Claimant

                        and

                THE MINISTRY OF TRUTH
                                                            Respondent

_____

                GROUNDS OF RESISTANCE
_____

1. Paragraphs 1 and 2 of the claim are admitted.
2. In or around May 2003 the respondent's senior management team decided [A] that for operational reasons it was desirable to merge the Croydon and Guildford Area Managers' Offices.

[A] request for additional information: *who took the decision?* request for discovery: *any written proposals, discussion papers, memos, agendas and minutes of relevant meetings, all e-mail correspondence leading up to the decision, etc*

---

7   This exercise is also likely to produce material that is better used for cross-examination than as the basis of requests for additional information: see paras 4.11–4.14 below for how to approach the choice between the two.

3. Detailed consultations took place with all staff who were likely to be affected by the proposed reorganisation [B]. The claimant told James Petrie, the Regional Administrator in a meeting on 30 June 2003 [C], that she had for some time been hoping for an operational position, ideally as Department Manager of the Central London Information Unit. She specifically said that she did not want to continue working in the Area Manager's Office after the reorganisation.

[B] additional information: *who was consulted, when, how and by whom?* request for disclosure: *all documentation of consultation process*

[C] request for dislosure: *any note or minute of that meeting, diary entry*

4. Suitable arrangements were made [D] to locate a suitable post at the claimant's grade into which to transfer her. Mr Petrie consulted colleagues [E] and formed the view that the claimant needed to improve her skills [F] before being ready to be appointed to an operational post.

[D] additional information: *who did what? when? with what results?*

[E] additional information: *minutes of any meetings, file notes of any conversations, any e-mail traffic*

5. The respondent identified as suitable a post at the Croydon Information Centre, but the claimant told Mr Petrie that she was not prepared to work at that location. To try to resolve the situation, Mr Petrie arranged to meet with the claimant on 28 September 2003 [G] for a discussion of the remaining options. In the course of that meeting, Mr Petrie told the claimant that it was his view, shared with other members of the Management Team, that she would not be ready for a Department Manager post until she had been through a re-training programme.

[F] request for additional information: *what skills did she need to develop?*

[G] disclosure: *any note or minute of that meeting, Mr Petrie's diary entry*

6. Mr Petrie met with the claimant again on 19 October 2003 [H]. Mr Petrie told the claimant what arrangements

[H] disclosure: *any note or minute of that meeting, Mr Petrie's diary entry*

had been made for training [I] to
equip her to take up an operational
post, and he promised her that in
March 2004 he would take a final decision as to her permanent redeployment would be taken in March 2004.

> [I] additional information: *what training*

7. The respondent denies that the
   claimant was at any time redundant.
   She was employed in a mobile grade
   in which she could have been redeployed anywhere in the UK, and there
   were vacant positions at her grade in
   several locations that she could have
   been appointed to on request.
8. The respondent denies that it acted in
   breach of the claimant's contract of
   employment as alleged or at all.

Written requests and cross-examination

4.11   There are always decisions to be taken about whether to seek information before the hearing by way of a request for further particulars or
written answers, or to save it for cross-examination. The best way of
approaching this is to think about the likely answer in each case, and
to decide which is more favourable to the claimant. For example: the
question 'How many of the staff of grade C3 and above are women?'
asked in cross-examination may elicit the answer 'Well of course I
don't have exact figures, but I'd say about half.' This will be very difficult for the claimant to challenge during the hearing unless she herself
can list the staff at that level. A request in advance for a list of all staff,
showing grade and sex, makes it much more difficult for the employer
to give anything but a straight and truthful answer.

4.12   On the other hand, if the question is put in correspondence 'What
factors did the dismissing manager consider before deciding to dismiss?'
the likely answer will be a textbook account, drafted by a lawyer, of all
the relevant and proper considerations that the manager should have
had in mind. By the time of the hearing, the manager in question,
having read this, may well have persuaded herself that she did indeed
have all those things in mind. The same question put to the manager
for the first time in cross-examination may produce a floundering
(and therefore extremely helpful) demonstration that she did not have

a clue what she ought to consider, and did not – for example – give the claimant any credit for his long unblemished service, or trouble to acquaint herself with his performance and past appraisal records.

4.13　As a rule of thumb, if the question is designed to elicit hard information that cannot easily be fudged or falsified, it is best to make it the subject of a request for additional information or written answers. If the aim is to embarrass a witness or to give him or her an opportunity to say something foolish, it is best to save it for cross-examination.[7a]

4.14　When requesting further detail of something that has been said in the employer's response, it is conventional – and helpful – to quote the relevant part.

Disclosure of documents[8]

4.15　There are two distinct ways in which the tribunal may approach disclosure of documents. One is to follow the practice that is prescribed by the Civil Procedure Rules in the ordinary courts. Here each party first provides the other (or others) with a list of *all* documents in its power or possession that are relevant to any of the questions to be resolved in the proceedings, and says which of those documents are privileged[9] and exempt from disclosure. This is followed either by provision of copies of those documents that the other party does not already have or the opportunity to view them and take copies.[10]

4.16　Alternatively, the tribunal may simply direct that each party disclose to the other all of the documents on which it intends to rely at the hearing. This is simpler and cheaper for the parties as it does not require them to conduct a search for relevant documents, draw up long lists, and admit to the existence of documents they do not particularly wish to disclose. The downside, especially for the employee (since in most employment cases the great bulk of relevant documents will be in the hands of the employer), is that the simpler process may fail to turn up relevant and helpful documents because the employer, having no intention of relying on them at the hearing itself, is not

---

7a With this in mind, it is worthwhile re-reading P4.1 and considering which of the suggested requests for additional information might be better saved for cross-examination. Some of them probably would.

8　Disclosure was called 'discovery' in previous versions of the rules, and practitioners are likely to continue to use the two terms interchangeably for some time.

9　See paras 4.28–4.36 below.

10　This tends to be inconvenient, and it is fairly rare for parties to choose to do it.

obliged to and does not choose to disclose them. It is suggested, therefore, that claimants' advisers should get into the habit of asking the respondent for *all* relevant (non-privileged) documents in their possession or control, and asking the tribunal to make an order in those terms if the respondent refuses.

4.17   If an order for general disclosure has been made, then both parties have a serious obligation to comply with it fully and honestly, and in particular not to suppress relevant documents which they regard as embarrassing or harmful to their case. The tribunal can be expected to take a very dim view of any failure to make full disclosure that emerges at the hearing, especially by a party that has been professionally represented: legal representatives have their own duty to ensure that their clients understand and have complied with the duty of disclosure. It is worth being aware that tribunals and lawyers appearing before them will sometimes appear to believe that that duty applies in full even if no order for general disclosure has been made. The term 'document' is not confined to material that already exists in paper form: computer files, e-mails, etc, should be disclosed if relevant.

4.18   Even if an order for general disclosure has been made, the claimant's adviser should never assume that the duty has been properly complied with on the other side. The duty is poorly understood by non-lawyers, and often inadequately explained by lawyers to their clients. It will almost always be necessary to make specific requests for documents that the respondent does not deem relevant, or to whose relevance the respondent has not turned its mind.

4.19   If no order for general disclosure has been made, there is no reason why the claimant should not nevertheless ask the respondent to carry out a search for all relevant documents, and ask them to confirm that they have done so.

Checklist for disclosure request

4.20   All organisations document their business differently, so there could be no comprehensive list of the kinds of documents that it might be helpful to request. The following list may serve as a helpful reminder of some of the possibilities, however.

- company or staff handbook
- contract of employment
- statement of particulars of employment
- claimant's personnel file

- personnel records of other employees[11]
- redundancy selection criteria
- written records of process leading to decision to make redundancy
- other employee's score sheets from the redundancy section[12]
- application forms, including the application forms of other candidates for the post
- job advertisements
- interview notes
- written guidance for interview panel
- requests from managers for human resources (HR) advice
- HR advice on conduct of interview, consultation or disciplinary meeting[13]
- letters
- memos
- file notes
- e-mails
- minutes of disciplinary or appeal meetings (including any handwritten notes taken at the time)
- minutes of other relevant meetings
- appraisal records
- reports
- discussion papers
- diary entries (including electronic diaries)
- log-books

---

11 Employers will often be reluctant to provide this on 'confidentiality' grounds; sometimes they will refer to the Data Protection Act 1998. Sometimes identifying details can be deleted from confidential documents, but if information about another employee is important then the tribunal should be willing to order discovery even if the employee says it is 'confidential'. The Data Protection Act 1998 does not prevent disclosure of relevant documents in legal proceedings and is irrelevant: employers who seek to rely on it for this purpose should be asked to quote the specific provisions they rely on. If necessary, the tribunal has power to hold a hearing in private for the purpose of hearing evidence that has been communicated to the witness in confidence: Procedure Rules r16.

12 There is likely to be a tussle for these, which the employee will often lose. Claimants should read *British Aerospace plc v Green* [1995] IRLR 433, CA and be ready to deal with the argument that the score sheets of other candidates are not relevant. There will be a better chance of obtaining them if very specific allegations can be made of the respects in which certain other employees must have been scored over-generously.

13 Employers may wish to claim privilege in respect of internal personnel or HR advice. Communications with in-house lawyers are privileged, but advice from personnel professionals who are not qualified lawyers is not and should be disclosed: see paras 4.28–4.35 below.

- timesheets
- rotas
- pay records
- sales records
- receipts
- accounts
- bank statements
- clocking records
- tacograph records
- insurance claims
- accident book
- order book
- telephone bills
- call logs (some organisations log each telephone call received in a book held at reception)
- text messages
- 'history' or 'statistics' files associated with any suspect document

4.21   The employee him or herself will usually be an excellent source of information about the kind of question it is useful to ask, and the kind of documents her employer may have. The trick, for an adviser, is to harness his or her own knowledge of how to get information out of an employer with the claimant's knowledge of his or her employer's working practices. One technique is simply to remember to ask the questions: 'How can we prove that? Will the employer have any documents?' at intervals while taking the statement. Another is to give the client a first draft request for discovery, etc, and to ask for ideas about what else it might be useful to ask for.

4.22   E-mail correspondence is particularly important, and is still often overlooked. Much that a few years ago would have been the subject of a quick chat on the phone or in person is now dealt with by e-mail. People tend to express themselves informally and candidly by e-mail, and they are more likely to forget that their e-mails may come under scrutiny: often they will say in an e-mail things that they would not dream of putting in a letter or even a formal memo. For this reason, e-mail correspondence can be extremely revealing. Mobile phone text messages may also be revealing, but a printed list of such messages may or may not be in the 'control' of the sender or recipient depending on the nature of the agreement with the mobile phone company. This is relevant because a document is only subject to the duty of disclosure if it is in the possession or *control* of a party.

P4.2 Request for discovery of documents – redundancy dismissal

Mike Hardwick was dismissed for redundancy, but he believes that there was no genuine redundancy situation and the real reason for his dismissal was a personality clash with a senior manager. He was employed as 'Engineering Process Manager'. Shortly after his dismissal, the company appointed an 'Engineering Design Manager'. Mr Hardwick believes that this is his post in disguise.

George Bean
Carrot & Marrow Solicitors
21 Lower St
Islington
London N12 3AB

Our ref: NC 1234/2004
Your ref: GB/ar 6789

28 July 2005

Dear Mr Bean

Mike Hardwick v ADAL Ltd

REQUEST FOR DISCOVERY OF DOCUMENTS

Please provide copies of the following:
1. All appraisals from the claimant's personnel file done in the years 2003, 2004 or 2005.
2. Monthly engineering department order summaries for the months January 2004 to May 2005 inclusive.
3. All documentation of the process that led to the respondent's decision to make the post of Engineering Process Manager redundant, including:

   (a) minutes of any meetings;
   (b) file notes recording any telephone conversations;
   (c) any reports, letters, memos or e-mails.

4. Any notes or minutes taken at the consultation meeting held between the claimant on 24 March 2005 and Ben Ledgerman.
5. Any notes or minutes taken at the meeting of 31 March 2005 between Ben Ledgerman and the claimant.

6. Any notes or minutes taken at the appeal meeting on 7 April 2005.
7. All documentation of the process that led to the respondent's decision to create the new post of Engineering Design Manager in May 2005, including:

    (a) minutes of any meetings;
    (b) file notes recording any telephone conversations;
    (c) any reports, letters, memos or e-mails.

8. All documentation of the recruitment process that led to the appointment of Terry Seaman as Engineering Design Manager in May 2005, including:

    (a) job description;
    (b) person specification;
    (c) notes or minutes of interview or any informal discussion between Mr Ayers and more senior management;
    (d) letter offering the new post;
    (e) contract of employment.

9. The report presented by Ben Ledgerman to the respondent's Board of Directors in the summer of 2004 concerning the company's potential for growth over the following five years.

Please list any other documents in your possession or control that are relevant to any issue between the parties, saying in respect of which documents you claim privilege. Please confirm that your client has carried out a reasonable search for relevant documents.[14]

Please provide these documents by 12 noon on Wednesday 11 August, failing which I shall apply to the tribunal for the appropriate order.

Yours sincerely

Natalie Cummings

---

14 This request echoes the requirement of a 'disclosure statement' by rule 31.10 of the Civil Procedure Rules. This is not compulsory, or even common practice, in the employment tribunals but there is no reason why the claimant should not ask for it.

P4.3 Request for disclosure of documents – constructive dismissal

George Bean
Carrot & Marrow Solicitors
21 Lower St
Islington
London N12 3AB

Our ref: NC 1234/2004
Your ref: GB/ar 6789

3 August 2004

Dear Mr Bean

Claudia Champion v Ministry of Truth ET/123456/04

REQUEST FOR DISCLOSURE OF DOCUMENTS

Please provide copies of the following documents:

1. Any minutes of Area Management Board meetings containing any reference to the claimant or her post during the 18 months from 1 May 2002.
2. All documents retrievable from Dawn Morvern's computer mentioning the claimant or relating to her or her circumstances created between 1 May 2002 and 31 June 2004, together with their associated statistics files.
3. The business plan mentioned by Simon Maltby during the meeting with area Higher Executive Officers (HEOs) on 15 April 2003.
4. All documentation of the process leading to the decision to create a third HEO post at the London Area Office including memos, reports, minutes of meetings, file notes, e-mails or any other documents.
5. Any minutes or other record of any meeting that took place between Sean McKitterick and James Petrie in accordance with Mr McKitterick's letter to Mr Petrie of 15 March 2003.

Please list any other documents in your possession or control that are relevant to any issue between the parties, saying in respect of which documents you claim privilege. Please confirm that your client has carried out a reasonable search for relevant documents.[15]

Some of these requests may take a little time to meet, so I should be grateful for your response within the next 28 days,[16] that is by close of business on 31 August. Please let me know promptly, however, if you are unwilling in principle to comply with any of these requests so that I can apply for an order without delay.[17]

Yours sincerely

Natalie Cummings

Faked documents

4.23　Claimants' advisers should not disregard the possibility that the respondent or some of its witnesses have created after the event the documents that they think will assist them in defending the case. This is not an allegation that should be made lightly simply because a document is embarrassing, but if there are real grounds for thinking that it may have been done then it should be investigated. A point to bear in mind in this context (as in many others) is that organisations are made up of a number of different individuals who do not all have the same information or interests. The middle manager who dismissed may have created fake documents – unknown to the more senior manager who confirmed the dismissal on appeal – as much to protect himself from criticism as to defend the employer from unfair dismissal proceedings. A faked document certainly does not mean that the employer's whole approach to the proceedings is dishonest, less still that their lawyers are in on the conspiracy.

4.24　Creating a convincing back-dated document is surprisingly difficult, and if a document is under suspicion the first step is obviously to examine it carefully for internal evidence that it is not what it purports to be. For example: a handwritten document that is said to have been created over a period by different individuals may be suspiciously

---

15　See note 14 above

16　14 days is a more usual time limit, but a claimant who is aware that his or her request is on the heavy side will be well advised, if possible, to allow a more generous time limit

17　See para 4.9 above.

uniform, giving the impression that it was in fact written by one person, using the same scratchy ballpoint pen, in a single sitting. Notes supposedly taken in the course of a heated meeting by one of the participants may be implausibly perfect. A writer recording what is supposed to have been the present when the document was written may inadvertently use a past tense, or betray knowledge of information that was not available until later than the purported date of the document. Dates may be wrong. If the document is one that is supposed to have been given to the applicant at the time, the applicant may even have a different version.

4.25   Three specific techniques for testing the genuineness of suspect documents are worth keeping in mind. First, any typed document put forward as a contemporaneous record of a meeting or telephone call will almost certainly have been typed up from handwritten notes. These should be requested as well, so that comparisons can be made.[18]

4.26   Secondly, documents created on a computer will have an associated 'history' or 'statistics' file showing when the document was created, edited and printed. If the respondent discloses what the claimant believes are fake documents, it can be helpful to make a supplementary request for the statistics file. This too may be faked, of course, if the respondent has the know-how and the will to do so, but if the request is dealt with by someone who believes the document to be genuine, or indeed by a lawyer who takes his or her professional responsibilities seriously, then a statistics file that seriously damages the credibility of the original document may be disclosed. Alternatively, if the respondent makes thin excuses for failing to disclose it, this in itself may usefully damage their credibility.

4.27   Finally, if a document is sufficiently important, it may in rare cases be proportionate to call in a forensic computer expert to examine the computer, or to have the original document analysed by an expert in techniques such as electro-static document analysis (a method of recovering faint imprints on paper from the pages above them, suitable for hand-written documents under suspicion).[19]

---

18 If the respondent claims that the handwritten notes were discarded once the typed document had been created, this can be pursued in cross-examination. Any reasonably sophisticated employer can be expected to know – especially if they have ever been through tribunal proceedings before – that the original documents should be filed alongside the typed transcript as a matter of course.

19 See paras 5.46–5.47 below on how to find and instruct an expert witness.

Privilege

4.28   A document is said to be 'privileged' if, although relevant, it is exempt from disclosure or cannot be relied on as evidence. There are three kinds of privilege that commonly affect employment tribunal proceedings: they are the 'without prejudice' rule and legal advice privilege and litigation privilege. The first relates to communications in the course of negotiation and is dealt with at 6.10 below. The last two are superficially similar, but it is important to understand the differences between them.

Legal advice privilege[20]

4.29   Legal advice privilege protects all communications passing between a lawyer and his or her client in connection with giving and receiving legal advice, whether or not there are current or contemplated legal proceedings. This means, for example, that the claimant has no right to see a letter from the employer to its solicitor seeking advice on the best way to dismiss the claimant, or the solicitor's reply.

4.30   However, in the employment tribunal context, what the rule does not cover is at least as important as what it does cover. Some employers may try to claim privilege in respect of every document they do not wish to disclose because they regard it as confidential, but legal advice privilege is defined more narrowly than that.

4.31   Legal advice privilege does *not* extend to advice given to either the employer or the employee by a person who is not a lawyer, even if that person is acting in a role that is very similar to a lawyer's role. So, for example, advice given by the employer's human resources department to a manager on how to conduct a disciplinary hearing, how to approach a capability or sickness procedure, how to select for redundancy, etc, will not normally be privileged.[21] Similarly, legal advice privilege does not extend to advice from external personnel consultants if they are not legally qualified,[22] nor to communications in the course of a disciplinary process between the claimant and his or her union representative. These kinds of communications should be disclosed by each side.[23]

---

20 See also ETP 3 10.37-10.38.
21 Although the situation is different if the advice comes from an in-house lawyer.
22 *New Victoria Hospital v Ryan* [1993] ICR 201.
23 The sharp distinction between communications with qualified lawyers, and communications with unqualified advisers whose role is very similar to that of a lawyer has been the subject of some criticism, but until the Court of Appeal or the House of Lords revisits the question the distinction stands.

4.32   This is widely misunderstood by both employers and employees. Employers especially will often assume that they cannot be expected to show the claimant what they regard as 'confidential' human resources advice to managers. They may refer to legal advice privilege in arguing that they should not have to disclose this material; or they may simply omit it from their list of documents altogether because they believe that it is none of the claimant's business. Claimants who believe that this kind of material exists will often have to make a considerable fuss before they get it. The fuss is worth making, because if at the time the advice was sought and given both the manager and the human resources adviser believed that what they said to each other would not come out in tribunal proceedings, the communications between them will be unguarded and may contain material that is very helpful for the claimant.

Litigation privilege

4.33   Litigation privilege protects from disclosure any document that was created for the purposes of current or future litigation, and it protects communications between unqualified advisers and their clients as well as between lawyers and their clients.

4.34   The key distinction to understand, therefore, is between: (a) documents that were created at the time of the acts or processes that have *since* become the subject of employment tribunal litigation; and (b) documents that have come into existence because of, and for the purpose of, the litigation itself. Documents in class (a) will only be privileged if they are communications between a qualified lawyer and his or her client for the purpose of legal advice. Documents in class (b) will always be privileged.

4.35   It is worth observing here that notes of a hearing taken by one party or its legal or other advisers are not privileged.[24] This will most often be relevant if there is an appeal for which notes of evidence are needed,[25] or a remitted hearing[26] after an appeal at which the claimant wishes to rely on evidence given previously by the respondent.[27] However, if a hearing is not completed in the time allotted and has

---

24 Because they are a record of what has taken place at a public hearing – and this by definition, cannot be confidential. See *Lambert v Home* [1914] 3 KB 86, CA.

25 See paras 11.52–11.56 below.

26 See paras 11.39–11.46 below.

27 Where, for example, one of the respondent's witnesses made helpful admissions under cross-examination.

to be adjourned for some weeks or months before it can be finished, then a party who has not been able to take accurate notes of the hearing may wish to seek discovery of the other party's notes. This is an application that both the tribunal and the respondent may find surprising, but there is no reason in principle why it should not succeed. The claimant should remind the tribunal if necessary that the overriding objective at regulation 3 of the Employment Tribunals (Constitution and Rules of Procedure) Regulations 2004[28] requires, among other things, 'ensuring that the parties are on an equal footing'. Where the claimant has represented him or herself – and the respondent has attended with counsel and a solicitor (and larger legal teams are not uncommon) – the justice of this should be evident.

Requests for additional information

4.36   These, as explained above at para 4.4, are requests of the general form 'When you said XYZ in your Response, what did you mean?' It is almost always necessary to request disclosure of documents from the respondent, but claimants need not assume that a request for additional information is required unless there is something about the Response that leaves them in genuine doubt about what it is the respondent is alleging. Unnecessary requests may leave them at risk of a costs order.

28 SI No 1861.

P4.4 Request for additional information

George Bean
Carrot & Marrow Solicitors
21 Lower St
Islington
London N12 3AB

Our ref: NC 1234/2004
Your ref: GB/ar 6789

14 October 2004

Dear Mr Bean

Claudia Champion v Ministry of Truth ET/123456/04

REQUEST FOR ADDITIONAL INFORMATION

Under paragraph 3:

Of: *It is admitted that in or around May 2003, a decision was taken to merge the Croydon and Guildford Area Managers' Offices.*

1. Please say who took the decision to merge the Croydon and Guildford Area Managers' Offices.

Of: *As part of the implementation, all staff affected were consulted in order to take into account, where possible, the wishes of individuals in re-allocating posts.*

2. Please say who was consulted.
3. Please say in each case who carried out the consultation.
4. Please say when and where the consultation took place.
5. Please say whether the consultation was carried out by way of meetings, by correspondence or otherwise.

Under paragraph 4:

Of: *It was considered by the respondent that the claimant needed to develop the required skills before being able to take up an operational post.*

6. Please say what skills it was thought the claimant needed to develop before being able to take up an operational post.

Of: *Accordingly, arrangements were made to find her another post at her grade.*

7. Please say what arrangements were made.
8. Please say who made them.

Please provide this information by 12 noon on 28 October 2004, failing which I will apply to the tribunal for an order.

Yours sincerely

Natalie Cummings

Requests for written answers

4.37   The comments at para 4.4 above on requests for additional information apply here too: the tribunal has power to order written answers to questions, but it does not follow that in every case a request for written answers must be made.

Applying for an order for disclosure, additional information or written answers

4.38   An application for an order should normally be made as soon as the deadline set for voluntary compliance with the request has passed. If the respondent requests extra time, that request should be granted if it is reasonable and can be granted without jeopardising the claimant's chances of getting an order from the tribunal if the respondent fails to meet the new deadline. So, for example, if a request is made with a 14 day time limit seven weeks before the hearing and the respondent asks for another week to comply, there is no reason not to agree: the tribunal will not hesitate to make an order four weeks before the hearing if it turns out in the end that it is needed. On the other hand, if the request is made four weeks before the hearing with a 14 day time limit, it will be prudent to request the order as soon as the time limit has expired even if the respondent is promising imminent voluntary compliance.[29] An application that is received in the last seven days before the hearing is most unlikely to be granted.

4.39   The application should explain briefly the relevance of the documents or information sought, and say how granting the application will help the tribunal deal with the case efficiently and fairly. It should also contain the usual instructions for the respondent about how and when to oppose the application, and it must of course be copied to the respondent. Sometimes the relevance of the request is self-evident, in which case the request for an order can be brief. In other cases, the need for the requested documents or information will require careful explanation, or if the respondent has put in a reasoned objection to complying this may need to be dealt with at some length.

DO4.1 Applying for an order for disclosure

Identify the order sought, and refer to (and enclose) the letter of request

Explain the relevance of the requests

Deal with the respondent's objections, if any

Explain how an order will help the tribunal to deal with the case efficiently and fairly[30]

Give the respondent instructions for opposing the request[31]

---

29 It does not hurt in these circumstances to explain to the respondent that the application is made protectively and will be withdrawn if the respondent complies voluntarily in the meantime.

30 This is required in order to comply with rule 11 of the Procedure Rules.

31 This is required in order to comply with rule 11 if the claimant is legally represented, but it will save time in any case since the alternative is for the tribunal to give the other party those instructions after receiving the application.

P4.5 Request for an order for discovery – unfair redundancy (straightforward)

The Regional Secretary
London Central Employment Tribunal
19–29 Woburn Place
London WC1H 0LU

Your ref: 123456/2004
My ref: NC/1234

11 August 2005

Dear Madam

Mike Hardwick v ADAL Ltd

I should be grateful if you would put before a Chairman my request for an order that the respondent comply with my requests for discovery of documents as set out in my letter of 28 July, of which I attach a copy. I have received no reply.

A central issue between the parties is whether there was a genuine redundancy situation affecting Mr Hardwick's post. The relevance of the appointment of Mr Seaman as Engineering Design Manager is that Mr Hardwick believes that the new post of Engineering Design Manager was in reality the same as the post of Engineering Process Manager from which he had been dismissed.

In the circumstances disclosure of the requested documents will clarify the matters in dispute between the parties and will assist the tribunal in dealing with the case efficiently and fairly.

This letter is copied to the respondent. The respondent should note that if it objects to the application, it must write to the tribunal within seven days of receiving this letter, or before the date of the hearing (whichever date is the earlier)[32] explaining the reasons for its objection, and should copy that letter to me. Rule 11 of the Procedure Rules has been complied with in relation to this application.

Yours faithfully

Natalie Cummings

---

32 See note 31 above.

P4.6 Request for an order for discovery – constructive dismissal (more complex)

The Regional Secretary
London Central Employment Tribunal
19–29 Woburn Place
London WC1H 0LU

1 September 2004

Dear Madam

Claudia Champion v Ministry of Truth ET/123456/04

I should be grateful if you would put before a Chairman my request for an order that the respondent comply with my requests for discovery of documents as set out in my letter of 3 August, of which I attach a copy together with the reply received today.

The respondent has refused to provide items 1 and 2. The claimant asserts that her wish to return an operational post, and in particular the post of Department Manager in the Central London Information Unit, was realistic and had previously been discussed with management as a feasible medium-term option. She believes that Area Management Board Meeting minutes from the period before the reorganisation will support this contention. She further believes that Area Management Board Meeting minutes from the period around and immediately after the reorganisation will show that the respondent had no coherent plan for her redeployment after the reorganisation.

As to item 2, Dawn Morvern is James Petrie's personal assistant and would have typed the notes of the meetings in September and October 2003 which James Petrie has put forward as his contemporaneous notes of those meetings. The claimant does not accept Mr Petrie's account of the meeting and does not believe that the notes were typed up at the time. She believes that the notes were created some time after the event. For this reason item 2, including statistics files showing when each document was created, edited and printed, are highly relevant.

The requested documents are relevant to important issues between the parties, and granting this application will therefore assist the tribunal in dealing with the case efficiently and fairly.

I am sorry that this request is made close to the hearing date. In my letter of 3 August I asked the respondent to notify me at once if it objected in principle to providing any of the disclosure sought so that I could apply for an order in good time if necessary. I received no reply to that letter until today, when the respondent complied with my requests 3–6 but refused to comply with requests 1 and 2. In the circumstances I suggest that there is no unfairness to the respondent granting the order sought.

This letter is copied to the respondent. The respondent should note that if it objects to the application, it must write to the tribunal within 7 days of receiving this letter, or before the date of the hearing (whichever date is the earlier)[33] explaining the reasons for its objection, and should copy that letter to me. Rule 11 of the Procedure Rules has been complied with in relation to this application.

Yours faithfully

Natalie Cummings

Questionnaires

4.40   The questionnaire procedure is unique to discrimination claims. In any discrimination claim, the claimant may either before or after commencing proceedings serve on the respondent (or potential respondent) a list of questions. The respondent is not obliged to answer the questions, and the tribunals have no power to order replies to a questionnaire; but the tribunal that hears the case will have regard to the questionnaire and any reply and may draw inferences from a failure to reply or from evasive or incomplete replies.

4.41   Before 1993, the employment tribunals had no general power to order a party to give written answers to questions: it could order further particulars (what is now called 'additional information') of an employer's response to the claim, and it could order disclosure of documents already in existence; but it could not order a respondent to provide specific information such as statistics on the make-up of its workforce, or lists of employees dismissed in the last year or so broken down by reason for dismissal and ethnic origin.

33 See note 31 above.

4.42 This meant that before 1993 the questionnaire procedure was very important indeed. The tribunal's power to draw inferences from inadequate replies provided a sanction to encourage – although not compel – employers to respond. After the 1993 Rules came into force the importance of the questionnaire procedure diminished somewhat: general questions aimed at casting light on how an employer treats ethnic minority staff, or women, for instance, can be put as requests for written answers, and if the tribunal thinks the question is relevant it can order the employer to respond.

4.43 However, there are two important respects in which the questionnaire procedure can still provide significant tactical benefits. The first is that it is available *before* proceedings start, and can be used by an employee thinking of making a claim to decide whether or not the claim is well founded. This can be particularly useful in recruitment cases, where an applicant for a job may have an uneasy feeling that he or she may have suffered unlawful discrimination, but has very little hard information about the employer or its practices or even about the successful candidate for the job. In those circumstances, the decision whether to proceed with a claim may well depend on the reply to a questionnaire: the employer may in fact have, and give, a convincing and legitimate explanation for its failure to recruit the aggrieved candidate and that may be the end of the matter.

4.44 The other strength of the questionnaire procedure is probably more important. Ironically, the fact that the tribunal has no power to order replies to a questionnaire makes the questionnaire in one way a *more* powerful weapon in the hands of the claimant. An employer faced with a list of requests for discovery of documents or written answers which it considers excessively long and detailed, or questionably relevant, can say to the claimant 'We consider that your requests are irrelevant and oppressive, and we are not prepared to answer them without an order from the tribunal.' The decision whether the questions are relevant is then left to the tribunal, and if the tribunal refuses to order answers then the employer cannot subsequently be criticised for failing to respond. In other words, by this means the employer can safely pass to the tribunal the decision whether or not the questions need to be answered.

4.45 Faced with a long and detailed questionnaire, the employer does not have this option. It cannot pass the decision about whether or in how much detail it should reply to the tribunal: it must make the judgment itself. This means it will, if it is well advised, play safe. It will normally be better for an employer to give more information than would ever have been ordered than to risk giving the claimant the opportunity to invite the tribunal to draw adverse inferences from incomplete answers. Questionnaires, therefore, will often be a way of digging up more information than a tribunal would be likely to order an employer to disclose.

4.46   This is deliberate. It is recognised both in the way the legislation is drafted[34] and in discrimination case law that discrimination cases are difficult to prove and the relevant information will often be elusive.[35] The standard case law on disclosure makes it clear that 'fishing expeditions' will not normally be permitted.[36] Discrimination is an exception: in discrimination cases, claimants are provided with line and hook.

The form for the questionnaire

4.47   Unfortunately there is no single website that provides links to the forms for all of the questionnaires, and several of the websites on which the individual questionnaires appear are difficult to navigate or search. The following table sets out where each is most readily to be found; hard copies should be obtainable from a Job Centre or Citizens Advice Bureau. Each of the questionnaires appears as part of the statutory instrument that gives it its effect. Where a booklet including the questionnaire and relevant guidance is available, a website address has been given that provides this.

---

34 Especially the reverse burden of proof at, for example, Sex Discrimination Act 1975 s63A.

35 See, for example, *King v Great Britain–China Centre* [1992] ICR 516, CA..

36 See *British Aerospace plc v Green* [1995] IRLR 433.

Ground of discrimination	Legislation	Website
Sex	Sex Discrimination (Questions and Replies) Order 1975 SI No 2048	www.eoc-law.org.uk[37]
Race	Race Relations (Questions and Replies) Order 1977 SI No 842	www.cre.gov.uk[38]
Disability	Disability Discrimination (Questions and Replies) Order 2004 SI No 1168	www.drc-gb.org[39]
Sexual orientation	Employment Equality (Sexual Orientation) Regulations 2003 SI No 1660	www.dti.gov.uk[40]
Religion or belief	Employment Equality (Religion or Belief) Regulations 2003 SI No 1661	www.dti.gov.uk[41]
Equal pay	Equal Pay (Questions and Replies) Order 2003 SI No 722	www.womenand equalityunit.gov.uk[42]

4.48   Each form includes a number of standard questions that must be completed in all cases. Each (with the exception of the equal pay questionnaire) follows a very similar pattern. The claimant[43] gives his or her name and address and the name and address of the person or body whose conduct is the subject of complaint, and sets out the substance of the complaint: this is at box 2 of the race, sex and disability questionnaires, and box 1.2 of the religion or belief and the sexual orientation questionnaires. Claimants' advisers almost invariably

---

37 Go to the homepage and follow the link to 'online forms.'

38 The website is difficult to navigate, search for 'rr65 race relations questions procedure' using a search engine and follow a link to the correct page of the CRE site.

39 The document is called 'DL56: The Questions Procedure'. The DRC site is difficult to navigate, so the easiest way to find this is to search for 'dl56 questions procedure' using a search engine.

40 This site too is difficult to navigate. Search for 'sexual orientation questionnaire guidance' or similar using a search engine and then choose the specific dti page.

41 See note 40 above.

42 There is a direct link to this questionnaire on the Unit's homepage.

43 Or potential claimant. A questionnaire may be served either before or after a claim has been presented to the tribunal, but for simplicity it is assumed in what follows that there is already a complaint in existence.

repeat here the whole of the complaint as it appears in the claim to the tribunal.[44]

4.49   At box 3[45] there is a standard statement: 'I consider that this treatment may have been unlawful because' and a box for the insertion of the reasons why the treatment complained of is considered unlawful. Most advisers routinely cross out 'because' and leave the box blank. This is sensible. The legal basis of the claim will need to be made clear in the claim form submitted to the tribunal, but as that is in a different format there is no need to take on the extra work of re-drafting it for the questionnaire.

4.50   There then follow two standard questions which the claimant need not alter, and at box 6[46] there is space[47] for further specific questions.

4.51   Box 6[48] is the point at which the real work of drafting the questionnaire is done. It can be tempting to assume that it is good to ask as many questions as possible at this point; or that a brief questionnaire is somehow inadequate. Neither assumption is justified. There is no necessity to dream up questions for the sake of making the questionnaire look substantial. In some cases it will not be necessary to serve a questionnaire at all, and a claimant (or adviser) who cannot think of any questions that it is useful to ask at this stage will do better not to serve a questionnaire than to serve a questionnaire putting a number of questions that either do not help his or her case or positively hinder it.

4.52   The advice at paras 4.11–4.13 above on making a careful choice between questions to put in writing and questions to save for cross-examination applies here too. A claimant will not be restrained by the tribunal from attempting to cross-examine on paper by means of the questionnaire procedure, but it does not follow that this is a good thing to do. If the case is strong enough, demonstrating to the employer by way of a questionnaire that there are difficult and pointed questions to which they do not have good answers can help to lever a settlement out of them without going to tribunal, but this is a high risk strategy. If the case does still proceed to a hearing, much of the bene-

---

44   See chapter 3 above. It is not obvious that this is really necessary, but as it is nearly universal practice and has been for many years it is probably as well to conform.

45   Box 1.3 in the case of sexual orientation and religion or belief.

46   Box 4 in the case of sexual orientation and religion or belief.

47   The box is small, and claimants will almost always need to attach their box 6 questions as a separate sheet or sheets.

48   Or 4 as the case may be.

fit of effective cross-examination will be lost if the respondent is given the chance to deal with the hardest questions at leisure and with the advice of its lawyers.

4.53   It is common practice to request documents as part of the questionnaire procedure. The legislation permits tribunals to draw inferences from a failure to reply to questions, or from evasive or incomplete replies to questions. It is not obvious that this also applies to a failure to provide documents on request: probably an employer is entitled simply to say 'Here are my answers to your questions; if you wish for disclosure of documents, you must deal with that after you have presented a claim under the tribunal's power to order disclosure.' However, requests of these kind can operate as an effective bluff: the only way for an employer to find out for sure whether the tribunal will draw adverse inferences from its decision to withhold documents is to withhold them. Most employers will not take the risk, so requests for documents in a questionnaire are worthwhile.

Checklist of subjects to cover in a questionnaire

4.54   As usual with checklists in this book, this is not and could not be exhaustive. It is intended to suggest ideas and give claimants an idea of the kinds of questions that it can be useful to ask. In this list, for simplicity in illustrating the ideas, examples are restricted to sex and disability discrimination, and in the former case it is assumed that the victim of discrimination is a woman. These topics can easily be adapted to fit complaints of discrimination on grounds of race, sexual orientation, or religion or belief.[49]

- the respondent's equal opportunities policy, what it covers, when and how often staff have been trained on it;
- the respondent's workforce profile – that is, the proportions in which women/people with disabilities are found in the organisation, and what levels of seniority;

---

49 For more extensive lists of sample questions, see the Commissions' websites; Tamara Lewis's excellent booklets *RRA Questionnaires* (Central London Law Centre, 2003); *RRA Questionnaires* (Central London Law Centre, 2004); *DDA Questionnaires* (Central London Law Centre, 2001); *SDA Questionnaires* (Central London Law Centre, 1996, a new edition is waiting for legislation expected in 2005) and *Discrimination Questionnaires* (Central London Law Centre, 2004); and *Disability Discrimination Claims: an adviser's handbook* by Catherine Casserley and Bela Gor (Jordans, 2001).

- the proportion of applicants for the job in question or similar jobs over a defined period who were female or had disabilities;
- if the complaint is about an allegedly discriminatory requirement or practice (that is, indirect discrimination) the relative proportions of male and female employees who were adversely affected;
- whether the respondent has been the subject of any previous complaints of sex/disability discrimination or whether a particular individual has previously been accused of sexual harassment;
- what adjustments to the workplace/the claimant's job description/working practices/the recruitment process have been considered to deal with the claimant's disability;
- the reasons why the claimant was treated in the way that he or she is complaining about;
- the reasons why other individuals have not been treated in the same way as the claimant;
- who made the decision to treat the claimant in the way that he or she is complaining about;
- the manner in which other employees have been treated, and if different the reasons why;
- in a recruitment or promotion case, the qualifications of the successful candidate;
- in a reasonable adjustments case,[50] the cost of any adjustments the claimant says should have been made and the employer's resources; it may sometimes be productive to explore the employer's expenditure on non-essentials if the employer is pleading poverty.

---

50 That is, a complaint under the Disability Discrimination Act 1995 that the employer failed to comply with a duty to make reasonable adjustments.

P4.7 Questionnaire – sex discrimination[51]

These answers follow the format of the SDA 1975 questionnaire which is available from the Equal Opportunities Commission website[52] a blank copy of which is reproduced at appendix B.

To: Bristol Advocacy Project
Of: 2 Hillock Way, Clifton, Bristol B2 1AB

1. I | Yasmin Creasey |

   of | 23A St Matthew's Hill, Bristol, B1 2CD |

2. consider that you may have discriminated against me contrary to the Sex Discrimination Act 1975.

> (i) I was employed by the Bristol Advice Project as a receptionist and filing clerk. I was told on starting work that I was on a nine month probationary period from 19 April 2004, but no arrangements were made for appraisal or review.
> (ii) On 15 June 2004, I told my line manager, Mary Smiling, that I was four months pregnant.
> (iii) As far as I was aware, my work was satisfactory. All my colleagues seemed friendly and no-one made any complaints.
> (iv) I started my maternity leave on 1 November 2004. On Friday 29 October, my last day at work, my colleagues gave me a card and a bunch of flowers. Mrs Smiling wished me good luck and said 'See you next year.'
> (v) On 7 January 2005, I received a letter dated 5 January from Reuben Fitzwell informing me that as my performance during my probationary period had been unsatisfactory, my employment would not be confirmed and would accordingly come to an end on 14 January 2005.

3. I consider that this treatment may have been unlawful ~~because~~:

Questions 4 and 5 are standard questions printed on the form

---

51 See P3.5 above and P11.2 below.
52 www.eoc-law.org.uk.

6. Other questions (if appropriate):

> (i) Does the respondent have an equal opportunities policy? Please provide a copy.
>
> (ii) Does the respondent have a maternity leave policy? Please provide a copy.
>
> (iii) When was the decision taken that I was not to be confirmed in post?
>
> (iv) Who took the decision?
>
> (v) What information did he or she rely on? Please provide copies of any written information relied on.
>
> (vi) How many new employees have you recruited in the last five years? In each case please specify:
>
> > (a) whether the recruit was male or female;
> >
> > (b) the date of recruitment;
> >
> > (c) whether he or she was subject to a probationary period, and if so of what duration;
> >
> > (d) what appraisals or progress reviews were conducted during the probationary period; and
> >
> > (e) whether the recruit was confirmed in post, and if not, the date when the decision not to terminate the employment was taken.

P4.8 Questionnaire – disability discrimination

In this precedent only the questions at part 6 of the form are reproduced. The claimant is Pauline Phelps of P3.1 above, and the statement of the basis for her belief that she has suffered discrimination would closely follow the statement at box 6.1 of her claim form.

6. Other questions (if appropriate):

   (i)   Do you have an equal opportunities policy? Please provide a copy.

   (ii) Have any of your partners or staff received training on the Disability Discrimination Act 1998? Please give names and dates.

   (iii) Do you accept that I am disabled for the purposes of the Disability Discrimination Act 1998 in that (a) I have a facial disfigurement and (b) I suffer from depression and agoraphobia?[53]

   (iv) Who made the decision that I should go to work in the pool of secretaries after Mr Gentleman's retirement in July 2004?

53 It is worth asking this now in order to have advance notice of whether there is any need for medical evidence on either point.

(v) What alternatives, if any, were considered?

(vi) Why was my suggestion that I should work full-time for Miss Grey from August 2004 rejected?

(vii) What adjustments did you consider making from August 2004 to prevent the arrangements for working in the pool of secretaries from placing me at a substantial disadvantage compared to persons who were not disabled?[54]

(viii) What steps were taken to investigate my condition or to assess what adjustments might helpfully be made to prevent working in the pool of secretaries from placing me at a substantial disadvantage?

(ix) Why was there no reply to my GP's letter of 17 February 2005?

(x) Who took the decision that morning reception should be covered during the maternity leave of Alison Sheppard by members of the pool?

(xi) Who took the decision that I should be included on the reception rota?

(xii) What arrangements did you consider making to prevent the arrangements for morning reception cover from placing me at a substantial disadvantage compared to persons who were not disabled?

Data Protection Act requests

4.55 The Data Protection Act (DPA) 1998 provides a means by which individuals may require disclosure of certain kinds of information held about them by any person or body. In many cases the employment tribunal's power to order disclosure of relevant documents will be an adequate means of getting hold of information for an employment tribunal case, but a DPA 1998 request will occasionally be helpful, particularly where the employee wants the information (for example, for the purposes of an internal grievance) before employment tribunal proceedings have started.

54 This question is deliberately broad. A series of detailed questions at this stage about whether the employer considered this or that specific adjustment may prompt to the employer to claim that each was considered and think of convincing reasons why each was rejected. If they are not going to answer the questionnaire honestly, a question in this form at least leaves them to do the work of thinking of the adjustments they could or should have considered at the time. It will be difficult for them to claim at any later stage that they considered any adjustment that they do not mention in answer to this question.

4.56   The two main limitations on what an employer (or other body) can be compelled to disclose under the DPA 1998 concern (a) the manner in which the information is held and (b) the nature of the information. Since a ruling of the Court of Appeal in *Durant v Financial Services Authority*[55] in 2003 a restrictive view has been taken of both.

4.57   Information is only covered by the DPA 1998 if it is either held on a computer or as part of a sufficiently structured paper filing system.[56] The effect of the judgment of the Court of Appeal in *Durant* is that information held in paper filing systems will not come within the right of access provided by the DPA 1998 unless the filing system is sophisticated enough that it can be readily discovered whether personal data are held in relation to a particular individual, and if so, where in the files specific information about specific individuals will be found. Paper files will not be covered unless the information in them is similarly accessible to computerised files. This means that only highly structured and well-organised paper files are subject to the right of access.

4.58   The other limitation is the kind of information that is covered. The right of access is not to every piece of information held on a computer or a sophisticated paper file that mentions the individual making the request: the information has to be *about* the individual in question, or to have him or her as its focus. Suppose, for example, Mark Bowland of P3.2 above makes a subject access request to the Hospital, and the Hospital keeps computerised personnel records. A search of those records by reference to Mr Bowland's name will turn up his own personnel file, but also Mr Rahman's and no doubt several others, because he line-manages Mr Rahman and has been mentioned in the latter's employment tribunal claim against the Hospital. Mr Bowland's own personnel file is clearly about Mr Bowland and he can demand to see it. Mr Rahman's file only mentions him in passing, and he is not entitled to see it or even the parts of it that mention his name.

---

55 [2003] EWCA 1746.

56 Claimants who are employees of a public body who find limb (e) of the definition of 'data' at section 1 of the Act may be led to think that this means that they are entitled to a much broader category of information from their employers than other employees, but the impression is misleading. Section 33A(2) excludes employment-related data from this definition, and the net result is that public employees are entitled to the same amounts and kinds of information from their records *about themselves* as any other employees. Other information held by their employers may be accessible under the Freedom Of Information Act 2000, and in this respect they may be better-placed than private sector workers: see note 1 above.

4.59   Under the DPA 1998, the person seeking information about him or herself is called the 'data subject' and the body holding (or believed to be holding) information is the 'data controller.'

Making a request under the DPA 1998

4.60   Despite these limitations, a request[57] for information under the DPA 1998 may have its uses. The data subject does not have to know first what kind of information is held about him or her, or where or how it is held: the data controller must reveal its existence when asked.

4.61   The data controller may charge a fee of up to £10[58] for providing the information, and must provide the information within 40 days of receiving the request and the fee. The sensible course is to enclose £10 with the request.

---

57 Known as a 'subject access request'.
58 For most kinds of information.

P4.9 Data Protection Act 1998 request to employer

Sarah Feldman has worked for Glad Rags plc, a national retail clothing chain, for 15 years. Her career progressed well for most of that time, but for the last five years she has made a series of unsuccessful applications for promotion. She has not been able to discover why her progress has suddenly stopped, although she is now one of a small number of women at her level of seniority and she has started to wonder if she has reached a 'glass ceiling'. However, a manager recently told her that he thought it ought to be obvious to her why she has stopped making progress. He said that there were certain kinds of things on a person's record that would always stop them from reaching the highest levels. Ms Feldman was completely baffled by this and demanded to know what he meant. He refused to explain, saying only that she 'must be realistic in all the circumstances'.

The Legal Department
Glad Rags plc
25 Budgerigar Wharf
London E1 7QB

5 April 2005

Dear Madam/Sir

Data Protection Act 1998: subject access request

Please provide me with the following information, to which I am entitled under section 7 of the Data Protection Act 1998:

1. A description of what personal data is held by Glad Rags plc of which I am the data subject.
2. The purposes for which these data are being processed.
3. To whom these data are or may be disclosed.
4. The information constituting any personal data of which I am the data subject.
5. Any information available to Glad Rags plc as to the source of that information.[59]

I enclose £10 and look forward to hearing from you as soon as possible, and in any event within 40 days.

Yours faithfully

Sarah Feldman

---

59 These categories are parallel to the relevant subsections of section 7.

The claimant's disclosure of documents

4.62   The claimant is under the same duty as the respondent to comply properly with whatever order the tribunal has made for disclosure of documents – that is, to disclose all relevant documents in her or his possession or control, or to disclose all documents on which she or he proposes to rely at the hearing as the case may be (see paras 4.14–4.16 above). Claimants in employment tribunal disputes will typically have far less to disclose than respondents: normally it is the employer that holds the great bulk of the relevant documentary evidence, but advisers should be careful to ensure that claimants have understood the scope of the duty to disclose. The idea that there might be a duty to show a former employer personal diaries, private letters or e-mails, bank statements, telephone bills, etc, will come as a surprise to many claimants.

4.63   Again, attention needs to be paid to the form of the tribunal's direction (if any) on disclosure: if disclosure of all relevant documents in each party's power or control is ordered, then the claimant as much as the respondent must comply with it fully. The tribunal is likely to react badly if it becomes clear in the course of the hearing that the claimant has relevant documents that she has not disclosed.

4.64   The safest course in fact will normally be to disclose all relevant documents (other than privileged documents)[60] whichever order the tribunal has made. A decision to withhold a particular document because the claimant does not wish to rely on it and does not wish the respondent or the tribunal to see it needs to be approached with great caution. The parties and their advisers have a duty not to mislead the tribunal, so it will never be permissible to withhold a document that flatly contradicts an assertion in the witness statement. There may be a relevant document in the claimant's possession that gives a misleading impression, but even so it will normally be better to disclose and explain it than to attempt to suppress it.

4.65   Moreover, because there is always a duty of full disclosure in litigation in the ordinary courts (with which the chairman at least is likely to be familiar), the tribunal itself cannot necessarily be relied upon to understand that the same duty does not automatically apply in the employment tribunal. A claimant who has withheld a relevant document because she considers it misleading may find herself in hot water with the tribunal if she is subsequently forced to admit to its existence. If this happens, the adviser should be ready to argue that in

---

60 See paras 4.28–4.35 above.

the absence of a specific direction by the tribunal, there can be no duty of general disclosure in employment tribunal proceedings because there is nothing in the rules to impose it, but even if this is accepted the claimant's credibility is likely to have been damaged.

4.66   Claimants in employment tribunal cases will tend to have far fewer relevant documents than respondents, and in most cases the simplest course will be to make copies of all relevant documents and send them to the respondent. If the volume of relevant documents is large, the parties may agree (or the tribunal may order) disclosure by exchange of lists of documents in the first instance.

P4.10 Claimant's list of documents

The claimant worked for a small local charity. An e-mail dispute with the chair of the management committee, Tony Byrd, about her workload escalated to the point that she went sick with stress and then resigned. The full e-mail correspondence with Tony Byrd and other management committee members is clearly relevant and should be disclosed – although it is almost certainly in the respondent's possession already. What may come as a surprise to the claimant is that her contemporaneous e-mails about the dispute to her friend Carol Parker and her husband, David Manley, and any relevant diary entries, also have to be disclosed.

IN THE EMPLOYMENT TRIBUNAL
LONDON CENTRAL

BETWEEN

BELINDA MANLEY

Claimant

and

LOCAL ACTION PROJECT

Respondent

CLAIMANT'S LIST OF DOCUMENTS

Date	Description
19 Aug 04	e-mail BM/Tony Byrd (TB)
19 Aug 04	e-mail TB/BM
19 Aug 04	e-mail BM/David Manley (DM)
20 Aug 04	e-mail BM/TB
20 Aug 04	e-mail TB/BM
20 Aug 04	e-mail TB/Carol Parker
20 Aug 04	e-mail BM/DM
20 Aug 04	e-mail DM/BM
20 Aug 04	BM's personal diary page
24 Aug 04	e-mail TB/BM, cc management committee (MC)
24 Aug 04	e-mail BM/TB, cc MC
24 Aug 04	BM's personal diary page
25Aug 04	e-mail Tola James (TJ) /BM
25 Aug 04	e-mail BM/TJ
26 Aug 04	e-mail TJ/BM
27 Aug 04	e-mail BM/MC
27 Aug 04	e-mail TB/BM, cc MC
4 Oct 04	e-mail BM/MC
5 Oct 04	e-mail TJ/BM, cc MC
11 Oct 04	BM's notes of meeting with TB and TJ
11 Oct 04	BM's personal diary page
11 Oct 04	e-mail BM/DM
13 Oct 04	letter BM/TJ, cc MC
18 Oct 04	memo TJ/BM
12–30 Oct 04	extract from BM's itemised phone bill
20 Oct 04	GP's certificate
21 Oct 04	letter TJ/BM
9 Nov 04	letter of resignation
Nov 04 – Jan 05	privileged correspondence with the CAB

Responding to requests for additional information

4.67   Some solicitors, when acting for respondents, will invariably make a request for additional information, however much detail the claimant has put in the claim. Normally it will be more economical for the claimant simply to answer unnecessary questions than to get into a debate about whether or not they are legitimate at this stage. Occasionally the claimant will refuse to answer questions on the grounds that they are requests for evidence or an attempt to conduct a written cross-examination. Broadly, questions that seek additional detail on *what it is the claimant alleges* are legitimate; questions that explore *why the claimant thinks the tribunal ought to believe his or her allegations* are not.

4.68   It is helpful to repeat each request before answering it so that the letter is a self-contained document that the tribunal can understand without constantly referring back to the letter of request. If there have been reasonably co-operative dealings with the respondent, it is sensible to ask for the request letter to be e-mailed so that this can be done by cutting and pasting the relevant portions of the request.

P4.11 Letter responding to requests for disclosure and additional information

George Bean
Carrot & Marrow Solicitors
21 Lower St
Islington
London N21 3AB

30 September 2005

Dear Mr Bean

James Dodd v Pineapple Plant Hire Ltd

Thank you for your letter of 31 August to the Citizens' Advice Bureau. I apologise for the delay in responding to your requests, which has been caused by the transfer of the case from the CAB to the Law Centre.

RESPONSE TO REQUEST FOR ADDITIONAL INFORMATION

1. Request
Of *My GP warned that for a couple of weeks I might suffer side effects*

Please state:

(a) when the claimant's GP advised him that he would suffer side effects;
(b) the nature of the side effects.

1. Response
(a) 13 December 2004, the day on which the medication was changed.
(b) That it would take two weeks for his body to adjust to the new medication and that in that period he was liable to suffer hyper-glycaemic episodes.

2. Request
Of: *I advised management and others at Pineapple accordingly*

Please state:

(a) whom the claimant advised at Pineapple;
(b) when the claimant allegedly advised the management and others.

2. Response
(a) The claimant told his manager Sue Slight.
(b) 14 December 2004.

Yours sincerely

Natalie Cummings

CHAPTER 5

Witnesses

5.41   **Expert witnesses**

P5.6 Letter requesting direction for medical evidence

5.46   Choosing an expert

5.48   Paying for the report

5.50   Drafting the letter of instruction

DO5.3 Letter of instruction to expert

P5.7 Letter of instruction to medical expert

Civil Procedure Rules (CPR), Part 35

Some definitions: evidence in chief, cross-examination and leading questions

5.1   Three technical terms are needed first. *Evidence in chief* is the evidence given by a witness in his or her own statement or under questioning by the advocate on his or her side; *examination in chief* is asking questions of one's own witness. *Cross-examination* is the questioning of a witness by the other party's advocate.

5.2   *Leading questions* are questions that indicate the expected answer: 'Did Mr Smith then hit you on the head with a blue ring binder?' is a leading question. 'What happened next?' is not. Leading questions are strongly discouraged in examination-in-chief, because the tribunal wants to hear the witness telling the story in their own words rather than simply agreeing with whatever the advocate on their own side suggests. In cross-examination, leading questions are essential, and will not be discouraged: for example 'You did not look at the claimant's personnel file at all before you decided to dismiss him, did you?'

5.3   It is worth noting that none of these terms is defined or used in the employment tribunal rules of procedure: they are concepts borrowed from the ordinary criminal and civil courts. They are widely used in the employment tribunals nevertheless, and they are such fundamental concepts for trained lawyers that tribunals will often seem oblivious to the fact that they may be new to parties acting in person or to inexperienced lay advisers.[1]

The role of witness statements

5.4   Witness statements – that is, a typed narrative that tells the story according to that witness – are expected in England and Wales.[1a] There will normally have been a direction to exchange statements with the other side some days or weeks before the hearing, but even if this is not the case the tribunal will expect to see typed witness statements on the day. Some tribunals will refuse to hear from a witness for whom no written statement has been prepared, or will order an adjournment (with the risk of costs) in order for this to be done.

---

1   See note 5, introduction pix above.
1a Curiously, the practice is different in Scotland, where witnesses give their evidence by way of examination-in-chief: that is, the advocate on their side asks them a series of questions – which should not be leading questions – aimed at giving them the chance to tell their story.

5.5   The witness statement will normally be read aloud by the witness, and the witness will then be questioned by the respondent's advocate and the tribunal. If time is short or the statements are long the tribunal may take time at the beginning of the hearing to read the statements. Then when the witnesses come to give evidence they can simply be asked to confirm that the statement is theirs and is true, and can then be cross-examined. If the witness cannot read or is nervous reading aloud, the tribunal will ask the representative to read the statement aloud.

5.6   The aim in drafting a witness statement is to give, clearly and in a logical (usually chronological) order, the whole of the story the witness has to tell. However, there is very often a need to expand orally on the witness statement, either because the statement is not as complete as it should have been or because the witness wishes to comment on allegations that have been made for the first time in the respondent's witness statements. Tribunals should always permit supplementary questions in chief[2] to deal with matters raised for the first time in the other side's witness statements.

5.7   Tribunals will often also permit an advocate to ask supplementary questions even where the additional information sought could have been included in the statement, but it is not safe to assume this. The statement should therefore be drafted to include all the detail that the party wants the tribunal to hear. Sometimes in complex cases the tribunal will direct the parties to exchange supplementary witness statements after the main statements have been exchanged. Again, if this is done it is important to include the *whole* of the claimant's comment on the respondent's statements in the supplementary statement: if supplementary statements have been permitted, there is a real risk that supplementary questions in chief will be strictly limited.

Relevance

5.8   Relevance is difficult. What the witness thinks is important may be very different from what the tribunal considers relevant. Material is relevant if it is directly about the subject-matter of the complaint, or if it tends to suggest that the claimant's central allegations are true.

---

2   That is, questions from the claimant or his or her advocate.

Example

Suppose the complaint is of a number of separate instances of sex discrimination.

The claimant feels that she has been undervalued for years, and has a series of complaints against a number of different managers about failures to promote on a number of different occasions. She has had particular difficulties at work since returning from a period of maternity leave two years ago.

Most of the individual acts are more than three months before her complaint, but the tribunal has agreed to extend time for events over the last two years because they concern the same individuals and are connected. The claimant is still very aggrieved about what happened when she worked for a different branch of the same employer four years ago, but the tribunal has refused jurisdiction to hear those complaints. The claimant may still want to talk about what happened four years ago, and may feel that it is all part of the same pattern. If it involves different individuals at a different workplace, the tribunal will almost certainly say that this story has no bearing on whether or not they should believe the claimant's more recent allegations.

If on the other hand the claimant says that the same manager who failed to promote her also bullied a colleague into resigning shortly after her return from maternity leave, this is plainly relevant. It is not part of the claimant's complaint, but it tends to suggest that this manager has a bad attitude to new mothers.

5.9 A significant part of the adviser's task in drafting the claimant's witness statement is to exclude irrelevant material, and at the same time to explain to the claimant why it is irrelevant. If this is not handled sensitively, the claimant may feel he or she has been stifled and prevented from telling the full story, and may be keen to put that right under cross-examination. Most tribunals will be tolerant up to a point, but if they are presented with a large volume of irrelevant material they are likely to become impatient and to start imposing strict limits on what they are prepared to listen to. It is far better for the claimant to have his or her adviser make carefully-judged decisions before the hearing about what to include and what to leave out than to have a tired, bored and impatient tribunal make those decisions in haste.

5.10 As well as excluding irrelevant material, the statement must cover the relevant material in full. This advice is easier to give than to follow.

It is necessary to have a clear idea of what conclusions the tribunal will have to come to if the claimant is to succeed, and then to ensure that the claimant (or his or her witnesses) give evidence in support of each.

> **Example**
> Saifur Rahman (of P3.2 and P5.2 below) complains of unfair dismissal. He will succeed if the tribunal concludes that the reason for his dismissal was that he made a protected disclosure. He will also succeed if the tribunal concludes that although the employer's belief in his misconduct was genuine, that was not a belief for which they had reasonable grounds and/or there were procedural faults with the dismissal.
>
> Mr Rahman's evidence therefore needs to establish the following key points:
>
> - that he made a public interest disclosure – so he needs to tell the story of his complaint about what he heard Sister Winston say;
> - that it was Sister Winston whose complaint about him got him into trouble;
> - that her complaint was untrue;
> - that the disciplinary panel dismissed him because of what Sister Winston had said;
> - that the panel did not investigate the complaint against him properly;
> - that he was not given an effective right of appeal.

Hearsay

5.11   Hearsay is a much misunderstood concept, but there is no real mystery to it. Evidence is not hearsay evidence just because the witness is reporting what someone else said: in P5.2 below, Saifur Rahman's allegation that he heard Lorraine Winston say 'Give him some Somnex' is not hearsay. Hearsay evidence is evidence of a statement of another person *given for the purpose of proving the truth of that statement.* 'Give him some Somnex' is not a statement at all and is not capable of being true or false. Saifur's assertion that Penny Short had told him that no-one had asked her what she had seen or heard of the alleged incident is hearsay: the purpose of telling the tribunal that Penny said this is to persuade the tribunal *that no-one had asked Penny what she had seen or heard.* Clearly the best witness of this is Penny, not Saifur, and it is for that reason that there has always been a suspicion of this kind of second-hand evidence.

5.12   There are procedural rules in the ordinary courts that have to be satisfied if hearsay is to be admitted. These do not apply in the employment tribunal, which is entitled to hear any evidence it considers relevant. Nevertheless, it is fair for the tribunal to be sceptical of hearsay evidence unless there is some good reason why the maker of the statement in question could not herself be called to give evidence.

5.13   The claimant in an employment tribunal case may be at a tactical advantage here. If Saifur Rahman failed to call Penny Short, he might be criticised for that by the hospital's counsel, who would say that the tribunal should place little weight on this evidence because Penny was not there to be cross-examined. However, if Saifur has failed to persuade Penny to attend and give evidence because she is still employed by the hospital, he has a good answer to this: 'I cannot persuade Penny to attend because she is worried about souring relations with her employer. You are her employer, so if you say I am misquoting her, or her statement is untrue, why have you not called her?'

5.14   If a claimant wants to rely on hearsay evidence, it may be a useful tactic[3] to alert the respondent to this in advance and invite them to call the witness themselves. It will be difficult for the respondent to protest that the tribunal should place little weight on the statement of a witness who is not available for cross-examination if it is the respondent's own fault that the witness is not available. The letter should be copied to the tribunal.

---

3 Inspired by the Civil Procedure Rules: see rule 33; and on the relevance of the CPR generally, see paras 1.29–1.31 above.

P5.1 Letter notifying respondent of intention to call hearsay evidence

Carrot & Marrow Solicitors
2 Lower Street
Islington
London N12 3AB

17 January 2005

Your ref: GB/ar 6789
Our ref: NC 1234/2004

Dear Mr Bean

Saifur Rahman v St Julian's Hospital NHS Trust

You will note when witness statements are exchanged that Mr Rahman will give evidence that a care assistant at the Hospital, Penny Short, has told him that although she was present on the Coventry Ward when the incident for which he was dismissed was alleged to have taken place, no-one asked her what she had seen or heard. If asked, she would have confirmed that Mr Rahman's collection of Mrs Goody had passed without incident.

Because Ms Short still works for the Hospital, it has not been possible to persuade her to attend the hearing to give evidence for Mr Rahman. It is of course open to you to call her if you wish.

Yours sincerely

Natalie Cummings

cc the Employment Tribunal

Evidence distinguished from argument

5.15   The witness statement is not the place for legal argument, which should be dealt with in submissions at the end of the hearing. For example, Alice Fearon[4] describes the treatment she has suffered and how it has affected her, but she does not go on in her statement to say why she thinks it amounts to sex discrimination: that is argument, which she or her representative will put in closing submissions[5] to the tribunal. If the respondent's witness statements contain legal argument, the claimant's representative should resist the temptation to cross-examine on it. If in doubt, there is no reason why an adviser should not check with the chairman that he or she agrees that a particular assertion is legal argument and a matter for submissions on both sides rather than cross-examination.[6]

Example

An employer says 'The Claimant refused an offer of the same job only four miles away from her home. All my other staff agreed to the move, and they all lived more than four miles from the new office. I offered to pay her bus fares and change her hours so that she did not have to travel at lunch-time, but she refused everything and insisted she had to be within 10 minutes' walk of home in case her mother needed her. I know her mother is old and frail, but I am running a business and I do not have to make a good worker redundant just because she refuses to commute a short distance to work.'

The first three sentences here are assertions of fact, and if the claimant agrees that they are accurate then the employer need not be cross-examined on them. The final sentence is a statement of opinion as to the law. It is wrong, but there is no need for the claimant's adviser to take this up with the respondent in cross-examination.

---

4   See P5.3 below.
5   See paras 9.24–9.29 below.
6   Chairmen can be unhelpful when faced with a question of this nature, and say something like 'It is a matter for you what questions you want to put to the witness.' Qualified lawyers and advisers acting for a fee or employed by an advice agency probably have to take this. A claimant acting in person, or an unqualified person acting for a friend or relative on a one-off basis may wish to point out that they do not have legal expertise and the chairman does: part of his or her function is to guide the parties through the hearing.

The style of writing

5.16   The statement is a formal document, and where lawyers are involved it will normally have been drafted by a lawyer. It is worth making sure that the witness is aware that this is standard practice. Sometimes a witness is asked in cross-examination: 'Did you write this yourself?' and the witness, suddenly fearing that it will be thought improper for her to have signed a document drafted by someone else, may be rattled enough to answer 'Yes' when in fact it is obvious that cannot be true.

5.17   The aim in drafting a witness statement should be to write a clear, logical and reasonably formal account, but in words that are within the witness's own vocabulary. A balance must be struck between attempting a close imitation of the witness's natural speaking style – which in most cases will be excessively informal – and drafting a document parts of which, because of complex vocabulary or syntax, the witness cannot comfortably read aloud or even does not understand. The witness's credibility will be severely damaged if it turns out in the course of questioning that she does not understand the meaning of some of the words used in her 'own' statement: although there is no expectation that she has written it herself, she certainly should have read it carefully and made sure that she agreed with it all. If in doubt, it is probably better to err on the side of informality.

5.18   It is important to make the statement concrete and specific. If the claimant is a kitchen assistant whom the chef has victimised by allocating her to all the dirtiest and most unpleasant jobs, her statement should not say 'The chef treated me unfairly in the allocation of kitchen tasks' – it should say 'From [approximate date when the victimisation started] the chef started allocating me only to the pot-wash, cleaning the chip-fryers, and filling the pig bins. These were all hot, smelly and unpleasant tasks, and everyone hated them. I was never put on floor mopping, wiping the kitchen surfaces or table clearing, which were the end of service tasks that everyone preferred.' Similarly, if the claimant's manager called her a 'useless fuckwit,' her statement should not say 'My manager shouted and swore at me' – it should spell out the allegation in full. Sometimes claimants are hesitant to quote abusive language in the formal setting of a tribunal; they can be assured that the members of the tribunal are used to hearing such stories, and will want to know exactly what was said in any relevant exchange.

5.19 Tribunals have different preferences when it comes to referring to individuals by name, and no approach will please all tribunals. Here each individual's full name is used when she is first mentioned; subsequently she is referred to in whatever manner is habitual with the witness, thus:

> 'The next day I found a note on my desk from my line manager, Jennifer Bennett (Jenny) telling me that I was not to work from home in the future without her express permission. Jenny was not in that day ...'

5.20 If a statement mentions 'Jennifer Bennett' once and then refers consistently to 'Ms Bennett' it will be confusing for the tribunal if the witness, in answer to questions, speaks of 'Jenny.' It is easier to make the statement conform to whatever name comes naturally to the witness than to expect the witness, under the stress of cross-examination, to remember to refer to the person she knows as Jenny as 'Ms Bennett' or 'Jennifer Bennett.'

5.21 A statement should be set out in numbered paragraphs, double spaced so that there is space for notes. The 'statement of truth' is a formality that has become common in the employment tribunals because it is required in the ordinary courts. There is no technical necessity for it in an employment tribunal, but there is no harm in conforming either.

Accuracy

5.22 The accuracy of the statements is extremely important. The adviser should make sure that the claimant (or other witness) understands very clearly that the statement is his or her statement, not the adviser's, and he or she must be sufficiently sure that it is all true to be willing to swear to it. It is essential that the witness has had a sufficient opportunity to check the statement for accuracy before it is signed. If possible, it is preferable to send the witness away with a draft to read at leisure rather than asking him or her to read it in an interview room while the adviser waits: many people simply cannot give the task the attention it needs if they are conscious that someone busy is waiting for them to finish.

5.23 It is necessary to remember that giving evidence in a tribunal is a once-in-a-lifetime experience for most people, and witnesses are often confused about exactly what their role is. One of the most heart-sinking things that can happen for a representative listening to her witness give evidence is to hear the employer's advocate say 'The state-ment at paragraph 24 is not true, then?' and the witness reply 'No, it's not.' There is worse to come. The next question goes, 'So why did you put it in your statement?' and the witness answers 'Because Miss Cummings told me to.'

5.24   Now of course Miss Cummings did not think she was telling the witness what to say. She drafted a witness statement that she believed reflected what the witness had told her. What she failed to do was make it sufficiently clear to the witness that ultimate responsibility for the contents of the statement lay with the witness, not with the adviser; and that the task she was attempting was to draft a true account of what the witness told her, and not to tell the witness what she ought to say.

DO5.1 Witness statement

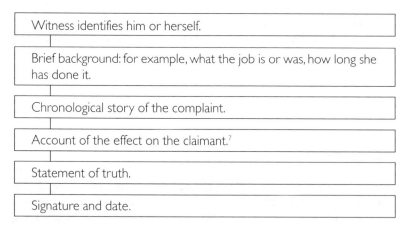

Witness identifies him or herself.
Brief background: for example, what the job is or was, how long she has done it.
Chronological story of the complaint.
Account of the effect on the claimant.[7]
Statement of truth.
Signature and date.

---

7 If it is clear by the time the statement is drafted that there will need to be a separate remedy hearing, this can go in a separate statement for the purpose. It should not be assumed that remedies will be dealt with separately unless the tribunal has said so.

P5.2 Witness statement – unfair dismissal for whistleblowing

IN THE EMPLOYMENT TRIBUNAL　　　　　Case No 123456/05
LONDON CENTRAL

BETWEEN

SAIFUR RAHMAN

Claimant

and

SAINT JULIAN'S HOSPITAL NHS TRUST

Respondent

STATEMENT OF SAIFUR RAHMAN

I, Saifur Rahman, of 25a Pepper Lane, London E11 2LL, make this statement in support of my complaint to the tribunal of unfair dismissal:

1. I came to the UK from India to join my wife and baby son in July 1998. [A] After a short period working for a family business, I applied for a job at the Hospital as a porter and started working there in December 2000. My job was to transport patients and equipment from one part of the hospital to another, as instructed by medical staff.

   > [A] *The claimant's immigration history is not strictly relevant, but it sets the scene.*

2. I was employed on an initial probationary period of six months. In about May 2001 I attended a probationary review meeting with my line manager, Mark Bowland (Mark). Mark congratulated me on my performance. He said that he had heard very good things from all the medical staff I had worked with, and he said that the patients liked me because I

was gentle and respectful with them. He said my employment would be confirmed. [B]

3. I got a letter from Mark confirming me as a permanent employee the next day. I did not have any other formal appraisals, but it continued to be clear that Mark and the medical staff I worked with were very happy with my work. I also got on well with patients.

4. In November 2001 I was promoted to the position of supervising porter.

5. Sometime in January or February 2005 I had a conversation with one of the Sisters, who asked me about my career intentions. She said she thought I was wasted as a porter and seemed to be picking up a lot about the patients and their care. She asked me if I had ever thought about getting qualified as a nurse. I had not thought about that before, but I discussed it with my wife that evening and began to think about it seriously. I did not know this Sister's name except that I think she was known as Shaz, but she was in charge of the ENT ward until about the end of March 2004. Last month I applied for a part-time nursing diploma course and I am waiting for the outcome of my application.

6. On 7 May 2005 I was sent to Coventry Ward, a geriatric ward, to collect a patient, Lisa Goody (Mrs Goody), for physiotherapy. Mrs Goody was well into her eighties and frail and quite deaf, but she was still mentally very sharp. [C] She greeted me by name and said 'How's

[B] *The point of paragraphs 2, 3, 4 and 5 is to establish Mr Rahman as a good, reliable and caring employee whose employers think well of him – this is directly relevant because it suggests that Sister Winston's allegations are inherently implausible and the Hospital should have regarded them with scepticism and investigated them more carefully than they did.*

[C] *Mrs Goody's mental acuity is relevant, because her age notwithstanding she could and should have been asked what had happened.*

my favourite [D] boy nurse?' She knew I was not a nurse [E], but she liked to tease.

7. As I reached the ward I heard the Ward Sister, Lorraine Winston, say to a junior nurse 'Give him some Somnex, it's the only way we'll get any peace round here. Don't put it on his chart or the doctor will create.' I think she was referring to a patient I knew as Roy. Roy was quite far gone with dementia and could be bad-tempered and difficult. Lorraine then looked up and saw that I had heard what she had said. She looked flustered, and said 'Only joking. You'd have to be a saint not to be tempted with some of them.'

8. I was very worried about this. I knew about Somnex because my mother-in-law, who is in her eighties, suffered a serious stroke last year while she was on the drug. It is a powerful prescription sedative, and it is dangerous for old people. I did not believe that Lorraine had been joking, and I was afraid that what I had heard meant that Roy was being given Somnex, without a prescription or proper record-keeping, to keep him quiet. I knew Roy was on a low salt diet, and I thought that might mean he was thought to be at risk of a stroke, so I was worried that Somnex might be particularly dangerous for him. [F]

9. I reported what I had heard to Mark. I did not tell him about my own family experience of Somnex because I am not an expert, but I thought it was bad if a patient was

being given prescription drugs without the doctors' knowledge. Mark refused to take any action. He said 'Don't worry, Lorraine's been at the Hospital forever. She would never do anything like that.' When I pressed him he said, 'What do you know about drugs?' [G]

10. On 12 May 2005 I wrote to the Chief Executive of the Hospital about what I had overheard. [H]

11. On 17 May 2005 the Chief Executive replied promising that my allegation would be looked into, and on 24 May I had a letter from Martin Ogunfowora, a human resources manager, saying that my allegation had been thoroughly investigated and no evidence of unauthorised medication had been found. [I]

12. That afternoon, I went to Coventry Ward to collect Mrs Goody for another physiotherapy session. Sister Winston was on the desk doing paperwork. She looked up and said to me, 'You're toast.' [J] I asked her what she meant, but she just repeated, 'You're toast. Just you wait.'

13. On 27 May 2005 I got a letter dated 26 May from Maisie Lee, another human resources manager. The letter said that I had been accused of swearing at a Sister in the presence of patients and junior nurses. It said I was suspended with immediate effect, and there would be a disciplinary meeting at 10.30 on 3 June 2005.

14. Enclosed in the letter were copies of written statements signed by Lorraine and two other nurses from

[G] *As this does not seem to have resulted in any action, it is not the relevant disclosure itself, but it is relevant to explain that Mr Rahman started by raising his concerns at the appropriate level and did not go straight to the Chief Executive.*

[H] *This is the disclosure.*

[I] *This explains, implicitly, how Sister Winston became aware of the allegation.*

[J] *This is not hearsay: Mr Rahman does not quote it in order to persuade the tribunal that he is toast, but to persuade them that Sister Winston had it in for him.*

the Coventry Ward, Sharon Foster and Michelle Brown. All the statements said that when Lorraine had asked me why I was late to collect a patient on 24 May 2005 I had shouted, 'I've had enough of your fucking nagging. Why don't you take the fucking patient yourself if you're in such a hurry?' The statements said I had then wheeled Mrs Goody's wheelchair out of the ward so fast that she had been frightened and had cried out, and that I slammed the door behind me. [K]

15. I was shocked and astounded by these allegations. I have never sworn at work in my life, and I would never shout at a nurse. I do not think I was late to collect Mrs Goody, and I am sure Lorraine did not accuse me of being late at the time. I am always careful to move patients gently so that they are not frightened. I am especially careful with elderly patients because I know hospital can be very frightening for them. I always try to treat elderly patients as I would like my own parents to be treated. [L]

16. I thought, and I still think, that the only possible explanation for the accusation was that this was what Lorraine meant when she said 'You're toast.' She meant that she was intending to make up a story to get me sacked. [M]

17. I went to the disciplinary hearing on my own because although the letter had said that I could ask a colleague to accompany me I did not want to tell a colleague about these horrible

[K] *These two paragraphs are centrally relevant: they deal with what Sister Winston did to victimise Mr Rahman for his complaint.*

[L] *This emphasises again why the employer should have found Sister Winston's allegations implausible.*

[M] *Strictly speaking Mr Rahman's opinion on this subject is not relevant, but this explains the basis for his complaint of automatically unfair dismissal and it would feel artificial to leave it out just because it is opinion.*

accusations. I thought it would be all around the hospital if I told anyone and I was afraid some people might believe it. [N] I arrived for the hearing at 10.10 because I was anxious not to be late, but the meeting did not start until 10.45. No-one told me why it was starting late or apologised.[O] They just called me in at 10.45 and started the meeting.

> [N] *This is of marginal relevance, but it bolsters Mr Rahman's insistence that it would be completely out of character for him to behave as alleged.*

> [O] *This shows a cavalier attitude to proceedings by the employer.*

18. I told the panel that the allegations against me were completely untrue. I said that Mrs Goody would remember if anything like this had happened. One of the panel said it would be completely inappropriate to ask a geriatric patient that sort of question, and anyway there were three witnesses who all said the same thing. This was the elder of two women on the panel: I think it must have been Elaine Watson. They seemed to think that because there were three nurses saying one thing and only me saying the other, the nurses must be telling the truth.

19. I tried to tell the panel that I thought this was Lorraine's way of getting back at me for writing to the Chief Executive about her giving Somnex to an elderly patient. [P] The chairman of the panel said this was a completely separate matter that had been investigated already. He said it was not relevant. Another member of the panel started to ask me a question about this, but the chairman stopped her and said again that it was a separate matter and had been dealt with. [Q] The panel member who wanted to ask the

> [P] *In other words, the employer was alerted to the fact that Sister Winston might have an axe to grind ...*

> [Q] *... but refused to take this into account.*

question looked very much the youngest member of the panel. She seemed quite nervous and blushed when the chairman spoke to her. [R] From the paperwork I have seen since I think she was Leah Tuckey.

20. Towards the end of the meeting the chairman of the panel said that this was a very serious allegation and they would be bound to consider dismissing me. He asked me if I would apologise to Lorraine if they decided not to dismiss me. I did not see how I could apologise for something that I had not done, and I told them that.

21. At about 11.20am they told me to go outside and wait while they decided what to do. I was given a cup of tea by someone in the personnel office, but I had hardly started it when they called me back in. I do not think I can have waited more than 5 minutes. When I went back in, the chairman told me that they had decided to dismiss me without notice for gross misconduct. I asked if there was a right of appeal, but the chairman said 'It is all in the letter, but there's not much point appealing unless you are prepared to apologise.' I remember that this is exactly how he put it because I thought it was a bit odd that he referred to the dismissal letter as if it already existed. I did not think they had had time to write anything.

22. I was sent outside again. The chairman told me to wait while he wrote the dismissal letter, but the personnel officer who had made me

[R] *In other words: there was a member of the panel who was sympathetic to Mr Rahman, but she was powerless.*

a cup of tea brought it almost at once. I had the impression that they must have had it ready before the meeting began. The letter said that I had a right of appeal and could exercise it by writing to the Director of Human Resources. I did not appeal because of what the chairman had said. [S] I could not apologise to Lorraine because I was not prepared to admit to having behaved in a way that was inconceivable.[T]

[S] *It will be argued for Mr Rahman that in this way he was effectively denied any right of appeal. Even if this is not accepted, it is important to explain why he has not exercised his right of appeal in order to avoid being penalised for that failure if and when the tribunal comes to consider the level of his award.*

23. I left the Hospital in a state of shock and went home to tell my wife what had happened. She was very upset and cried on and off all afternoon and evening. [U]

[T] *The course of the disciplinary hearing is crucial to whether the dismissal was fair or not, so as full an account of it is given as possible.*

[U] *Strictly irrelevant, but might help the sympathy vote along.*

24. My wife and I are friendly with Penny Short, a care assistant at the Hospital. She lives close by and has a young daughter at the same nursery as our son, and we baby-sit for each other sometimes. When she heard that I had been dismissed she came round for tea. [V] She told us that she had seen me arrive to collect Mrs Goody on 24 May and she could have confirmed if she had been asked that I had collected her quietly and without incident. She said she knew it was 24 May because that was her first day back from leave. She said to me that no-one had asked her about the allegations that had been made against me [W]

[V] *It might be said by the employer that Penny is only supportive because she is a friend, so it is better to admit to the friendship up front than to give the impression that she is a purely neutral onlooker.*

[W] *This is hearsay: Mr Rahman seeks to establish that no-one did ask her about the allegations.*

25. I have not yet been able to find another job, although I have made many applications. I have had a lot of interviews, but employers always want to know what my last job was and why I have left it. When I tell

them I do not hear from them again.
I am now wondering if I should apply
to do the nursing diploma course
full-time as there is no point in
studying part-time if I do not have a
job. [X]

26. This statement is true to the best
of my knowledge and belief.

> [X] *This explains the level of Mr Rahman's loss, set out more fully in his schedule of loss.*

Signed _____ Dated _____

P5.3 Witness statement – sex discrimination[8]

IN THE EMPLOYMENT TRIBUNAL   Case No 12345/2005
LONDON NORTH WEST

BETWEEN

ALICE FEARON

Claimant

and

NAFF TAT PLC

Respondent

STATEMENT OF ALICE FEARON

I, Alice Fearon of 2 Pond Lane, Hackney London N17 2BD make this statement in support of my complaint to the employment tribunal:

1. On 5 April 2005 I was interviewed for a job as a sales assistant at the Naff Tat on Tottenham High Road. The interview was set up by Helen Wale (Nell), my Disability Employment Adviser at the Tottenham Job Centre. I have a learning disability.
2. I was offered the job, and I started work the next day.
3. There were several things about the new job that I was a bit worried about. I was told that Sunday working on a rota was compulsory. I did not really want to work Sundays because I am a regular member of

8 The story makes it clear that the employee had been treated badly, but the argument that the treatment amounted to sex discrimination is far from clear-cut.

a local church, but as I had been out of work for three years I accepted the job. I was also worried once I started work about some safety issues. I was expected to climb a wobbly ladder to ceiling level, and some of the fire exits were blocked. I tried to talk to my manager, James Barfield (James) about these worries, and I also told him that I was not happy about being made to stay at work sometimes after 6pm when I was supposed to finish. He just said I could take the job or leave it.

4. I was particularly unhappy about the company's insistence on searching me every time I left the premises, up to four times a day. A manager did the search in the public area of the shop, asking me to lift up my top and my trouser leg showing my bare skin to demonstrate that I was not stealing any of the company's goods. These searches were almost always carried out by a male manager or supervisor. The only time the search was done by a woman was on my last day when the regular manager was not there and the relief manager was a woman.

5. I found this search procedure extremely humiliating. I would have found it unpleasant if the search had been conducted in private by a woman, but I found it particularly upsetting to be searched like this by a man in public. I talked to Nell about it, and she contacted the company's head office and was told that it was company policy to conduct searches and to insist on Sunday working. She also came to see James at the shop, and he demonstrated to her how the search was done.

6. On 19 and 20 April I had two days off, and I went to see Nell at the Job Centre. She contacted the Naff Tat head office and spoke to someone who promised that in future the searches would be done by a woman and away from the public area of the shop. I do not believe that they can have intended to keep this promise because most days I worked in the shop there was no female manager or supervisor present.

7. On 21 April for the first time there was a female relief manager. I went to see Nell in my lunch break. I was searched on my way out, as usual in the public area of the shop. I told Nell that I had decided that I was not going to put up with the searches any more. I asked her to be there with me when I told the manager this.

8. A little while after I got back from lunch, Nell came into the shop. I told the relief manager in front of her that I was not going to let them search me any more. The relief manager said it was company policy and she would make me. Nell asked her how she intended to do this, and I said she could call the police if she wanted.

9. The relief manager telephoned Michael Sugar, the regional manager after Nell had left. He came at about 5pm, looking very angry. He called me upstairs and said that I was on a trial period and they were dismissing me because my work was unsatisfactory. I asked him to put the reason for my dismissal in writing, but he said it was not company policy. He then escorted me off the premises.

10. Before my dismissal no-one had criticised my work in any way. I am convinced that I was dismissed because I refused to submit to the searches.

11. I found the searches extremely upsetting. I had been very excited when I was offered the job at Naff Tat and asked to start work the next day because I had been out of work for so long. I was happy to have a job at last and I was looking forward to earning a wage and having some money to spend. This meant that I was particularly upset when the job did not work out. For the fortnight that I worked at Naff Tat I cried most days because I was so upset about the searches, and I only put up with the situation for as long as I did because I was not confident about my chances of getting another job. I put on weight while I was at Naff Tat because I was so unhappy that I went to Macdonald's every day for lunch to cheer myself up. The whole situation made me feel very low and damaged my confidence.

12. When I was dismissed by Naff Tat, I was worried that I would be out of work again for a long time. I thought any other employer would want to know why I had been dismissed from my previous job.

13. This statement is true to the best of my knowledge and belief.

Signed _____ Dated _____

Witness orders

5.25 The tribunal has power under rule 10(c) of the Procedure Rules to order the attendance of witnesses. The power is mainly exercised on the application of a party, most often in circumstances where the witness is willing to give evidence but is concerned that without an order his or her employer may not give him or her time off to attend the hearing. An application for a witness order is made by writing to the tribunal. The letter should explain briefly the relevance of the witness's evidence and the reason why an order is needed – for example, that the witness is unwilling to attend without an order, or that the witness is afraid his or her employer will not give him or her time off. The letter should also give the full name and address of the witness.

5.26   Rule 11 of the Procedure Rules states that any application to the tribunal must say how the order will assist the tribunal in dealing with the proceedings efficiently and fairly. In the case of a witness order, that follows from the fact that the witness has relevant evidence to give, so it is suggested that this should be included.

5.27   An application for a witness order is the only interlocutory application to a tribunal that need *not* be copied to the respondent with instructions about how and when to object if they wish to. A witness order is a private matter between the party seeking it, the witness and the tribunal, and will not be disclosed to the other party.

DO5.2 Application for a witness order

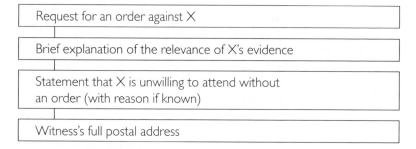

Request for an order against X

Brief explanation of the relevance of X's evidence

Statement that X is unwilling to attend without an order (with reason if known)

Witness's full postal address

P5.4 Application for a witness order

The Regional Secretary
Employment Tribunals (London South)
Montague Court
101 London Rd
West Croydon CR0 2RF

Your ref: 12345/2003
Our ref: NC/1234/03

15 December 2005

Dear Madam

Mr R Rahman v St Julian's Hospital NHS Trust

I should be grateful for an order for Ms Penny Short to attend the hearing as a witness in this case at the hearing listed for 13–15 January 2006.

Ms Short's evidence will assist the tribunal in dealing efficiently and fairly with the case because she was present on the occasion on which the respondent alleges that Mr Rahman was guilty of the misconduct for which he was dismissed. Ms Short will give evidence that the alleged misconduct did not take place, and that she had no involvement in the respondent's investigation into the allegation.

Ms Short's address is 123 Rodney Road, London N17 9EQ. She works for the respondent as a care assistant and is unwilling to attend unless ordered to do so.

Ms Short is due to sit an examination at 10am on the first day of the hearing. I propose to call the claimant first, and I think it is most unlikely that his evidence will be completed until after lunch, so I should be grateful if Ms Short could be ordered to attend from 2pm only.

Yours faithfully

Natalie Cummings

Tactical considerations on witness orders

5.28   The difficulty for the claimant in an employment tribunal case is that witnesses who might be able to give helpful evidence will more often than not be employees of the respondent. They may well be unwilling to give evidence because – rightly or wrongly – they fear victimisation by the employer. There is only a limited amount of comfort the claimant's adviser can give such a witness: it is not accurate to say 'Your employer cannot dismiss you or victimise you for giving evidence.' The employer can do either, and some will. It is true that dismissal for such a reason would give the witness a strong employment tribunal claim of his or her own; but most employees will feel that a job is a better thing to have than a strong employment tribunal claim.

5.29   A witness who is genuinely unwilling to attend the hearing and give evidence presents a difficult problem. There are two kinds of unwilling witnesses a claimant might seek to call. The more common kind is someone who is (or is believed to be) essentially supportive of the claimant, but is unwilling to be involved in tribunal proceedings, often out of concern for her or his own employment position. Sometimes a witness will first agree to give evidence, and provide a statement, but then change his or her mind; sometimes he or she will simply refuse to give a statement at all. It is risky to apply to the tribunal for an order even if the witness has previously provided a statement: a judgment will need to be made whether the witness will stick to her statement if forced to attend against her will. If the witness has not provided a statement and refuses to do so, the risks are even greater: the claimant has no way of knowing what she will say.

5.30   More rarely, a claimant may wish to seek a witness order compelling the attendance of someone she knows will wish to support the respondent's case, but whom she wishes to cross-examine. Both situations are potentially difficult.

Hostile witnesses

5.31   If the claimant calls a witness whom she believes to be supportive, but who either denies that she has any relevant information, or, worse, offers positive support to the respondent's witnesses, the claimant's adviser will wish to cross-examine her. It may, for example, be necessary to ask her why she has changed her story, or suggest to her that the employer has put pressure on her.

5.32   Here the adviser may well find him or herself up against another of the unwritten rules of the employment tribunals: 'This is your witness,' she will be told, 'so you cannot cross-examine her.' This will be news to most non-lawyers, and it is nowhere to be found in the Procedure Rules. It reflects the practice in the ordinary courts, and it is a practice that, broadly speaking, it is useful to follow in the employment tribunals.

5.33   A very large part of cross-examination is asking a series of leading questions. If parties were routinely allowed to cross-examine their own witnesses, the evidence obtained that way would be of little use. If the adviser asks the claimant 'Did so-and-so happen?' and 'So then you did so-and-so?' and 'That was because you felt ... so-and-so?' the tribunal will not feel it has heard the story from the claimant at all. Instead they will have heard the claimant obediently agreeing to everything her adviser has suggested.

5.34   On the other hand, if a witness is clearly unwilling to give evidence helpful to the party that has called him or her, then it does need to be open to that party to cross-examine. In those circumstances, if the cross-examination is effective, the evidence wrung out of the witness may be telling.

5.35   In the ordinary civil and criminal courts there is a body of rules, drawn from both legislation and decided cases, on the circumstances in which a party is to be permitted to cross-examine his or her own witness. In the tribunals there are no comparable established rules, but it is clearly within the tribunal's general case management powers under rule 10 to permit cross-examination of a hostile witness if necessary. Any assertion (from the tribunal or the other side) that the tribunal has 'no power' to do so is simply wrong: if necessary the tribunal can be reminded of rule 14(2) of the Procedure Rules:

> So far as it appears appropriate to do so, the chairman or tribunal shall seek to avoid formality in his or its proceedings and shall not be bound by any enactment or rule of law relating to the admissibility of evidence in proceedings before the courts.

5.36   Slightly different questions arise in relation to the witness, known to be supportive of the employer's case, whom the claimant wishes to cross-examine but whom the respondent does not propose to call. The best way of dealing with this, if it works, is to pressurise the respondent into calling the witness: it is perfectly fair to warn a respondent that if they do not call a particular witness who plainly has relevant evidence to give, the claimant will make much of this failure in submissions and ask the tribunal to draw inferences from that witness's absence. If the respondent buckles under pressure and calls the witness the goal is achieved.

5.37   If the respondent refuses to call the witness, there are various options. The claimant can simply carry out the threat and draw the tribunal's attention to the letter. Most tribunals will see the point.[9]

5.38   A second possibility is to request a witness order, but invite the tribunal to call the witness as its own witness. Since the tribunal has power to exercise any of its rule 10 case management powers on its own initiative, it is clear that it must have power to order the attendance of a witness who is not identified as either the claimant's or the respondent's witness. If the witness is known or firmly expected to be hostile, it is advisable to make it clear that the purpose of the request is to allow the claimant to cross-examine the witness.

5.39   A third possibility is to ask the tribunal to order the witness to attend for cross-examination by the claimant. In the ordinary courts, where one party relies on hearsay evidence,[10] for example, there is a procedure under the Civil Procedure Rules for the other to apply to the court for an order that the maker of the statement relied upon should attend for cross-examination on the statement. The powers of employment tribunals to order the attendance of witnesses are broad enough to allow them to do this without a specific rule and there is no reason in principle why they should not adopt this procedure in an appropriate case where it seems clear that there is a witness who has highly relevant evidence to give but who has not been called by either party.

9   Although on one occasion when a FRU volunteer took this course, he returned from the hearing to report that the chairman had told him it was outrageous to suggest that inferences could be drawn from a particular witness's absence: if he thought that the witness had relevant evidence to give, he could have applied for a witness order. This illustrates something of a catch-22: if some tribunals will take this line, others will refuse to contemplate permitting the claimant to cross-examine his or her 'own' witness. It is suggested that an adviser in this situation should stand firm, insist that there is nothing improper about inviting the tribunal to draw inferences in these circumstances, and if the effect of the tribunal's refusal to do so is sufficiently important, appeal.

10   See paras 5.11–5.14 above.

P5.5 Application for an order for a witness to attend for cross-examination

The Regional Secretary
London Central Employment Tribunal
19-29 Woburn Place
London WC1H 0LU

Your ref: 123456/2004
My ref: NC/1234

15 December 2005

Dear Madam

Rahman v St Julian's NHS Trust

I should be grateful if you would put before a Chairman my application for an order for the attendance of Sister Lorraine Winston at the hearing of this case on 13–15 January 2006.

Sister Winston is the nurse who the claimant alleges made false accusations of misconduct against him. The respondent has indicated that it does not intend to call her. It is clear that Sister Winston has relevant evidence to give, and it is also clear that she will not be a willing or co-operative witness for the claimant. In the circumstances the tribunal is asked to order her attendance as a witness of the tribunal's, and to make her available for cross-examination by either party.

Sister Winston's professional address is:

Coventry Ward
St Julian's Hospital
Commerce Way
London E11 1LL

Yours faithfully

Natalie Cummings

Absent witnesses

5.40   From time to time the claimant will want the tribunal to receive evidence from a witness who has given a statement but who is unable (or unwilling) to attend the hearing. Tribunals will normally be willing to read the statement, but its weight will be severely limited by the fact that the witness is not available for cross-examination by the other party. Evidence from an absent witness should only be used if it is clearly relevant and important, and in that case the claimant should be ready with a clear and full explanation for the witness's inability to attend. Some claimants may prefer to put in an affidavit,[11] but there is probably little real advantage in an affidavit over an ordinary signed statement: either way, the problem remains that the witness is not available for cross-examination.

Expert witnesses

5.41   Sometimes it is necessary to instruct an expert witness in an employment tribunal case. This arises most often in disability discrimination cases where the claimant's disability is in issue, or in other discrimination cases where it is said that the claimant's health has suffered as a result of the discrimination. In an unfair dismissal there may be disputes about the extent of the illness of an employee dismissed for medical incapacity, or about what steps it was reasonable for the claimant to take to mitigate his or her loss.

5.42   Medical experts are not the only kind of expert it is ever necessary to call in the employment tribunal. If there is a dispute about the extent of a pension loss, then if the claim is large enough it may be necessary to instruct an actuary. A computer expert may be needed if there is a dispute about the implications of computer files or records. A handwriting or document analyst may be needed if there is a sufficiently important dispute about the genuineness of a document.

5.43   The only reference in the Procedure Rules to expert witnesses is at rule 10(2)(t): 'Examples of orders which may be made under paragraph (1) are orders ... (t) as to the use of experts or interpreters in the proceedings.'

5.44   As so often, the seeming simplicity of the rule is treacherous, and puts non-lawyers at a disadvantage. Expert evidence is an area in which

11 See glossary.

employment tribunals have a particularly strong tendency to conduct proceedings as if they were bound by the provisions of the Civil Procedure Rules. For this reason a claimant who thinks that a report from a medical or other expert is or may be necessary should always look at Part 35 of the CPR.[12]

5.45   The Employment Appeal Tribunal has also given guidance on expert evidence in the employment tribunals in *De Keyser v Wilson*.[13] The main points are as follows:

- A party seeking to rely on expert evidence should ask the tribunal for guidance and/or directions as to whether expert evidence will be acceptable and what arrangements are to be made.
- A joint expert is normally to be preferred.[14]
- If a joint expert is used, the parties should agree how the costs of the evidence are to be divided.
- If one party is unable to contribute to the cost, then the other party may reasonably choose their own expert. Even if this is the case, the tribunal may attach more weight to the evidence if the other party has been asked to approve or at least comment on the proposed letter of instruction to the expert before it was sent.
- The letter of instruction should tell the expert what questions he or she is required to answer.
- The letter should not take sides between the parties, but should ask the questions in a neutral form, and should emphasise that the expert's main duty is to the tribunal rather than to either party.

---

12 Reproduced at the end of this chapter; and see www.dca.gov.uk.

13 [2001] IRLR 324, EAT.

14 However, where medical evidence is needed the claimant will often have a strong preference to use an existing medical adviser – often a consultant – who already knows his or her medical history. The respondent will rarely agree to appoint the claimant's own consultant as a joint expert, so separate experts will often be unavoidable.

P5.6 Letter requesting directions for medical evidence

The Regional Secretary
Bristol Employment Tribunal

FAX ONLY 0117 925 3452

Your ref: 123456/2005
Our ref: NC ir/123

8 August 2005

Dear Madam

Pauline Phelps v Sharpe, Gentleman & Co Solicitors

I should be grateful if you would put before a Chairman my request for a direction for a medical report in this case.

Ms Phelps' complaint against the respondent is of discrimination on grounds relating to her disability. Ms Phelps has suffered from occasional bouts of moderate to severe depression throughout her adult life, and she has a serious facial disfigurement. The respondent in its notice of appearance denies that Ms Phelps suffers from a disability within the meaning of section 1 of the Disability Discrimination Act 1995.

In the circumstances, I suggest that medical evidence regarding Ms Phelps' condition will be essential to allow the tribunal to deal with the case efficiently and fairly.

Ms Phelps has for the last eight years been under the care of Mrs Roberta Toms, a consultant psychiatrist at St Matthew's Hospital, Bristol. Ms Toms has indicated that she is willing to provide a report. I should be grateful for the Tribunal's order that the claimant should be permitted to rely on expert evidence from Ms Toms on the question of the claimant's disabilities, and I suggest that it would be helpful to list the case for a case management conference to discuss detailed arrangements for this together with any other case management issues that arise.[15]

---

15   An alternative would be to propose detailed directions in this letter – especially if it has been possible to agree them in principle with the respondent first – but a case management discussion (CMD) will more often be necessary in a Disability Discrimination Act 1995 case.

My unavailable dates[16] during August and September are:
Week beginning 15 August
Week beginning 22 August
6, 15 and 21 September

Yours faithfully

Natalie Cummings

Choosing an expert

5.46   In the case of medical evidence, the choice of expert will often be obvious: the consultant who has been treating the claimant is likely to be best-placed to give evidence about his or her condition. In some cases it may be sufficient to ask the claimant's GP for a report. If the claimant is not under the care of a consultant, the claimant may need to contact her local hospital for a list of specialists in her condition; alternatively the Disability Rights Commission or a specific disability charity may be able to help.

5.47   If these sources fail to locate a suitable expert – or if a non-medical expert is required – two helpful websites that will put claimants in touch with experts in a wide variety of fields are www.jspubs.com and www.theexpertwitnessdirectory.co.uk.

Paying for the report

5.48   If a chairman orders a medical report, the tribunal service will normally pay for it, subject to certain limits. The claimant should first enquire how much the doctor will charge for a report, and then ask the tribunal to confirm that it will pay the fee. The claimant may need to pay the expert before recovering the money from the tribunal. Where an adviser is acting, instructions should not be sent to an expert without making sure that the claimant is willing, if necessary, to pay.

5.49   For other non-medical expert evidence, the parties will normally each have to pay the cost of their own experts, or share the cost of a joint expert. If the claimant cannot afford to share the cost of a joint expert, the respondent should be reminded of the suggestion in *de Keyser* that the evidence is likely to carry more weight if the instructions are agreed between the parties.

16 It is obviously preferable to tell the tribunal unavailable dates at this stage than to wait for a CMD to be listed and then ask for it to be postponed because it is inconvenient.

Drafting the letter of instruction

5.50   The letter should start with a short, clear summary of what the case is about and why expert evidence is needed. The questions on which the expert's opinion are sought should be spelled out, and the letter should end with guidance on what needs to be included in the report. It is helpful to enclose a copy of the Practice Direction that accompanies Part 35 of the CPR.[17]

5.51   The most important – and difficult – part of the task is drafting the questions for the expert. The starting point must be a clear under-standing of what it is that the claimant needs to prove in order to succeed in her claim. For example, in a Disability Discrimination Act (DDA) 1995 case where it is disputed that the claimant is disabled for the purposes of the Act, the claimant will typically[18] have to show:

- that she suffers from a physical or mental impairment;
- that the impairment affects mobility, manual dexterity, physical co-ordination, continence, ability to lift, carry or otherwise move everyday objects, speech, hearing, eyesight, memory, ability to con-centrate, learn or understand or perception of the risk of physical danger;[19]
- that the impairment has an effect on her ability to carry out normal day-to-day activities;
- that the effect is substantial;
- that the effect has lasted or is likely to last at least 12 months.[20]

5.52   The questions for the expert should be confined to matters on which she can be expected to have an opinion by virtue of her particular expertise. So, for example, a medical expert can sensibly be asked what the condition is, how long it is likely to last, what its effects are or can be expected to be on the claimant's ability to do specific things. She should not be asked whether the claimant is disabled within the

---

17 Reproduced at the end of this chapter.

18 The rules for what exactly the claimant has to show are complicated: see generally ELAH 5 paras 15.15-15.31.

19 The DDA 1995 makes meeting this requirement part of the definition of having an effect on the ability to carry out normal day-to-day activities: see DDA 1995 Sch 1, para 4. The result, for practical purposes, is that the claimant needs to prove *both* that the impairment affects one of these specific abilities *and* that it has a substantial and long-term effect on her ability to carry out normal day-to-day activities.

20 An effect that is likely to recur is treated as continuing for these purposes.

meaning of the DDA 1995, however, because that is a question for the tribunal to decide by applying the correct legal test to the facts as it finds them.[21]

DO5.3 Letter of instruction to expert

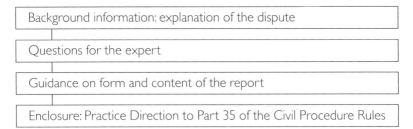

Background information: explanation of the dispute

Questions for the expert

Guidance on form and content of the report

Enclosure: Practice Direction to Part 35 of the Civil Procedure Rules

P5.7 Letter of instruction to medical expert

Roberta Toms
St Matthew's Hospital
St Matthew's Hill
Bristol BS1 2BZ

2 September 2005

My ref: NC ir 1234

Dear Ms Toms

Ms Pauline Phelps: instructions for medical report

BACKGROUND
Ms Phelps has made a complaint to the employment tribunal of constructive dismissal and discrimination contrary to the Disability Discrimination Act (DDA) 1995. She relies on depression and her facial disfigurement and she says that working practices imposed on her by her employer have placed her at a substantial disadvantage compared to workers who are not disabled.

Ms Phelps' former employer does not accept that she has a disability for the purposes of the DDA 1995.

---

21   See for example *Abadeh v British Telecommunications plc* [2001] IRLR 23.

QUESTIONS

I should be grateful if you would provide a medical report dealing with the following questions about the depressive illness for which I understand you are currently treating Ms Phelps:

1. What is Ms Phelps' current condition? How serious is it? [A]

2. What are the causes of Ms Phelps' depression? [B]

3. What treatment is Ms Phelps receiving for her depression? [C]

4. Does it affect any of the following:
   (i) Her mobility: ie, does it affect her ability to go to work, visit friends, go shopping, etc?
   (ii) Her memory?
   (iii) Her ability to concentrate?
   (iv) Her ability to learn?
   (v) Her ability to understand?
   (vi) Her perception of the risk of physical danger? [D]

5. If Ms Phelps is affected by her depression in any of these respects, please say to what extent in your opinion she is affected. [E]

6. To what extent would Ms Phelps' ability to do any of the things listed at question 2 be affected if she were not receiving any treatment for her depression? [F]

7. Has Ms Phelps suffered from depression in the past? Please give a brief account of her medical history in this respect, including any treatment. [G]

8. How long do you expect Ms Phelps' current depression to last? [H]

[A] *This will show whether or not she has a mental impairment.*

[B] *This may not be strictly relevant, but if depression has clear and comprehensible causes that is likely to help the tribunal to believe that it is real and substantial.*

[C] *The effects of medical treatment are disregarded for the purposes of assessing the seriousness of the effects of an impairment, so may be important to know what treatment is being received and what the condition would be without it – see question 6 below.*

[D] *The question deals only with the categories from schedule 1 that are relevant to Ms Phelps' case.*

[E] *It is important to show that the effects are 'substantial,' but the expert's view will carry more weight if she has not been prompted in the letter of instructions by a question of the form 'Would you describe the effects as substantial?' or similar. See paras 5.2 and 5.33 above on leading questions.*

[F] *See the comment on question 3 above.*

[G] *This is relevant to whether the effects are long term.*

[H] *As is this.*

FORM AND CONTENT OF REPORT

I attach guidance on the form and content of expert evidence from the applicable practice direction. Please note in particular that the report must contain the following two statements:

> 'I understand my duty to the Tribunal in writing this report and I have complied with that duty and will continue to comply with it.'

and

> 'I confirm that insofar as the facts stated in my report are within my own knowledge I have made clear which they are and I believe them to be true, and that the opinions I have expressed represent my true and complete professional opinion.'

My client will of course be responsible for your reasonable fee for this report.

Yours sincerely

Natalie Cummings

Civil Procedure Rules (CPR), Part 35

Part 35 of the Civil Procedure Rules and the accompanying Practice Direction are reproduced here because, although not technically applicable, they are essential reading for anyone considering calling expert evidence in the employment tribunal. See para 5.44 above.

Duty to restrict expert evidence

35.1   Expert evidence shall be restricted to that which is reasonably required to resolve the proceedings.

Interpretation

35.2   A reference to an 'expert' in this Part is a reference to an expert who has been instructed to give or prepare evidence for the purpose of court proceedings.

Experts – overriding duty to the court

35.3   (1) It is the duty of an expert to help the court on the matters within his expertise.

(2) This duty overrides any obligation to the person from whom he has received instructions or by whom he is paid.

Court's power to restrict expert evidence

35.4 (1) No party may call an expert or put in evidence an expert's report without the court's permission.

(2) When a party applies for permission under this rule he must identify –

(a) the field in which he wishes to rely on expert evidence; and

(b) where practicable the expert in that field on whose evidence he wishes to rely.

(3) If permission is granted under this rule it shall be in relation only to the expert named or the field identified under paragraph (2).

(4) The court may limit the amount of the expert's fees and expenses that the party who wishes to rely on the expert may recover from any other party.

General requirement for expert evidence to be given in a written report

35.5 (1) Expert evidence is to be given in a written report unless the court directs otherwise.

(2) If a claim is on the fast track, the court will not direct an expert to attend a hearing unless it is necessary to do so in the interests of justice.

Written questions to experts

35.6 (1) A party may put to –

(a) an expert instructed by another party; or

(b) a single joint expert appointed under rule 35.7, written questions about his report.

(2) Written questions under paragraph (1) –

(a) may be put once only;

(b) must be put within 28 days of service of the expert's report; and

(c) must be for the purpose only of clarification of the report, unless in any case –

(i) the court gives permission; or

(ii) the other party agrees.

(3) An expert's answers to questions put in accordance with paragraph (1) shall be treated as part of the expert's report.

(4) Where –
    (a) a party has put a written question to an expert instructed by another party in accordance with this rule; and
    (b) the expert does not answer that question, the court may make one or both of the following orders in relation to the party who instructed the expert –
        (i) that the party may not rely on the evidence of that expert; or
        (ii) that the party may not recover the fees and expenses of that expert from any other party.

Court's power to direct that evidence is to be given by a single joint expert

35.7 (1) Where two or more parties wish to submit expert evidence on a particular issue, the court may direct that the evidence on that issue is to be given by one expert only.

(2) The parties wishing to submit the expert evidence are called 'the instructing parties'.

(3) Where the instructing parties cannot agree who should be the expert, the court may –
    (a) select the expert from a list prepared or identified by the instructing parties; or
    (b) direct that the expert be selected in such other manner as the court may direct.

Instructions to a single joint expert

35.8 (1) Where the court gives a direction under rule 35.7 for a single joint expert to be used, each instructing party may give instructions to the expert.

(2) When an instructing party gives instructions to the expert he must, at the same time, send a copy of the instructions to the other instructing parties.

(3) The court may give directions about –
    (a) the payment of the expert's fees and expenses; and
    (b) any inspection, examination or experiments which the expert wishes to carry out.

(4) The court may, before an expert is instructed –
    (a) limit the amount that can be paid by way of fees and expenses to the expert; and

      (b) direct that the instructing parties pay that amount into court.

(5) Unless the court otherwise directs, the instructing parties are jointly and severally liable (GL) for the payment of the expert's fees and expenses.

Power of court to direct a party to provide information

35.9 Where a party has access to information which is not reasonably available to the other party, the court may direct the party who has access to the information to –

(a) prepare and file a document recording the information; and

(b) serve a copy of that document on the other party.

Contents of report

35.10 (1) An expert's report must comply with the requirements set out in the relevant practice direction.

(2) At the end of an expert's report there must be a statement that –

      (a) the expert understands his duty to the court; and

      (b) he has complied with that duty.

(3) The expert's report must state the substance of all material instructions, whether written or oral, on the basis of which the report was written.

(4) The instructions referred to in paragraph (3) shall not be privileged (GL) against disclosure but the court will not, in relation to those instructions –

      (a) order disclosure of any specific document; or

      (b) permit any questioning in court, other than by the party who instructed the expert,

unless it is satisfied that there are reasonable grounds to consider the statement of instructions given under paragraph (3) to be inaccurate or incomplete.

Use by one party of expert's report disclosed by another

35.11 Where a party has disclosed an expert's report, any party may use that expert's report as evidence at the trial.

Discussions between experts

35.12 (1) The court may, at any stage, direct a discussion between experts for the purpose of requiring the experts to –

    (a) identify and discuss the expert issues in the proceedings; and

    (b) where possible, reach an agreed opinion on those issues.

(2) The court may specify the issues which the experts must discuss.

(3) The court may direct that following a discussion between the experts they must prepare a statement for the court showing –

    (a) those issues on which they agree; and

    (b) those issues on which they disagree and a summary of their reasons for disagreeing.

(4) The content of the discussion between the experts shall not be referred to at the trial unless the parties agree.

(5) Where experts reach agreement on an issue during their discussions, the agreement shall not bind the parties unless the parties expressly agree to be bound by the agreement.

Consequence of failure to disclose expert's report

35.13 A party who fails to disclose an expert's report may not use the report at the trial or call the expert to give evidence orally unless the court gives permission.

Expert's right to ask court for directions

35.14 (1) An expert may file a written request for directions to assist him in carrying out his function as an expert.

(2) An expert must, unless the court orders otherwise, provide a copy of any proposed request for directions under paragraph (1) –

    (a) to the party instructing him, at least 7 days before he files the request; and

    (b) to all other parties, at least 4 days before he files it.

(3) The court, when it gives directions, may also direct that a party be served with a copy of the directions.

Assessors

35.15 (1) This rule applies where the court appoints one or more persons (an 'assessor') under section 70 of the Supreme Court Act 1981(1) or section 63 of the County Courts Act 1984(2).

(2) The assessor shall assist the court in dealing with a matter in which the assessor has skill and experience.

(3) An assessor shall take such part in the proceedings as the court may direct and in particular the court may –

    (a) direct the assessor to prepare a report for the court on any matter at issue in the proceedings; and

    (b) direct the assessor to attend the whole or any part of the trial to advise the court on any such matter.

(4) If the assessor prepares a report for the court before the trial has begun –

    (a) the court will send a copy to each of the parties; and

    (b) the parties may use it at trial.

(5) The remuneration to be paid to the assessor for his services shall be determined by the court and shall form part of the costs of the proceedings.

(6) The court may order any party to deposit in the court office a specified sum in respect of the assessor's fees and, where it does so, the assessor will not be asked to act until the sum has been deposited.

(7) Paragraphs (5) and (6) do not apply where the remuneration of the assessor is to be paid out of money provided by Parliament.

Practice Direction Supplementing CPR Part 35

Part 35 is intended to limit the use of oral expert evidence to that which is reasonably required. In addition, where possible, matters requiring expert evidence should be dealt with by a single expert. Permission of the court is always required either to call an expert or to put an expert's report in evidence.

EXPERT EVIDENCE – GENERAL REQUIREMENTS

1.1 It is the duty of an expert to help the court on matters within his own expertise: rule 35.3(1). This duty is paramount and overrides any obligation to the person from whom the expert has received instructions or by whom he is paid: rule 35.3(2).

1.2 Expert evidence should be the independent product of the expert uninfluenced by the pressures of litigation.

1.3 An expert should assist the court by providing objective, unbiased opinion on matters within his expertise, and should not assume the role of an advocate.

1.4 An expert should consider all material facts, including those which might detract from his opinion.

1.5 An expert should make it clear:

(a) when a question or issue falls outside his expertise;

and

(b) when he is not able to reach a definite opinion, for example because he has insufficient information.

1.6 If, after producing a report, an expert changes his view on any material matter, such change of view should be communicated to all the parties without delay, and when appropriate to the court.

FORM AND CONTENT OF EXPERT'S REPORTS

2.1 An expert's report should be addressed to the court and not to the party from whom the expert has received his instructions.

2.2 An expert's report must:

(1) give details of the expert's qualifications;

(2) give details of any literature or other material which the expert has relied on in making the report;

(3) contain a statement setting out the substance of all facts and instructions given to the expert which are material to the opinions expressed in the report or upon which those opinions are based;

(4) make clear which of the facts stated in the report are within the expert's own knowledge;

(5) say who carried out any examination, measurement, test or experiment which the expert has used for the report, give the qualifications of that person, and say whether or not the test or experiment has been carried out under the expert's supervision;

(6) where there is a range of opinion on the matters dealt with in the report—

(a) summarise the range of opinion, and

(b) give reasons for his own opinion;

(7) contain a summary of the conclusions reached;

(8) if the expert is not able to give his opinion without qualification, state the qualification; and

(9) contain a statement that the expert understands his duty to the court, and has complied and will continue to comply with that duty.

2.3 An expert's report must be verified by a statement of truth as well as containing the statements required in paragraph 2.2(8) and (9) above.

2.4 The form of the statement of truth is as follows:

'I confirm that insofar as the facts stated in my report are within my own knowledge I have made clear which they are and I believe them to be true, and that the opinions I have expressed represent my true and complete professional opinion.'

2.5 Attention is drawn to rule 32.14 which sets out the consequences of verifying a document containing a false statement without an honest belief in its truth.

(For information about statements of truth see Part 22 and the practice direction which supplements it.)

INFORMATION

3   Under Rule 35.9 the court may direct a party with access to information which is not reasonably available to another party to serve on that other party a document which records the information. The document served must include sufficient details of all the facts, tests, experiments and assumptions which underlie any part of the information to enable the party on whom it is served to make, or to obtain, a proper interpretation of the information and an assessment of its significance.

INSTRUCTIONS

4   The instructions referred to in paragraph 2.2(3) will not be protected by privilege (see rule 35.10(4)). But cross-examination of the expert on the contents of his instructions will not be allowed unless the court permits it (or unless the party who gave the instructions consents to it). Before it gives permission the court must be satisfied that there are reasonable grounds to consider that the statement in the report of the substance of the instructions is inaccurate or incomplete. If the court is so satisfied, it will allow the cross-

examination where it appears to be in the interests of justice to do so.

QUESTIONS TO EXPERTS

5.1 Questions asked for the purpose of clarifying the expert's report (see rule 35.6) should be put, in writing, to the expert not later than 28 days after receipt of the expert's report (see paragraphs 1.2 to 1.5 above as to verification).

5.2 Where a party sends a written question or questions direct to an expert, a copy of the questions should, at the same time, be sent to the other party or parties.

5.3 The party or parties instructing the expert must pay any fees charged by that expert for answering questions put under rule 35.6. This does not affect any decision of the court as to the party who is ultimately to bear the expert's costs.

SINGLE EXPERT

6 Where the court has directed that the evidence on a particular issue is to be given by one expert only (rule 35.7) but there are a number of disciplines relevant to that issue, a leading expert in the dominant discipline should be identified as the single expert. He should prepare the general part of the report and be responsible for annexing or incorporating the contents of any reports from experts in other disciplines.

ASSESSORS

7.1 An assessor may be appointed to assist the court under rule 35.15. Not less than 21 days before making any such appointment, the court will notify each party in writing of the name of the proposed assessor, of the matter in respect of which the assistance of the assessor will be sought and of the qualifications of the assessor to give that assistance.

7.2 Where any person has been proposed for appointment as an assessor, objection to him, either personally or in respect of his qualification, may be taken by any party.

7.3 Any such objection must be made in writing and filed with the court within 7 days of receipt of the notification referred to in paragraph 7.1 and will be taken into account by the court in deciding whether or not to make the appointment (section 63(5) of the County Courts Act 1984).

7.4 Copies of any report prepared by the assessor will be sent to each of the parties but the assessor will not give oral evidence or be open to cross-examination or questioning.

CHAPTER 6

Negotiation and settlement

6.48   Compromise agreements

DO6.2 Compromise agreement

P6.6 Compromise agreement – dealing with a point of priniciple

6.52   Consent order

P6.7 Consent order staying the case on agreed terms ('Tomlin order')

6.57   Settlement after partial victory

6.60   Negotiation and costs

P6.8 'Without prejudice save as to costs' settlement offer to respondent

P6.9 Response to a 'without prejudice save as to costs' offer from the respondent

Introduction

6.1　Most employment tribunal complaints end in settlement, and for good reasons. Hearings are stressful and expensive, and sometimes the claimant can achieve by negotiation a benefit that is more important than anything the employment tribunal could order. A favourable reference is the most common example of this: tribunals have no power to order an employer to provide a reference, but often an agreed reference is the key consideration for a dismissed employee keen to get back to work. From the employer's side, the costs of a hearing can often be considerably higher than the value of the claim, and the employer will only rarely recover any of its costs after an employment tribunal hearing. Even if the employer thinks the claim is completely without merit, it may be cheaper to settle than to fight.

6.2　The psychology of a negotiation is often more complex than this: it is always worth remembering that the practical and financial interests of the two opposing sides are not the only significant factors affecting the outcome. Where the employer is an organisation, the individual who is taking decisions about the tribunal case may be more concerned to protect his or her own position than to achieve the best outcome for the respondent. A manager who has no option but to authorise payment to the claimant if the tribunal makes an award may feel that it is safer to let this happen than to take the decision to settle the case. The question 'why did you pay Poppy Snook all that money?' can be laid very firmly to rest by the answer 'I had to because that was what the tribunal ordered.' The answer 'because I thought we would probably lose the case and anyway it was cheaper than paying our lawyers' locates responsibility for the decision with the manager.

6.3　The manager taking decisions about the case may be the same person who decided on dismissal, or upheld the dismissal on appeal. Here 'I thought we were likely to lose' would be very little different from 'I thought I had messed up.' The manager may prefer to expose the company to the risk of a large payment, after which he or she can grouse companionably to colleagues and superiors about the inherent employee bias in the tribunal system, rather than to limit the financial damage to the company by implicitly admitting fault.

The lawyers' role

6.4　Lawyers and advisers, of course, add another layer. Once negotiations have reached a point where settlement is looking more probable than not – and especially if negotiations are complex and are taking up a lot of time in themselves – it is very difficult for lawyers to remain fully focused on preparation for the hearing. This gives negotiations an added momentum: the closer the hearing approaches with a settlement in prospect, the more nightmarish it will be for both sets of lawyers if the deal falls through.

6.5   Claimants' advisers should be aware of this for two reasons. One is that there is the possibility of being badly caught out: the deal always can fall through at the last minute, and there is a limit to how much pressure it is proper or fair to put on a client to accept a settlement that the adviser considers good. In the end, it must be remembered that it is the client's case, not the adviser's, and the point of the whole exercise is to provide a result that the client is content with. If fighting a losing battle in the tribunal gives the client a better sense of 'closure' than accepting a settlement, then often the battle should be fought. There is also the theoretical risk that the other party's apparent willingness to negotiate is pure sham, intended to disrupt the claimant's preparation for hearing. This is a distant risk, but it is wise to proceed as if it could be the case if only because settlement is never certain until a deal is done.

6.6   The other reason to be wary of the momentum towards settlement is that, especially if most of the negotiation has focused on the financial side of the deal, it can put the claimant in a weak position when it comes to other aspects. This is best headed off first by taking instructions carefully about what the client cares most about; and then by making sure to open with a clear statement of what, other than money, the claimant is looking for.

Example

Suppose a reference is the key issue for the claimant, but the employer has an invariable policy of not providing references for employees they have dismissed. There is a long negotiation about money that finally produces a figure that is acceptable to both sides, and only then the claimant's adviser asks for a reference. The danger here is that by now both sides are behind with hearing preparation, and either side (depending which has stronger nerves) will be forced into a deal that is not genuinely satisfactory. Alternatively, the deal falls through and precious preparation time has been wasted on both sides negotiating about something that was not in fact the key issue.

Withdrawing free assistance

6.7   The position of voluntary sector advisers can be complicated by a need to focus services where they are most needed. This is a legitimate concern, and it is perfectly proper[1] for an adviser to warn a client early in proceedings that representation will be withdrawn if the client refuses an offer of settlement that the adviser considers good. Provided the client has time to make alternative arrangements it is fair to act on that warning. What is not fair is to withdraw representation on this basis within a few days of the hearing: by this time it will be far too late for the client to make any alternative arrangements, or to prepare adequately to represent him or herself. If settlement negotiations break down shortly before the hearing, even if the reason for that is unreasonableness on the part of the claimant, then an adviser who has previously promised to represent should not back out.

6.8   It is suggested that advisers who wish to impose this kind of limit on free services might tie the threat to the statutory conciliation period:[2] a sensible rule might be that if the adviser advises acceptance of an offer received within the conciliation period, and the claimant fails to accept it before the end of the period, then the adviser may cease to act. If it became known that voluntary sector advisers commonly applied this rule, that in itself would be a powerful incentive for respondents to make realistic offers within the conciliation period.

External factors

6.9   Finally, the potential power of seemingly wholly irrelevant factors should not be forgotten. If the hearing is listed for the same day as Tim Henman's first Wimbledon final, the party who is not a tennis fan and is represented by a lawyer who is not a tennis fan will be at a very significant advantage over a party who is – or whose lawyer is keen to see the match.[3]

---

1   Subject to applicable rules of professional conduct: barristers and solicitors should have regard to their respective codes.
2   See ETP3 paras 13.24–13.2 above.
3   Because the tennis fans will miss the match if the hearing goes ahead.

'Without prejudice' communications

6.10   Statements made – whether orally or in writing – in the course of negotiations cannot be referred to before the tribunal. This is what is known as the 'without prejudice' rule. Letters dealing with a proposed settlement are often headed 'without prejudice,' and lawyers may preface a conversation on the subject with a request for agreement that what is said should be 'without prejudice.' There is no magic in the words: whether or not they are used, settlement negotiations are exempt from disclosure to the tribunal. The reason for this is obvious: it is necessary that parties to litigation should be able to lower their guard for the purposes of negotiation without weakening their position in the event that negotiations fail. Sometimes letters are headed 'without prejudice save as to costs.' This means that although the contents of the letter and any response cannot be shown to the tribunal before or during the substantive case, one or other party may refer to these discussions after the case has been decided in the context of a costs application.

What should be included in a settlement?

6.11   The parties can make any lawful agreement to settle their dispute. The fact that a settlement can achieve a result that a contested hearing could not is often one of the key factors that persuades the parties to negotiate. Usually – but by no means always – the most important aspect of the settlement is financial, but very often a reference will be important too.[4] In many cases these two will be the only or main benefits in return for which the claimant agrees to drop his or her claim. It is important, however, to have an open mind to more creative solutions in a suitable case.

What the employee may want included

6.12   The following list is not – and could never be – exhaustive: it is intended only to suggest lines of thought

- money
- a reference

---

4 See paras 6.01–6.27 below.

- an apology
- an admission of liability[5]
- a commitment by the employer to change some aspect of its employment practices for the future
- a promise that some of the respondent's staff will be required to undergo some form of equal opportunities training
- a promise to adopt and publicise an equal opportunities policy, or re-draft its existing policy
- a promise to send the claimant on a particular course
- a promise to move the claimant to a different department or office
- a promise to move a colleague (eg, in a harassment case the harasser) to a different department or office
- a promise to short-list the claimant for the next vacant post of a certain description
- reinstatement to the claimant's old job or re-engagement to a different job[6]

6.13   In the very rare cases where it is possible to agree reinstatement or re-engagement of a dismissed employee, this should be done by way of a compromise agreement[7] or a form COT3,[8] or ordered by consent by the tribunal. An informal agreement to withdraw on terms, although adequate in many cases,[9] may fail to preserve continuity on reinstatement or re-engagement.[10] If continuity is not preserved, the resumed employment may be very insecure because it will be a year before the claimant has statutory protection from unfair dismissal.

What the employer may want included

6.14   There are certain familiar elements that employers often want to see included in an agreement.

---

5 See for example P6.9 below.
6 If this is a real possibility in a misconduct dismissal, the employer may wish to substitute a final warning for the decision to dismiss. There is no reason why this should not be agreed in a suitable case.
7 See P6.6 below.
8 See P.6.5 below.
9 See paras 6.35–6.40 below.
10 See *Harvey on Industrial Relations and Employment Law* (Harvey) (Butterworths, Looseleaf) notes to R1036.

'Without admission of liability'

6.15　Employers rarely want to admit liability. Unless there is a practical reason why the claimant needs an admission of liability, this should probably be conceded without too much fuss.

Confidentiality

6.16　Employers tend to want to keep the settlement confidential, probably because they do not want to give any encouragement to other employees who might consider making a similar claim in the future. Often this is not objectionable in principle to the claimant, but the confidentiality clause should not promise too much: claimants will invariably tell their spouse or immediate family about the settlement, so it is futile to ask them to sign an agreement that prohibits this.

Repayment of the settlement sum as a debt if the claimant acts in breach of the confidentiality clause (or other requirement)

6.17　This is a clause that rolls off the word-processors of many respondents' solicitors. It is included in order to frighten the claimant into compliance with the confidentiality (or other) clause, and it will almost always be unenforceable as a 'penalty clause'.[11] On one view this is a reason why claimants should sign up to it with a light heart: it is not worth the paper it is written on. However, it is suggested that this kind of clause should be resisted, because in reality the effect is likely to be to cause the claimant needless anxiety.

Settlement of any other claim that the claimant may have against the employer arising out of the employment or its termination or (sometimes) otherwise

6.18　These are very common, and some respondents will refuse point blank to settle a case without a general clause of this nature. They can be unobjectionable: if there is no other potential claim there is nothing to be lost. However claimants should give this some thought, because if they do have another claim against the employer this is likely to dispose of it. If this kind of clause is included, it is standard practice to qualify it with something along these lines: 'For the avoidance of doubt, nothing in this agreement affects any rights the claimant may have in respect of personal injury or accrued pension rights.'

11　See glossary and *Chitty on Contracts* (Sweet & Maxwell, 2004) paras 26.109–26.111.

6.19   The latter may be difficult to negotiate if the original claim has a personal injury element – if, for example, the claimant has alleged that harassment at work has made him or her ill. In that case, the solution may be to include in the settlement any personal injury of which the claimant is aware at the time, but not any latent injury. It is important that if, for example, the claimant falls ill years later from the delayed effects of some chemical she was exposed to at work, she should not be prevented from suing her employer for that.

References

6.20   References are sometimes treated by advisers as a side issue, to be tacked on to an agreement if possible at the last minute but not to be made a deal-breaker once a sum of money has been agreed. This can be a great mistake. The most serious concern of an employee who has been dismissed will very often be to get another job. A recent dismissal by an employer who is not prepared to provide a favourable reference will be a great handicap in the labour market, and an agreed reference will often be the most important aspect of the deal. It is often helpful to include an agreement that reference requests will be dealt with by a named individual at the previous employer, particularly if there is a suitable manager whom the claimant trusts.

6.21   The value of open references should not be underestimated. Many employers, particularly of low-paid workers, will expect job applicants to bring references with them to the interview, and will not themselves go to the trouble of taking up references from named referees.[12] An agreement to provide a number of open references should be included as a matter of course.

6.22   Respondents' attitudes to references vary widely. Some will simply refuse to provide any reference at all for employees they have dismissed for reasons of misconduct or poor performance, but many will be willing to give a factual reference in these circumstances.

Drafting a reference

6.23   It is a good idea for the claimant to take the initiative in providing the first draft of a reference, and, as tends to be the case in any negotiating

12 See P Toynbee, *Hard Work: Life in Low-pay Britain* (Bloomsbury, 2003).

situation, it is advisable to aim reasonably (but not absurdly) high and include more than you think the other side is likely to accept. In other words, it is sensible to build in some points for the respondent to win on that the claimant is prepared to concede.

6.24　　Drafting a reference for a dismissed employee that sounds satisfactory without being untruthful is something of an art. The model to follow is the over-priced boxed salad from a sandwich shop: three prawns, a crabstick and a squirt of pink salad cream carefully arranged on top of a large quantity of iceberg lettuce may fool the careless buyer into thinking she has bought a 'seafood salad' worth £4.30. Similarly, a bland account of job title, dates of employment, duties made to sound as extensive and responsible as possible, topped off with an endorsement of whatever can be honestly endorsed, can appear to the careless reader to be a good reference. Employers can be surprisingly flexible about this: even if the employee was dismissed for serious misconduct it is sometimes possible to secure a reference that talks up her few good points and draws a charitable veil over her misconduct or incompetence.

6.25　　If the question of a reference looks set to become a deal-breaker, the claimant should take careful stock. What needs to be remembered is that the tribunal cannot order a reference. Claimants sometimes assume that a positive tribunal finding will somehow 'clear their name' and may therefore help them get another job without a reference. Nothing could be further from the truth: if 'I was dismissed from my previous job' looks like bad news to a potential employer, 'I was dismissed from my previous job but I took my employer to an employment tribunal and won' is even worse news.[13]

6.26　　It follows that if the money offered is as much or more than the claimant can realistically hope to get at a hearing, it is futile to let the settlement founder on the employer's refusal provide a reference. It is sensible to let this happen *only* if the sum of money offered is independently unacceptable: in other words, if an agreed reference would be a sufficient benefit to persuade the claimant to settle the case at what is otherwise an undervalue.

6.27　　The document outline below suggests the questions that a reference might cover, in a logical order. Obviously it is better to leave a subject out altogether if the only truthful statement that can be made about it is damaging.

13　Because few organisations will be keen to recruit a new employee who has 'form' for suing his or her employer.

DO6.1 References

Heading – ex-employee's name

Job title and dates of employment

Responsibilities at termination

Performance and any promotions

Attendance, time-keeping, conduct, likeability

P6.1 Reference: genuinely good

Jane Close

Jane Close was employed by the company's Payroll Section for two periods separated by maternity leave and career break, from July 1988 to February 1995, and from July 1998 until October 2005. She was first employed as a Payroll Assistant (Scale 1/2) , and had progressed to the level of Senior Payroll Officer (SO1) by 1995.

By 2005 Jane had overall responsibility for payroll administration for over 150 staff, and for supervising the work of two Payroll Assistants, both of whom she had trained on their arrival in the Payroll Section.

Mrs Close was a highly competent and reliable employee who coped well under pressure. Her attendance, time-keeping and general conduct were exemplary. She took organisational, procedural and technical changes in her stride and proved a competent and tactful supervisor of more junior staff. She was well liked by colleagues, and we were sorry to lose her.

P6.2 Reference: superficially good

Richard Lightfoot was first employed by this Borough from 1982 until 1985 as a yardman at our Crowley Road depot. From 1982 to 1987 he was employed as Assistant Caretaker at the John Russell School, and from 1988 to 2003 he was Resident Caretaker at St George's School. In his last post, he had sole responsibility for the cleaning of the school (a total of over 15,000 square feet), and he was also willing to undertake minor maintenance and repairs. We found him to be punctual and reliable, and his attendance record was good.[14]

14 Note what the reference omits: it says nothing of the fact that although regular and punctual, Mr Lightfoot was all too often under the influence of alcohol, nor of the fact that he was dismissed for assaulting the deputy headmistress.

'Final' and time-limited offers

6.28 The claimant's adviser should always treat the respondent's assertion that an offer is 'final' or 'non-negotiable' with a degree of scepticism. Respondents' advisers often describe their opening offer as 'final' and proceed to make several more 'final' offers.

6.29 Sometimes there are good reasons for an offer to be strictly time-limited. Barristers' fees, for example, very often become payable at the point that the brief is delivered. Barristers need preparation time, so by 3 or 4 days before a hearing (or longer if the case is complex) the respondent's solicitor will be anxious to deliver the brief and let the barrister start preparing the case. Once this has happened, the respondent is committed to significant further costs and may well be unwilling to negotiate further: the money they might have been prepared to spend on a settlement has now been committed to legal costs.

6.30 If the respondent seeks to impose a tight time limit many weeks before the hearing, however, this can normally be taken with a pinch of salt: it may simply be an attempt to bounce the claimant into settling the case quickly. It is a good idea to meet the respondent's deadline for a response if possible, but if it is not possible – or not possible to take an adequately considered decision in the time – it will very rarely turn out that a day or so's delay several weeks before the hearing date causes the offer to be withdrawn.

Negotiating by letter

6.31 Negotiations frequently take place in a flurry of telephone calls in a short space of time, and only the final agreement is recorded in writing. It is often helpful, however, if the claimant fires an opening shot in negotiations by way of a letter setting out the strength (and sometimes admitted weaknesses) of the claim and attaching a schedule of loss.

6.32 This letter should make sense. There is no point drafting a schedule of loss showing a claim for £20,000 and writing a letter the gist of which is 'The claimant has a strong case, which she is willing to settle for £5,000.' If the claimant is willing to settle the claim for a quarter of its value, there has to be a reason why. If the letter fails to account for that, the respondent may conclude that the claimant knows she cannot prove her case, or has simply decided that she cannot face a hearing. There is a real sense in which a claimant needs an 'excuse' to offer settlement at a substantial discount, if that is what he or she has decided to do. If the weaknesses of the case are self-evident, then there is no benefit in being coy. As so often, one eye needs to be kept on the risk of a costs application: if the claimant's letters are reasonable and proportionate, the risk of a successful costs application on the strength of the failure of negotiations will be much reduced.

6.33   There are two negotiation errors that are common among beginners. One is to make it obvious that the respondent is not expected to agree to the proposal, by ending the letter with something along the lines, 'I look forward to hearing from you with your next revised offer' or 'the claimant's proposal is of course negotiable and I look forward to hearing from you.' While it is not recommended that advisers should assert that an offer is 'final' if it is not, it is also self-defeating to make an offer and at the same time spell out that a lower offer is likely to find favour. For the same reason, it is futile to suggest a range of figures for settlement: indicating that the claimant would accept an offer 'in the range £10-£15,000' will not elicit the answer from the respondent, 'We'll make that £15,000, then, shall we?' The preferred result for the claimant, on making a settlement offer to the respondent, is that the respondent accepts the offer. The respondent will not accept the offer if it thinks settlement for less may be possible, so an offer letter should never make it obvious that that is the case.

P6.3 Letter opening negotiations

George Bean
Carrot & Marrow Solicitors
21 Lower St
Islington
London N12 3AB

our ref NC 1234/2004
your ref GB/ar.6789

WITHOUT PREJUDICE

Dear Sir

Mr Matthew Pointer v Tailors of Gloucester Street

I enclose a schedule of loss in this case, which as you see shows a total claim of just over £10,000.

I have advised my client that his resignation under threat of dismissal for gross misconduct very clearly amounts, in law, to an actual dismissal. As he was denied a right of appeal against dismissal on the grounds that he had 'resigned,' the statutory disciplinary procedure was not complied with and his dismissal was unfair; again, there can be no serious doubt of this.

My client fully mitigated his loss within 11 weeks of his dismissal, so there can be no credible argument that he did not do enough to mitigate.

However, I have of course advised my client that he is vulnerable on contributory fault, and in the circumstances I have instructions to offer settlement for £5,000.

The conciliation period in this case has only a further week to run, so if the parties are to take advantages of the services of ACAS it would be helpful if you would take instructions on this offer as soon as you are able.

Yours faithfully

Natalie Cummings

Different methods of settling a claim

6.34   There are a number of ways that a claim once started can be disposed of before a hearing. Broadly, a claim may be withdrawn (either unconditionally or in return for some promise from the respondent), it may be settled by way of an ACAS conciliated agreement, or it may be settled by way of a compromise agreement drawn up in accordance with Employment Rights Act (ERA) 1996 s203. In addition, it may be dealt with by the tribunal in a manner agreed on by the parties. Each of these possibilities is considered below in turn.

Withdrawal

6.35   If for any reason the claimant decides not to pursue the claim, she or he can simply write to the tribunal to withdraw it. The effect of withdrawl is to bring proceedings to an end: see Procedure Rules r.25(3).

6.36   A decision to withdraw a claim does need caution, however, because if the claimant takes that course it is possible that the respondent will make an application for its costs[15] on the grounds that the claimant's conduct of the case has been unreasonable. Withdrawal itself cannot be said to be unreasonable conduct such as to give the tribunal power to make an award of costs against the claimant, but – especially if the claim is withdrawn at a late stage – withdrawal may lead the tribunal to consider that the claimant has behaved unreasonably in failing to withdraw sooner. Claimants who are in serious doubt whether to proceed with their cases should be advised to make that decision as promptly as possible. If a last minute withdrawal is unavoidable, they should be ready with a good explanation for why that is so.

6.37   It will sometimes be advisable to seek an ACAS settlement of the case on the basis that the claimant withdraws in return for the respondent's undertaking not to make any application for costs. This is certainly helpful if the respondent has previously threatened a costs application; in other cases the benefit may need to be weighed carefully against the risk of prompting the respondent to consider an application that they otherwise might not have thought of. This decision will depend in part on the claimant's assessment of the respondent's advisers: City solicitors Sharpe & Hardnose will not overlook the possibility of applying for costs on withdrawal; Bodge & Bluster Employment Consultancy Ltd may.

15   See paras 10.4–10.23 below.

6.38   Cases are sometimes settled by an exchange of correspondence, or a simple written agreement, in which the claimant promises to withdraw and the respondent promises to pay a sum of money, provide an agreed reference, etc. This is probably the most straightforward way of settling a case, and it is quite often used when settlement is reached on the day of the hearing. Otherwise it is surprisingly rare. Probably the reason for this is that it is widely known that an agreement to withdraw (or not to bring) an employment tribunal claim is not binding *on the employee* unless it is negotiated through ACAS or recorded in an agreement that conforms to the requirements of ERA 1996 s203 (a 'compromise agreement').

6.39   This is true, but it may have created a myth that goes further than the reality, and persuaded claimants and respondents that only a compromise agreement or an ACAS conciliated settlement is effective. Suppose the claimant promises to withdraw and the respondent promises to pay the claimant £5,000. The respondent pays up, but the claimant then changes her mind and continues with the claim. In this situation, ERA 1996 s203 has the effect that notwithstanding his promise to withdraw, the claimant cannot be prevented from continuing her claim – although she will certainly have to give credit for the £5,000 received against any compensation she is ultimately awarded, and depending on the circumstances she could be at risk of a costs order if the tribunal thinks her conduct of the case has been unreasonable. This means that an informal agreement under which the respondent pays first and the claimant then withdraws is a bad idea from the respondent's point of view, because it gives the respondent no certainty that that is the end of the case. Claimants have nothing to fear from this, but respondents will normally – and understandably – be unwilling to settle a case in this manner.

6.40   If on the other hand the agreement is that the claimant withdraws the claim first, and the respondent then pays within a set period of withdrawal, there is no such risk for the respondent. For the claimant, there is the same degree of certainty as there would be under an ACAS settlement or a compromise agreement: the agreement is a contract, so if the respondent fails to perform its side of the bargain the contract can be enforced, like any other contract, in the county court. This is exactly the situation where the case is settled in this manner at the door of the tribunal.

P6.4 Agreement to withdraw on terms

Carrot & Marrow Solicitors
24 Lower Street
Islington
London N12 3AB

17 January 2005

your ref GB/ar.6789
our ref NC 1234/2004

Dear Mr Bean

Andrew Tullet v The Big Shift Ltd ET/ 123456/05

As discussed just now, I should be grateful if you would sign and fax back to me the attached terms of settlement of this case.

Yours sincerely

Natalie Cummings

SETTLEMENT AGREEMENT

Andrew Tullet ('the claimant') and The Big Shift Ltd ('the respondent') have agreed as follows:

1. The claimant will by close of business on 18 January 2005 withdraw his complaint numbered 123456/05 of unfair dismissal and unauthorised deductions from wages from the tribunal.
2. On or before 30 January 2005 the respondent will pay to the claimant the sum of £6,750.
3. Each party will refrain from making or publishing any disparaging statement about the other, or any statement about the other calculated or intended to lower the other's standing or reputation with the public or in the eyes of any third party.
4. The fact of this agreement and its terms are confidential, save that either party may disclose them to his or its legal advisers or as required by law and the claimant may disclose them to members of his immediate family (that is, his wife, his parents, and his son).

Signed *Natalie Cummings*   Dated *17 January 2005*
for the claimant

Signed   Dated
for the respondent

ACAS conciliated settlement

6.41   Advisory, Conciliation and Arbitration Service (ACAS) is a government agency that has the job of trying to broker a settlement in all employment tribunal cases. ACAS receives a copy of every claim to the tribunal. A conciliation officer will be assigned to the case and will write to the parties at an early stage to offer his or her services. The form on which ACAS records an agreement is called COT3.[16] Until October 2004, conciliation officers had a duty to act to promote a settlement throughout the proceedings.

6.42   From 1 October 2004, fixed conciliation periods are introduced[17] during which the conciliation officer will have a duty to act. After the end of the conciliation period, there will only be a power to act. ACAS has said in its public consultation paper: Employment Act Proposals on Limiting Conciliation, 5 December 2003 that the power will be exercised only in exceptional circumstances: the aim of the fixed conciliation periods is to encourage parties to negotiate as early as possible, and ACAS has taken the view that this intention will be undermined unless there is a credible penalty for failure to do so. Nevertheless, until the fixed conciliation periods have been in operation for some time, it is impossible to say how strictly in practice they will be applied. If they are strictly applied, the result may be that parties negotiate sooner as intended; or it may simply be that more last minute settlements will be negotiated without the involvement of ACAS.

6.43   The ACAS officer is a neutral go-between who will convey offers and counter-offers between the parties, but will not offer advice on the merits or value of the claim.[18] Most ACAS officers are friendly and pleasant to deal with, but it must be remembered that they are strictly impartial and will convey any information given to them to the respondent, so claimants and their advisers should never say anything to ACAS that they would not be prepared to say to the other side.

6.44   The ACAS officer's practical role can seem like little more than a post-box, but there are potential benefits for the claimant. First, ACAS offers a simple way of settling a case that is widely understood: the claimant will have no difficulty in persuading the respondent that a settlement achieved through ACAS is valid and binding. Secondly, in

---

16   Generally pronounced 'cot 3'. The initials stand for Conciliation Officer of the Tribunal.

17   Except in discrimination and equal pay cases.

18   ACAS officers do occasionally volunteer an opinion on these matters, but they are not legally qualified and it is not part of their job to do so.

a case where feelings run high, using a neutral go-between is sometimes the only way of cooling the temperature sufficiently to negotiate at all. Thirdly, once ACAS notifies the tribunal that a settlement has been reached the tribunal will immediately take the case out of the list. Once the ACAS officer has confirmed that the case is settled – even if a settlement is reached after tribunal staff have gone home – the parties can be rest assured that the tribunal will be informed and the hearing will not take place. If the parties are negotiating at the last minute without the assistance of ACAS, they will not be able to get confirmation after hours that the case has been taken out of the list, so they may still need to attend.

6.45   If the parties approach ACAS after they have agreed a deal, the ACAS officer may refuse to become involved at the last minute, so if a COT3 settlement is desirable, the parties should approach the ACAS officer early in negotiations and keep in touch throughout. At the same time, the fact that negotiations are proceeding through ACAS does not prevent the parties from negotiating directly with each other when that is helpful.

6.46   As a rule, not much turns on whether a particular stage of the negotiations is conducted direct or through ACAS. Sometimes the psychology of negotiations is delicate, however, so the decision can be affected by a number of factors. The relationship with the respondent (especially if unrepresented) may be difficult, and the ACAS officer may be better able to keep tempers cool. Sometimes the claimant's adviser will wish to speak to the respondent's adviser direct to break a deadlock, or to persuade her that a clause she is insisting on is unnecessary. Sometimes the claimant's adviser will simply wish to bring home to the respondent how strong the claim is: an adviser who genuinely feels very confident about a case may be able to convey that confidence, and undermine the respondent's, better in a direct conversation than through an intermediary. On the other hand the claimant's adviser may be conscious of weaknesses in the case, and may prefer to keep the respondent's adviser at arm's length in order to avoid letting that slip. Or the conciliation officer's telephone may simply be engaged at the point that the claimant's adviser wants to put a counter-offer and they will contact the respondent's adviser directly.

6.47   Once terms of settlement are agreed, the conciliation officer will record them on the COT3 form, which will be sent out to the parties for signature. It is important to note that the settlement is binding as soon as both parties have agreed – usually over the telephone – to the words that will appear on the COT3. If the claimant changes his or her mind between agreeing on the telephone and receiving the COT3, it is too late: the case is settled.

P6.5 COT3 wording – money and reference

The claimant is a school caretaker who has been dismissed after a clearly unfair procedure for being drunk at work and assaulting the head teacher.

The parties have agreed as follows:

1. The respondent will pay without admission of liability the sum of £3,500 (three thousand, five hundred pounds) to the claimant in full and final settlement of his complaint before the Employment Tribunal numbered 123456/04 and any other claim arising out of his contract of employment or its termination, provided that nothing in this agreement affects any claim the claimant may have in respect of accrued pension rights or personal injury. The respondent agrees to make the payment under this agreement within 21 days[19] of receipt of copies of this agreement signed on behalf of the claimant.

2. On any request by any third party for a reference for the claimant, the respondent will provide promptly and duly signed and dated on its headed notepaper the reference attached as Schedule to this agreement, and only that reference, provided that in the event of a request in the form of a telephone inquiry or questionnaire, the respondent will respond in a manner fully consistent with the contents of the Schedule hereto. At or before the time for payment agreed at clause (1) above, the respondent will provide to the claimant six copies of an open version of the agreed reference on company notepaper, duly signed and dated and headed 'To whom it may concern.'

3. Neither party will disclose to any third party (including the maker of any request for a reference for the claimant), save as required by law or to their respective legal advisers and in the case of the claimant his immediate family, the existence or content of this agreement.

SCHEDULE

[See reference for Richard Lightfoot at P6.2 above]

---

19 It is essential to agree a date for payment: an agreement to pay a sum of money but not on any particular date is certainly unsatisfactory and could be difficult to enforce.

Compromise agreements

6.48   If the parties settle before the day of the hearing without using ACAS, the usual method is to draw up a compromise agreement that complies with the requirements of ERA 1996 s203. Section 203 requires an agreement in writing relating to the particular proceedings, which must identify an independent adviser who has advised the claimant on the effect of the agreement, and which must state that the conditions regulating compromise agreements under the ERA 1996 are satisfied. The adviser must be a qualified lawyer, or a person certified in writing by either a trade union or an advice centre as competent to give advice and authorised to do so. The adviser, whether a qualified lawyer or not, must be covered by insurance against claims in respect of negligent advice.[20]

6.49   Often the main reason for preferring to use ACAS rather than to enter into a compromise agreement will be that the respondent's adviser takes some persuading that the applicant's adviser, if unqualified, is a 'relevant independent adviser' for the purposes of section 203. This is a legitimate concern for the respondent: if the claimant's adviser is not a relevant independent adviser, then the agreement will still be enforceable against the respondent, but will not prevent the claimant from continuing with the case. If the claimant is unrepresented, it is common for the respondent to agree to pay his or her legal costs of getting the necessary independent legal advice to make the agreement binding.[21]

6.50   A compromise agreement, like a COT3 agreement, is a contract which the claimant can enforce in the county court if the respondent does not comply with its terms.

6.51   The substance of a compromise agreement can be as simple or as complex as the parties require: it is perfectly possible to draft a short, simple compromise agreement that merely settles the case for a sum of money, or a sum of money and a reference. The example below demonstrates the formalities required for a compromise agreement, but its subject matter is unusual in that it is dealing with a point of principle.

---

20   Most advice centres and other organisations that provide free representation will have arrangements in place that are sufficient to meet these requirements in respect of their paid staff and their volunteers.

21   It is worth approaching the local law centre for this purpose: even if it has not been able to take on the case, it may be able to advise on a compromise agreement for a moderate fee paid by the employer. A fee in the region of £300–£500 would be typical.

DO6.2 Compromise agreement

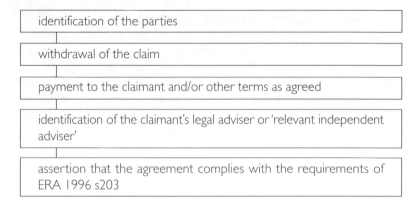

identification of the parties

withdrawal of the claim

payment to the claimant and/or other terms as agreed

identification of the claimant's legal adviser or 'relevant independent adviser'

assertion that the agreement complies with the requirements of ERA 1996 s203

P6.6 Compromise agreement – dealing with a point of principle

COMPROMISE AGREEMENT

This agreement is made between Alice Fearon ('the claimant') and Naff Tat plc ('the respondent'). The claimant and the respondent agree as follows:

1. The claimant's complaint to the Employment Tribunal numbered 123456/04 against Naff Tat plc is withdrawn.
2. The respondent affirms its commitment to the dignity of all its staff at work and undertakes to take the following steps to ensure and protect the dignity of its staff:
    (i) The respondent will within 14 days draw up a draft dignity at work policy dealing with personal privacy, sexual and racial harassment and any comparable mistreatment on grounds of sexual orientation, religion or disability, and submit the draft to the claimant for her approval. If the parties cannot agree within a further 28 days on a final draft of the policy, it will be finalised, taking the views of both parties into account, by Antonia Thwaite of the Humane Resources Consultancy Ltd. Once finalised the policy will be adopted by the respondent forthwith.
    (ii) The respondent undertakes to bring the dignity at work policy to the attention of all its staff within 14 days of its adoption, and to retain it in force for a period of three years without further revisions.
    (iii) The respondent will immediately institute a programme of equal opportunities training, to be provided by the Humane Resources

Consultancy Ltd, for all managers of the grade P2 and above. Naff Tat plc will ensure that all such managers have attended a two-day course by 31 December 2005.

(iv) The respondent will amend its disciplinary policy with immediate effect so that a manager who conducts a personal search of any staff member without specific grounds to suspect wrongdoing will be guilty of gross misconduct. It will bring this change to the attention of all its staff within 21 days of the date of this agreement.

3. On a mutually convenient date in June 2005 the Chairman and the Human Resources Director of the respondent will meet with the claimant and her legal adviser to review progress under this agreement.

4. The purpose of clauses 2 and 3 above are to mitigate the injury to feelings suffered by the claimant as a result of unlawful discrimination against her by the respondent. If these clauses are not fully complied with by 31 December 2005, the respondent will forthwith pay to the claimant the sum of £5,000 in compensation for her injury to feelings.[22]

5. The relevant independent adviser for the purposes of this agreement is Natalie Cummings of the North London Law Centre.[23]

6. The conditions regulating compromise agreements under the Employment Rights Act 1996 are satisfied.

SIGNED . . . .   DATED . . . .
FOR THE APPLICANT

SIGNED . . . .   DATED . . . .
FOR THE RESPONDENT

22 The point of this is to head off any future dispute about what damage the claimant has actually suffered if the respondent fails to comply with those parts of the agreement that do not directly affect her. This too – compare para 0.00 above – could prove unenforceable as a penalty, although the aim is that it should be a valid 'liquidated damages' clause. See glossary *Chitty on Contract* (Sweet & Maxwell, 2004) paras 26.109–26.111

23 Paragraphs 5 and 6 are essential if the agreement is to be valid as a compromise agreement under the Employment Rights Act 1996. Many respondents will also wish the agreement to spell out that Ms Cummings is a 'relevant independent adviser' for the purposes of ERA 1996 s203(3)(c) and that there was in force when she gave the advice a contract of insurance covering the risk of a claim by the employee in respect of loss arising in consequence of the advice. These things must be so, but if they are not, a false assertion that they are does not validate the compromise agreement.

Consent order

6.52   If the parties can agree to the terms of an order that they would like the tribunal to make, then provided it has power to do so the tribunal will almost certainly be willing to make the agreed order. Tribunals only have the powers that they have been given by legislation, so they cannot – for example – order an employer to provide a reference in certain terms even if both parties ask them to. If the parties' agreement is simply that the respondent admits liability and is to pay the claimant a certain sum of money, this can be embodied in a tribunal order without difficulty. It will be fairly rare that the respondent is willing to agree to this: more often, the respondent will be unwilling to admit liability and will wish the terms of any settlement to be confidential. The tribunal cannot of course order one party to pay the other a sum of money without finding that the paying party is liable.

6.53   If the parties wish to agree to terms that the tribunal does not have power to order, it is common to ask the tribunal to make what is known as a 'Tomlin' order. This is an order staying the case for a set period while the parties give effect to their agreement. If the respondent defaults on the agreement, then the claimant can apply to the tribunal to have the case re-listed. If no such application is received by the tribunal within the period of the stay, the tribunal will dismiss the claim.

6.54   The practical difference between this and immediate dismissal on agreed terms is that if the respondent defaults, the claimant can choose between applying to the tribunal to hear the case or enforcing the agreement in the county court. In fact, it is rare that returning to the tribunal is more preferable to enforcing the agreement in the county court: the claimant would presumably not have entered into the settlement agreement unless she or he considered it was preferable to having the case heard by the tribunal, and if that was so at the time the agreement was made, it will most likely still be so a week or so later when the respondent has failed to perform its side of the bargain.

6.55   Nevertheless, this does not mean that 'Tomlin' orders are useless. They have a psychological advantage in that the respondent knows that until it has paid the agreed sum (and performed any other part of the agreement), the tribunal case is not dead but only sleeping. The tribunal case was ready for hearing, and to bring it back to life the claimant has only to write to the tribunal: this is likely to seem more immediate to the respondent than the danger that it will be sued in the county court for breach of contract.

6.56   Occasionally tribunal chairmen express the view that they lack the power to make a 'Tomlin' order. This is mistaken: the tribunal has a wide power under rule 10[24] to determine its own procedure and to stay proceedings if it thinks fit, and there is no reason why it should not exercise that power for the purpose of facilitating settlement. However, if the tribunal is determined not to make a 'Tomlin' order, then dismissal on agreed terms will normally be an adequate alternative.

P6.7 Consent order staying the case on agreed terms ('Tomlin order')

IN THE EMPLOYMENT TRIBUNAL   CASE NO. 123456/2004
LONDON CENTRAL

BETWEEN

JANE CLOSE

Claimant

and

THE LONDON BOROUGH OF HOLBORN

Respondent

draft

_____

ORDER

_____

The parties having agreed to the terms set out in the attached schedule

IT IS ORDERED BY CONSENT:

That all further proceedings in this claim be stayed until 31 January 2004 except for the purpose of carrying those terms into effect, both parties being free to apply to the tribunal to restore the claim on or before that date.

24 Employment Tribunals (Constitution and Rules of Procedure) Regulations 2004 SI No 1861 Sch 1.

SCHEDULE

AGREEMENT

The parties have agreed as follows:

1. The respondent will pay to the claimant the sum of £7,500 in full and final settlement of her employment tribunal complaint numbered 123456/04, payment to be made within 14 days of receipt by the respondent of this agreement signed on behalf of the claimant.
2. The respondent will supply to the claimant, in a letter duly signed and dated by Mark Bertram on the respondent's headed paper and promptly on request by any third party, the following reference:

   [See reference for Jane Close at P6.1 at p201 above.]

3. Any request in the form of a telephone call or a questionnaire will be answered by Mark Bertram and only by Mark Bertram in a manner consistent with the agreed reference set out under paragraph 2 above.

Signed . . . .   Dated . . . .
for claimant

Signed . . . .   Dated . . . .
for respondent

Settlement after partial victory

6.57   If the claimant wins on liability at the hearing, or wins part of his or her claim, the tribunal will then very often invite the parties to try to agree between themselves what the level of any award should be. Often it is very sensible for both parties to settle at this stage. If the claimant has been receiving social security benefits for part of the period that the award will cover, settlement avoids recoupment of those benefits.[25]

6.58   However, if the finding on liability only represents a partial win for the claimant, she should first think carefully about whether there is any prospect that she might wish to appeal the tribunal's decision. Settlement without thought for this possibility will be likely to make any

25 See ELAH 5 paras 18.52–18.56

future appeal impossible; but if the claimant insists that the terms of any settlement must keep open her right to appeal, then this may well make settlement impossible.

Example

Sufiya Halai of P2.2 and P2.7 was aggrieved by her employer's decision to stop paying her enhanced rates for weekend work. Suppose the dispute culminated in her resignation and claim to the employment tribunal, complaining of unauthorised deductions from pay and unfair constructive dismissal.

The hearing runs for a day and a half, and after lunch on the second day the tribunal announces its decision that Ms Halai has suffered unauthorised deductions and has been constructively dismissed, but that she contributed to her dismissal by 50% by not being prepared to negotiate about the enhanced pay. Ms Halai was out of work and receiving social security benefits for just over three months before finding another job, and there is no suggestion that she has failed to do enough to mitigate her loss. The tribunal asks the parties if they would like 20 minutes to discuss whether they can agree the amount of the award.

Ms Halai is disappointed to be told that she is partly to blame for the loss of her job, but she knows that if the tribunal makes an award in respect of her lost earnings while she was unemployed she will lose the Job Seekers' Allowance she claimed during that period. She agrees to accept £2,400 in full and final settlement of her claim, and the tribunal duly records that 'terms of settlement having been agreed between the parties, the claimant's claim for a remedy is dismissed on withdrawal.'

Ms Halai goes to see her adviser at the law centre and asks about appealing against the decision that she was partly to blame for her dismissal, and she is told that she has settled her claim for a remedy and there is now no possibility of an appeal: the case is closed.

6.59   If Ms Halai had seen this problem coming, she would have had various options, but she would not necessarily have been able to solve it. She could simply have told the tribunal and the respondent that she was not prepared to settle because she wanted to take advice about appealing the finding of contributory fault. If she had done that, then the tribunal would have made an award in her favour and she would have lost money through recoupment.

Negotiation and costs

6.60   Respondents will often head settlement offers 'without prejudice save as to costs' and will threaten that, if the claimant does not accept the offer, they will rely on it as evidence of the claimant's unreasonable conduct in making an application for costs. This echoes the practice in the ordinary civil courts, where costs will normally be ordered against a party who has won the case but failed to recover more than has been offered. However, the Employment Appeal Tribunal (EAT) has made it clear that this rule does not apply in the employment tribunals: the power to award costs only arises if a party has behaved unreasonably, and misjudging by a moderate margin the amount that the tribunal will award is not in itself unreasonable conduct.[26]

6.61   The claimant may be at a real risk of a costs order if he or she has no reasonable prospect of recovering more than has been offered: in other words, where the offer is equivalent to the most that the tribunal can be expected to award if the claim is an unqualified success. This will be most likely in cases where the maximum value of the claim is modest, and will be less than the respondent's costs of fighting the case; or where the claimant's case is very strong and easily quantifiable.

6.62   A claimant who has received an offer of, or close to, the maximum the tribunal can realistically be expected to award should think carefully before refusing it because of the costs risk. There is authority that a claimant is entitled to continue with the case for the sake of a finding of liability,[27] but if that is the claimant's concern it is advisable to make it clear to the respondent that an admission of liability would make the difference.[28] Similarly, the respondent's insistence on a confidentiality clause may be a legitimate sticking point for the claimant: again, if that is so, it should be made clear in writing to the respondent.

6.63   There is no reason why the claimant should not turn this tactic on the respondent in a suitable case. If the respondent's defence is misconceived and the amount that the claimant will recover is very clear (in an unfair dismissal case where the claimant's losses clearly exceed the maximum award for such cases, for example, or in a claim for statutory redundancy pay), the claimant can write to the respondent offering to settle for that amount and warning that the claimant may seek costs (or a preparation time order)[29] if the offer is not accepted.

---

26   See *Kopel v Safeway Stores plc* [2003] IRLR 753, EAT.
27   See *Telephone Information Services v Wilkinson* [1991] IRLR 148, EAT.
28   See P6.9 below.
29   See ETP 3 paras 10.14–10.18 and 18.36.

P6.8 'Without prejudice save as to costs' settlement offer to respondent

The case is a complaint of automatically unfair dismissal for refusal to work on Sundays.[29a] It was not finished on the day of the hearing and has had to be listed for a further day some weeks later: the respondent's witnesses have finished giving their evidence but the claimant has yet to be heard. The claimant's adviser takes the view that the claim cannot now fail, but the claimant is anxious about giving evidence and wants to avoid completing the hearing if possible.

Carrot & Marrow Solicitors
24 Lower Street
Islington
London N12 3AB

6 April 2005

your ref GB/ar.6789
our ref NC 1234/2004

WITHOUT PREJUDICE SAVE AS TO COSTS

Dear Carrot & Marrow

Mr Pool v Savemore plc

In light of the evidence given by your client's witnesses at the hearing on 4 April, I invite you to consider urgently with your client whether your defence is misconceived.

Two of your client's three witnesses gave clear evidence that at the time of Mr Pool's dismissal they did not believe that he had any right to refuse Sunday work. One of them appeared to maintain this belief even at the hearing. Even more tellingly, Mr Harpar, who made the decision to dismiss my client, gave unequivocal evidence that the only reason for the dismissal was Mr Pool's refusal to work Saturday night shifts. As the Saturday night shift fell mainly on Sunday, your client's own evidence points conclusively to a dismissal for refusing Sunday work.

29a See the written submissions at P9.2 at p274 below for a fuller account of the story.

In the circumstances I take the view that persisting with the respondent's defence that Mr Pool was fairly dismissed for 'inflexibility' is unreasonable and/or misconceived: the only respect in which he was inflexible was his insistence on his right to refuse Sunday work.

Mr Pool's losses have been clearly quantified and are not open to any credible dispute. As you have seen from his statement and the bundle of applications and rejection letters that have been disclosed, he took immediate and vigorous action to mitigate his loss; and he secured a new job at slightly better pay than he was earning while employed by your client after only 15 weeks. I therefore have instructions to offer settlement of the case for the full sum claimed on his schedule of loss, failing which I will rely on this letter in an application to the tribunal for Mr Pool's whole costs, or alternatively his costs of preparing for and attending the resumed hearing.

Yours faithfully

Natalie Cummings

P6.9 Response to a 'without prejudice save as to costs' offer from the respondent

Mr Herbert has been dismissed because he refused to travel to the new location to which his employer moved its offices. He does not dispute the fairness of the dismissal, because his employer closed the office where he worked when they lost the lease, and they had no other job to offer him. The dispute is about whether he is entitled to redundancy pay, so the sum at stake is modest and exactly quantifiable. The respondent has offered the whole sum claimed, and has threatened a costs application if the offer is rejected.

Carrot & Marrow Solicitors
24 Lower Street
Islington
London N12 3AB

10 January 2005

> your ref GB/ar.6789
> our ref NC 1234/2004

FAO George Bean

WITHOUT PREJUDICE SAVE AS TO COSTS

Dear Mr Bean

David Herbert v Supaclean Ltd

Thank you for your letter of 4 January.

I am afraid that your offer of settlement 'without admission of liability' is unacceptable to my client. The reason for this is that Mr Herbert is in negotiations with his bank over the effect of an insurance policy covering loan repayments in the event of his dismissal for redundancy. The bank has told him that if the tribunal finds that he was dismissed for redundancy, or if your client confirms in writing that this was the reason for his dismissal, his repayments will be covered for the agreed period. If the case is settled without an admission of liability, he will not have the benefit of his insurance. Depending on how long he is out of work, the insurance may be of considerably more value to him than the redundancy payment which is the subject of the claim.

In the circumstances I am instructed that unless your client is willing to admit liability, this claim cannot be settled even for payment of the full sum claimed.

The position my client takes on this cannot be characterised as unreasonable: he is entitled to a finding of liability, and there is a compelling practical reason why he should insist on that entitlement. In the circumstances I have advised him that there is no significant risk of a costs order against him.

Yours sincerely

Natalie Cummings

CHAPTER 7

Case management discussions and pre-hearing reviews

Different types of hearing

7.1   Hearings divide into four different types:

- case management discussions
- pre-hearing reviews
- substantive[1] hearings
- review hearings

7.2   Case management discussions are held where the tribunal thinks that a meeting to discuss procedural and organisational aspects of the case will be useful. Pre-hearing reviews are rare, but are mainly held if a case seems on the papers to be very weak, to determine whether, if the tribunal thinks the claim has little or no prospect of success, it should be struck out or the claimant should be required to pay a deposit in order to be permitted to continue. Pre-hearing reviews are discussed at paras 7.10–7.18 below.

7.3   Substantive hearings deal with the legal or factual issues that will determine the case, and are discussed in chapter 9. Review hearings are occasionally held after the substantive hearing in order to give one party or the other the chance to attempt to persuade the tribunal to change its mind; they are discussed in chapter 10.

Case management discussions

7.4   Before the main hearing, the tribunal may think it necessary or desirable to hold a case management discussion. The tribunal can order this of its own motion, or on the application of one of the parties. There will almost always be a case management discussion in a discrimination case.

7.5   Case management discussions (CMDs) are heard by a chairman alone, and they are oral hearings to deal with the kinds of questions often dealt with by a chairman in correspondence. These are questions like:[2]

- whether or not a party should be permitted to amend the claim or the response;[3]
- whether a hearing date should be postponed;[4]

---

1   See glossary.
2   See Employment Tribunals Rules of Procedure rule 10(2) for a longer – but not exhaustive – list of the orders that can be made at this stage.
3   See paras 4.28–4.35 above.

- whether orders should be made for disclosure of specific documents or written answers to questions;[5]
- when witness statements should be exchanged;[6]
- who should be responsible for preparing the bundle and when this should be done;[7]
- whether expert evidence is to be permitted;[8]
- what are the issues for the main hearing.[9]

7.6 For once the 'plain English' of the rules reflects the reality quite well: these hearings can feel more like a discussion about what arrangements will be most convenient rather than a formal hearing. Often there is little or nothing that is seriously contentious at a case management discussion, and it is not at all uncommon for the parties to agree the issues and suitable directions before the hearing starts and propose them, jointly, to the chairman.

7.7 When push comes to shove, however (and it quite often does), the chairman is in control and can impose his view. Although often uncontentious and co-operative, a case management discussion can also be the forum for a serious dispute between the parties with far-reaching consequences for the final outcome of the case. It is important to be aware of which issues are likely to be contentious, and to be ready with arguments on any that are. Matters of timing, for example, or who is to be responsible for the preparation of hearing bundles, will usually be able to be agreed without much difficulty. Disputes about whether a particular document or class of documents should be disclosed by the respondent may be hotly contested, on the other hand.[10] Any significant amendment to the claim or response may be strongly opposed by the other party. An application for costs may be made at a case management discussion, and this too will almost always be strongly contested.

7.8 It is always a good idea to draw up, and if possible agree with the other side, an agenda for a case management discussion. This focuses the parties' (and the chairman's) minds on what needs to be considered,

---

4 See paras 8.7–8.9 below.
5 See paras 4.38–4.39 above.
6 See para 5.4 above.
7 See paras 8.11–8.12 below.
8 See paras 5.43–5.45 above.
9 See P7.2 below.
10 As a rule of thumb, the more vigorously the respondent defends its right not to disclose a document, the more important it will be to the claimant to get hold of it if possible.

and helps with preparation for the hearing. Rule 10(2)[11] can be used as a check-list for the questions that may arise in addition to the clarification of the questions for the main hearing.

7.9   A proposed list of issues for the main hearing is a good idea, as is a set of proposed directions. Occasionally it will even be appropriate to prepare a skeleton argument for a directions hearing. Skeleton arguments might be desirable at this stage if there is a serious dispute about whether or not a particular document in the possession of one party or the other is privileged, for example, or whether proceedings should be stayed pending the outcome of a related appeal or other proceedings.

P7.1 Agenda for case management discussion

IN THE EMPLOYMENT TRIBUNAL   Case No 123456/2004
LONDON CENTRAL

BETWEEN

SAIFUR RAHMAN

Claimant

and

SAINT JULIAN'S HOSPITAL NHS TRUST

Respondent

AGENDA FOR CASE
MANAGEMENT DISCUSSION
ON 16 DECEMBER 2004

---

1. Clarification of issues for the main hearing.
2. Claimant's application to amend the claim.
3. Respondent's application to amend its response.
4. Claimant's application for an order for disclosure of all communications between personnel and management relating to the disciplinary proceedings.[12]

---

11 Of the Employment Tribunals Rules of Procedure 2004 (found at SI No 1861 Sch 1).
12 This might need a short skeleton argument if the respondent argues that the material is covered by litigation privilege.

5. Witness statements.
6. Hearing bundle.
7. Listing.

P7.2 List of issues and suggested directions for case management discussion

IN THE EMPLOYMENT TRIBUNAL   Case No 123456/2004
LONDON CENTRAL

BETWEEN

SAIFUR RAHMAN

Claimant

and

SAINT JULIAN'S HOSPITAL NHS TRUST

Respondent

PROPOSED LIST OF ISSUES
AND DIRECTIONS

Limitation
1. Was it reasonably practicable for SR to present his complaint by 2 September 2004?
2. If not, did he present it within such further time as was reasonable in all the circumstances?

Unfair dismissal
3. Did SR make a protected disclosure in informing the Chief Executive of the Trust of his concerns about what Sister Winston had said on 7 May 2005?
4. If so, was the fact that he had made a protected disclosure the reason or a significant part of the reason for SR's dismissal?
5. If not, what was the reason for SR's dismissal?
6. Was that an admissible reason for dismissal?
7. If so, was the dismissal (a) substantively fair; (b) procedurally fair?
8. If SR's dismissal was unfair, what loss has he suffered because of his dismissal?

Wrongful dismissal
9. Was SR guilty of gross misconduct?[13]

Suggested directions

- Updated schedule of loss to be provided by claimant on or before 6 January 2005.
- Hearing to be listed for three days.[14]
- Witness statements to be exchanged 28 days before the hearing.
- Index to hearing bundle to be agreed between the parties 14 days before the hearing.
- Bundle to be compiled and copied by the claimant,[15] and one copy to be provided to the respondent seven days before the hearing.

Pre-hearing reviews

7.10   Under the rules in force until 1 October 2004, the purpose of a pre-hearing review (PHR) was clear. It was to determine, on the basis of the claim and response and any oral or written representations (but not evidence), whether the contentions of either party had any reasonable prospect of success. If they did not, the tribunal could order that party to pay a deposit of up to £500 as a condition of being permitted to take part in the proceedings. If the other party was subsequently successful in an application for costs, the deposit would go towards the amount ordered.

---

13 The respondent's position is that he was dismissed without notice for gross misconduct. It follows that the only issue on wrongful dismissal is whether or not he was guilty of gross misconduct. Note that here the question is not what the employer reasonably believed, but what actually happened. In light of Mr Rahman's future career plans, it could be very important to him to have the tribunal come to a conclusion on this – even though his damages for wrongful dismissal will be limited to his net pay for the duration of his contractual notice period – because a dismissal for gross misconduct in the circumstances alleged could have him placed on a register of persons prohibited from working with vulnerable adults.

14 See paras 8.3–8.5 below.

15 Or respondent, if they can be persuaded to take the task on.

7.11   Under the new rules 18 and 19,[16] PHRs have (at least in theory) a much expanded role. At a pre-hearing review a chairman may:

(a) determine any interim or preliminary matter relating to the proceedings;

(b) issue any order in accordance with rule 10 or do anything else which may be done at a case management discussion;

(c) order that a deposit be paid in accordance with rule 20 without hearing evidence;

(d) consider any oral or written representations ...[17]

7.12   There is no requirement that the tribunal must notify the parties in advance of the questions it intends to deal with at a PHR. The likelihood is that they will nevertheless do so, but the rules create an uncertainty that means a claimant who receives notice of a PHR should approach it with caution. If there are any preliminary questions in dispute – whether the claimant was an employee, for example, whether the claim was presented in time, etc – then there is a danger these will be considered at the pre-hearing review. A letter to the tribunal asking it to clarify the questions that will be considered at the pre-hearing review may be helpful, but there is no guarantee that the tribunal will answer the question.

7.13   Pre-hearing reviews will normally be heard by a chairman sitting alone. If either party requests a full tribunal 10 days or more before the hearing, and a chairman considers that 'substantive issues of fact' are likely to be considered at the pre-hearing review, then the chairman may order that the pre-hearing review should be heard by a chairman. If the claimant thinks there is a danger that a significant preliminary issue will be decided at the pre-hearing review, then he or she should always request that it be heard by a full tribunal. The same letter might usefully seek some clarity about what will be decided at the review.

---

16   Which came into force on 1 October 2004 as Employment Tribunals (Constitution and Rules of Procedure) Regulations 2004 SI No 1861, Sch 1 (the 'Employment Tribunals Rules of Procedure').

17   Employment Tribunals Rules of Procedure 2004 r18(2).

P7.3 Letter requesting that a pre-hearing review should be heard by a full tribunal

The Regional Secretary
London Central Employment Tribunal
19–29 Woburn Place
London WC1X 0LU

my ref NC/ir.123
your ref 123456/04

FAX ONLY 020 7273 8686

6 December 2005

Dear Madam

Gilbert Rutledge v Dick Whittington Newsagent Ltd

Thank you for your letter of 3 December giving notice of a pre-hearing review in this case on 10 January 2005.

I should be grateful if you would let me know whether it is intended that any substantive issues should be considered at the pre-hearing review. Specifically, it has been alleged by the respondent that the tribunal lacks jurisdiction because (a) the claimant's claim was presented out of time; and (b) that the claimant was not a worker for the purposes of the Working Time Regulations.

If it is intended to deal with either of these issues, I request that the review should be conducted by a full tribunal. This will assist the tribunal in dealing with the proceedings efficiently and fairly because it is undesirable that substantive issues of fact on which the claimant's entitlement to bring proceedings rests should be determined by a Chairman sitting alone.[18]

This letter is copied to the respondent. The respondent should note that if it objects to the application, it must write to the tribunal within seven days of receiving this letter, or before the date of the hearing (whichever date is the earlier) explaining the reasons for its objection, and should copy

---

18   Rule 11(3) of the Procedure Rules requires a statement of 'how the application will assist the chairman or tribunal in dealing with the case efficiently and fairly' to be included in every interlocutory application. The provision is ill-judged, and inevitably invites bland and formulaic treatment. This statement or something very like it will be adequate for most if not all amendment applications.

that letter to me. Rule 11 of the procedure rules has been complied with in relation to this application.[19]

Yours faithfully

Natalie Cummings

Making use of the pre-hearing review procedure

7.14   Paragraphs 7.11–7.13 above are precautionary: the theoretical scope of pre-hearing reviews has expanded a great deal, and claimants need to be aware of the range of things that *could* be decided at a pre-hearing review. It seems likely,[20] however, that pre-hearing reviews will continue to be rare, and will mainly be confined to their old purpose of deciding whether the contentions of either side are so weak that they should be made to pay a deposit as a condition of being permitted to proceed.

7.15   Pre-hearing reviews are normally seen as a method by which respondents and tribunals may deter weak claims from going ahead. However, the power to order a deposit is equally available against respondents if they put forward unsustainable contentions.

7.16   There are two ways that claimants can occasionally use the pre-hearing review procedure to their advantage. One is to request a pre-hearing review on the grounds that the respondent's contentions are self-evidently weak. It must be remembered that a pre-hearing review is an *extra* hearing unless it deters one party or the other from continuing, so it needs to be capable of producing a significant benefit in order to be worthwhile. One situation in which it might be beneficial is where the employer's case is weak, but the claimant is very anxious about giving evidence. If the tribunal can be persuaded at a pre-hearing review to order the respondent to pay a deposit, this will be a strong signal to the respondent that it ought to offer a realistic settlement of the case.

---

19 This quotes rule 11(4)(b). The rule is unsatisfactory, because it is not clear whether the alternative date to 'within seven days of receiving' the letter is merely 'before the hearing' or 'seven days before the hearing'. However, the party applying for an order cannot be faulted for giving the respondent ambiguous instructions if the ambiguity is the ambiguity of the rules themselves.

20 Because habit is a strong force, and although the new rules make it possible for tribunals to use pre-hearing reviews much more widely, they do not make it compulsory.

P7.4 Letter requesting a pre-hearing review

The Regional Secretary
London Central Employment Tribunal
19–29 Woburn Place
London WC I X 0LU

my ref NC/ir. I 23
your ref I 23456/04

FAX ONLY 020 7273 8686

I 4 January 2005

Dear Madam

Monica Bannon v Easy Peasy Driving School Ltd

I should be grateful if you would put before a Chairman my request for a pre-hearing review in this case to consider the following question:

> *Should the respondent should be required to pay a deposit as a condition of being permitted to pursue its contention that the tribunal lacks jurisdiction to consider the claim on the grounds that the claimant is not an employee of the respondent's?*

The claim is one of sex discrimination involving serious allegations of sexual harassment over a substantial period. The respondent's contention that Ms Bannon cannot bring a complaint against it because she is not an employee has no reasonable prospect of success. It is clear on the face of Ms Bannon's contract with the respondent that she is engaged as a 'self-employed driving instructor,' but that she is under a contract 'personally to do ... work' for the respondent and is therefore within the extended definition of an employee for the purposes of the Sex Discrimination Act 1975. The respondent's argument appears to rest on a failure to grasp that this definition has a wider scope than the common law definition of an employee.

A pre-hearing review on this question will assist the tribunal in dealing efficiently and fairly with the case[21] because the respondent has not to date engaged with the substantive allegations, relying solely on its insistence

---

21   See note 18 above.

that Ms Bannon is not an employee. A clear indication from the Tribunal that the respondent is mistaken in this belief may permit the parties to focus on the real issues on which the case will be decided, and possibly also facilitate negotiations.

Ms Bannon is unfortunately unlikely to be well enough to attend a hearing and give evidence for two to three months, so a preliminary hearing on this issue in the near future is unlikely to be practicable. Please refer to the attached report from Ms Bannon's consultant.

This letter is copied to the respondent. The respondent should note that if it objects to the application, it must write to the tribunal within seven days of receiving this letter, or before the date of the hearing (whichever date is the earlier) explaining the reasons for its objection, and should copy that letter to me. Rule 11 of the procedure rules has been complied with in relation to this application.

Yours faithfully

Natalie Cummings

7.17   The other tactical use a claimant may make of the procedure is in response to a threat of costs. This may be particularly powerful in the hands of an unrepresented claimant.

Example 1
Suppose the respondent has said that the case is misconceived and threatened to apply for costs of up to £10,000[22] if it is not withdrawn. The claimant does not believe his case is misconceived, but is not a lawyer and has not been able to get any legal advice on the strength of his claim. He cannot possibly afford to lose £10,000, so he is extremely worried by the threat. He therefore writes to the tribunal enclosing a copy of the respondent's letter and proposes a pre-hearing review, so that he can, in effect, get the tribunal's preliminary advice on the strength of his claim.

---

22   This is often the form in which the threat is made by respondents, but it is important to note that it is only the limit on what the tribunal can assess itself. It is *not* an absolute limit on the costs that can be ordered: the tribunal can order a detailed assessment of a party's whole costs – without limit – in the county court.

7.18   Letters making a threat of this nature are sometimes headed 'without prejudice save as to costs'[24] and this could give rise to objections from the respondent[25] that the letter should not be shown to the tribunal before the hearing. There are two possible answers to this. The first is that if the letter is nothing more than a threat that if the claimant does not withdraw the claim the respondent will apply for costs, then it is not a genuine attempt at negotiation: this means that it is not entitled to the benefit of the 'without prejudice' rule in the first place. If that argument is not accepted, it can still be argued that the question that the tribunal is invited to determine at a PHR is whether the claimant should be required to pay a deposit against a possible future costs order. It follows from that that the PHR is 'as to costs' and is therefore a hearing at which a letter headed 'without prejudice save as to costs' can properly be produced.[26]

Hearing separate complaints together

7.19   Often what is essentially a single workplace dispute gives rise to a number of different claims. Sometimes it is not possible to put all the claims on the first claim form that is presented to the tribunal. This may be because the limitation period[27] for one claim expires during the waiting period after raising a grievance in respect of the other,[28] or because the employer commits acts of victimisation because the original complaint was presented to the tribunal, or just because the claimant realised – or was advised – that there were further possible claims only after having presented the first complaint.

7.20   In these circumstances it will normally be cheaper and less stressful for both sides if the tribunal hears the various related complaints together. This is often referred to as 'consolidating' the claims; the tribunal has power to do it, at the request of either party or of its own accord, by rule 10(2)(j) of the procedure rules.

---

24 See para 6.10 above.

25 Or possibly the tribunal itself.

26 If the tribunal finds these arguments unconvincing it may send the respondent's 'without prejudice save as to costs' letter back to the claimant on the grounds that it is not something that can properly be retained on the tribunal file and should not be seen by the tribunal that decides the case. No harm will have been done.

27 See glossary.

28 See para 1.62 above.

7.21 It is necessary to be realistic when asking the tribunal to order that a new claim should be heard together with an existing claim. The respondent will need time to put in its written response to the new claim, to prepare new witness statements or at least alter existing statements to deal with the new allegations, and possibly to take other additional preparatory steps. If a new claim is presented shortly before the hearing fixed for an existing claim, the claimant will have to decide whether it is preferable to have the case postponed so that the cases can be heard together, or to go ahead with the existing hearing date but accept that the two cases will have to be heard separately. This can be an important tactical decision.

Example 2

Suppose the claimant says that she has been subjected to racial harassment and abuse by her manager and, after an internal grievance fails to solve the problem, complains to a tribunal of race discrimination. Her manager has never abused her in the presence of anyone else, and strenuously denies her allegations. The case is listed for a hearing on 1 December 2005. On 5 November 2005 the claimant is given notice of a disciplinary hearing on 12 November to discuss an allegation that she has been fiddling her expenses, and at the end of the hearing on 12 November she is dismissed without notice for gross misconduct. Someone anonymously sends her a copy of an e-mail sent by her manager to a colleague in accounts saying 'Can you take a close look at that mouthy cow's expenses claims? There must be something we can get her for.'

She presents a tribunal claim about her dismissal, which she says is (a) unfair and (b) an act of discrimination by way of victimisation, on 22 November 2005. It is clearly not possible to get this claim consolidated with the existing claim and heard with it on 1 December: if the claims are consolidated then the inevitable result will be a postponement of the hearing. On these facts, that is probably what the claimant prefers: she is in a strong position to prove her victimisation claim, and the damage that her evidence will do to the credibility of her manager should assist her in persuading the tribunal that she is telling the truth (and he is lying) when it comes to the first claim.

Example 3
The claimant has presented an unfair dismissal claim, and subsequently been advised that he has good grounds for a disability discrimination claim as well. The unfair dismissal case is straightforward and is listed for one day, but the claimant is advised that his Disability Discrimination Act (DDA) 1995 claim will take at least four days to hear. The claimant has an offer of free representation in his unfair dismissal case, but his representative is unable to offer representation for a four day case.

In this situation, the claimant may wish to complete the unfair dismissal claim first: if he wins that and recovers a significant award, he may then be able to afford representation at the hearing of his DDA claim.

7.22   It should be remembered that the other party may apply for two related claims to be consolidated, or the tribunal itself may even be sufficiently wide awake to consider this without an application from either side. In either case, the decision to consolidate should not be taken before both sides have had an opportunity to make their views known. In this kind of situation the respondent may also prefer a single hearing to two separate hearings, so it will be worth contacting the respondent before applying for consolidation to find out whether they are prepared to support the application.

P7.5 Letter requesting consolidation of new claim and consequential postponement

The Regional Secretary
London Central Employment Tribunal
19–29 Woburn Place
London WC1X 0LU

FAX ONLY 020 7273 8686

22 November 2005

Dear Madam

Ngosi Nbuka v Ambience plc

I enclose the claimant's claim form.

The claimant has previously presented a complaint of race discrimination against the same employer. That claim, number ET/123456/04 is currently listed for hearing for three days from 1 December 2005.

The new claim relates to the claimant's dismissal with effect 12 November. The claimant believes that she was dismissed because of her pending race discrimination claim, and therefore that her dismissal was an act of discrimination by way of victimisation, and also unfair.

There are substantial factual issues in common between the two claims. Both are predominantly concerned with the conduct towards the claimant of the same individual and the same witnesses are likely to be required for both. In the circumstances I suggest that it will be more economical for the tribunal and for the parties if the new claim is heard together with the existing claim. Unfortunately there is insufficient time now for the respondent to respond to the new claim before 1 December. I suggest that in the circumstances it would assist the tribunal in dealing fairly and efficiently with the case if the hearing listed for 1 December is be postponed and the case re-listed for a consolidated hearing in the New Year.

This letter is copied to the respondent. The respondent should note that if it objects to the application, it must write to the tribunal within seven days of receiving this letter, or before the date of the hearing (whichever date is the earlier) explaining the reasons for its objection, and should copy that letter to me. Rule 11 of the procedure rules has been complied with in relation to this application.[29]

Yours faithfully

Natalie Cummings

---

29 This paragraph, or something to the same effect, is necessary to comply with rule 11 if the claimant is professionally represented, and desirable in any event. If it has been possible to secure the respondent's agreement to the application, substitute something to the effect: 'I have discussed this proposal with the respondent's solicitor, who supports this application and will write separately to confirm that.'

Approaching the main hearing

Fixing the date

8.1   The tribunal will sometimes – but not always – invite the parties to list their unavailable dates before assigning a hearing date (usually referred to as 'listing'). If this is done, the claimant's adviser should take care to provide unavailable dates for the claimant, any witnesses, and (assuming he or she intends to represent the client at the hearing) him or herself. If unavailable dates are given in advance, then provided they are not too extensive they will rarely, if ever, be questioned by the tribunal. Voluntary sector or volunteer representatives sometimes doubt whether it is permissible to take their own convenience into account, so it is worth spelling out that it is: many Free Representation Unit volunteers, for example, are still students, and should not feel shy to give as 'unavailable' dates on which they have exams to sit, or imminent exams or assessments to prepare for.

8.2   This is also the moment to tell the tribunal if you think its time estimate is wrong. This is important because cases are listed for a set number of days, and if the case is not completed in the allotted time the tribunal will not be able to continue on consecutive days: it will be necessary to find another date, often several months ahead, when all three members of the tribunal, the parties, their representatives and any remaining witnesses can be present. This is very undesirable: the tribunal's recollection of the evidence will fade, and depending on the order in which the evidence is given the tribunal may be left with strong and immediate recollections of the respondent's evidence as against distant and incomplete memories of the claimant's.

Estimating the length of the hearing

8.3   That said, estimating the length of hearing is an inexact process even for experienced practitioners. Much depends on the way the witnesses answer questions, and the way the chairman runs the hearing. The following factors have to be considered:

- *The subject-matter of the case.* If it is about a single event – a dismissal for gross misconduct, for example, or a failure to promote or appoint – then it will be shorter than a complaint that a course of conduct over a long period was discriminatory, or that a whole series of different acts added up to a fundamental breach of contract.
- *The amount of relevant documentation.* If there is a great volume of paper that the tribunal will need to read, and that the witnesses

will need to answer questions on, then the hearing will take longer than if the bundle is only 30 or 40 pages long.

- *The number of witnesses.* This is relevant, but it is less important than it may seem at first sight. The factor that makes most of the difference is how long and complicated a story the witnesses have to tell, not how many of them there are.
- *Whether any of the evidence will have to be taken through an interpreter.* If so, the estimate for that witness's evidence needs to be doubled at least.

8.4   Most wages or contract claims are finished in a day or less. A straightforward unfair dismissal claim where the reason given is redundancy or gross misconduct will not usually take more than a day. Discrimination claims tend to take longer, although they can sometimes be finished in a day if the facts are simple and the complaint does not involve the telling of a long story.[1]

8.5   For more substantial claims a picture can be built up by considering each witness in turn. In a discrimination or constructive dismissal case, a helpful starting point might be to assume that the claimant's evidence will take two hours for the first 100 pages of bundle and an additional hour for each 100 pages after that. If there are supporting witnesses, their evidence is likely to be shorter: allow say 20 or 25% of the time taken by the claimant for each supporting witness, but unless there is a very large number of them, assume that the supporting witnesses will not take longer in aggregate than the claimant. Then add a similar time for the respondent's case, or a little less if they are calling fewer witnesses, plus a day for submissions and preliminary issues, etc. For a long case, it is always worth suggesting at a directions hearing that the tribunal should take the first day to read the statements and key documents. The parties should be ready to agree between them what the key documents are.

8.6   If something changes that affects the likely length of the hearing after it has been listed, it is important to draw the fact to the tribunal's attention as soon as possible.

---

1 For example, 'failure to appoint' cases tend to be much more straightforward than other discrimination cases because there is no story to tell about the previous relationship between the parties.

Postponement requests

8.7   Once the case is listed, the tribunal is likely to be less accepting of reasons given for unavailability than it would have been if they had been drawn to its attention in advance. If the parties have not been invited to give their unavailable dates, then a prompt request for a postponement on the grounds that the claimant, a witness or the representative is unavailable will probably be granted, at least for the first time. The more previous postponements there have been, and the closer to the hearing a postponement request comes, the harder the tribunal is likely to look at the reasons before granting it. If it is essential to request a postponement close to the hearing, or after the case has been previously postponed, the request should deal carefully with the reasons why the need could not have been foreseen earlier, and why it is essential that that witness – or that particular adviser – should be able to be present.

8.8   Where the problem is with the representative's availability, a claimant relying on free advice has a slight advantage. Tribunals will be reluctant to postpone a case because of the unforeseen unavailability of the respondent's counsel or solicitor: they will take the view that there are plenty of barristers and solicitors in the world and the respondent can choose another. The same cannot be said of free representation: demand greatly outstrips supply, and a claimant whose law centre adviser or FRU representative, for example, is unavailable on the day of the hearing is unlikely to have any other options. This was recognised by the EAT in *Yearwood v Royal Mail*.[2]

8.9   If an application for postponement is opposed by the other party, or is made at short notice, the party applying should be ready to provide evidence of the need for it – including medical evidence if the reason for the request is illness. A medical certificate simply signing the claimant off work for a period is likely to be insufficient, so the GP (or other medical adviser) should be asked to deal specifically with whether the claimant is well enough to attend a hearing – see *Andreou v Lord Chancellor's Department*.[3]

---

2   EAT/843/97; May 1998 *Legal Action* 15; reproduced at appendix A below
3   [2002] IRLR 728, CA. See also *Teinaz v London Borough of Wandsworth* [2002] IRLR 721; ICR 1471, CA.

P8.1 Application for postponement – illness of representative

The Regional Secretary
London Central Employment Tribunal
19–29 Woburn Place
London WC1X 0LU

your ref 123456/04
my ref JS/ir.321

FAX ONLY 020 7273 8686

22 February 2005

VERY URGENT PLEASE: HEARING TOMORROW

Dear Madam

Ngosi Nbuka v Ambience plc

I am afraid it is necessary for me to make an urgent application for a postponement of this hearing, listed for three days from tomorrow.

I have just heard that Natalie Cummings, who has conduct of this case for Ms Nbuka and was intending to represent her at the hearing, has been taken into hospital today with suspected appendicitis. Ms Cummings was off work yesterday, but had put her symptoms down to a 'tummy bug' and had expected to be able to return today. I understand that an operation is scheduled for tomorrow morning.

The case raises complicated issues of discrimination law and there is a substantial volume of documentation. Ms Cummings is the only employment lawyer employed by the Law Centre, and there is no-one who can represent Ms Nbuka in her place. Moreover the papers are currently with Ms Cummings as she took them home to work on over the weekend. Ms Nbuka herself has not of course yet made any preparations to represent herself, and cannot reasonably be expected to be able to do so adequately between now and tomorrow.

For these reasons I suggest that it is strongly in the interests of the efficient and fair disposal of the case that the hearing should be postponed.

This letter is copied to the respondent. The respondent should note that if it objects to the application, it must write to the tribunal today[4] explaining the reasons for its objection, and should copy that letter to me. Rule 11 of the procedure rules[5] has been complied with in relation to this application.

Yours faithfully

Jennifer Selscombe

8.10   For an application as urgent as this, it is a sensible precaution to telephone the tribunal 10 or 15 minutes after sending the fax to check that it has arrived and is legible, and ask the clerk to make sure that it goes before a chairman at the earliest opportunity.[6]

The bundle

8.11   Once both sides have disclosed all their relevant documents, it will be necessary to agree the content of a hearing bundle. This is something that the parties or their advisers should normally be able to handle co-operatively, although occasionally there may be a dispute about whether a document that one side says is privileged[7] should be included. Agreement that a particular document should be included in the bundle does not amount to agreement that the document is genuine. If one side doubts the authenticity of a document it is prudent to make that doubt clear but agreeing that since the other side wants to refer the tribunal to it, it should be included in the bundle.

8.12   There are differing views about whose job it is to prepare the bundle, but this will rarely, if ever, be worth a serious battle. It is in the interests of both sides that it should be competently done in good time before the hearing. If the respondents are represented by solicitors who clearly know what they are about, it is probably worthwhile trying to charm them into doing it. If the respondents are incompetently represented the consequence of persuading them to do it may be an incomplete

---

4   The usual instruction to write to the tribunal seven days before the hearing is meaningless here, so the standard paragraph is adapted.

5   Employment Tribunals (Constitution and Rules of Procedure) Regulations 2004 SI No 1861 Sch 1.

6   This is a request to a member of tribunal staff to go out of his or her way to help, so charm – and a willingness to explain the problem – is in order.

7   See glossary and paras 4.28–4.35 above.

bundle, in random order and with crucial pages either missing or illegible, and the claimant's copy not provided until the day of the hearing. The benefit of a clear well-organised bundle which the claimant's adviser has had a couple of days to decorate with highlighters, notes and sticky notes before the hearing is well worth the price of some quality time with the photocopier. (It is for the same reason that respondents' solicitors will often be willing to take on the job: they will want it done properly, and in good time, and they may not trust the claimant or his or her advisers on either point.)

P8.2 Letter proposing a joint bundle

George Bean
Carrot & Marrow Solicitors
24 Lower Street
London N12 3AB

my ref NC/1234/04
your ref CB/fc. 1234

5 January 2005

Dear Mr Bean

Yasmin Khan v First Call Cleaning Services Ltd 123456/2004

I enclose a draft index for a joint bundle of documents. I suggest that we can leave out all but a short extract of the company handbook, as indicated, and I do not think that it will be necessary to refer to more than one payslip as they are the same in the relevant respects. Please let me know if you disagree, or if there are any other documents that you would wish to see included.

The Law Centre is a small charity and has no secretarial back-up, so it would be very helpful if you would be willing to arrange for the bundle to be compiled and copied.

I will compile a short separate bundle of documents relevant to my client's efforts to find work after his dismissal, and the expenses he incurred in doing so. I do not imagine that you will have any documents that you wish to add to this bundle, but please let me know if I am wrong in this.

Yours sincerely

Natalie Cummings

The content of the bundle

8.13   The bundle should be limited to the documents that one side or the other wishes the tribunal to read and should not be any longer than necessary. 'For completeness' is an inadequate reason to include any document: if there is no better reason, it should be left out. There will rarely be any need to include much of the pre-hearing correspondence between the parties or their advisers. Long documents – such as company handbooks, redundancy and redeployment policies, etc – should, if possible, be reduced to a short relevant extract instead of being included whole. Repetitive documents – such as time-sheets, rotas, payslips – will sometimes need to be included at length if they need to be considered in detail, but often a representative sample will do.

8.14   Preparing bundles is a tedious and time-consuming task, but it is a mistake to delegate it to someone who does not properly understand the case. This is probably more often done by the respondents' representatives: The bundle is compiled by a trainee or paralegal who lacks the confidence to make judgments about what is and what is not relevant and includes everything in sight 'just in case'. The result is a bundle running to several hundred pages, only a dozen or so of which the tribunal is actually asked to read at the hearing. This is inconvenient and annoying for everyone concerned.

8.15   The conventional order for the bundle is the claim and response first (plus requests for additional information and responses, etc), followed by dated documents in chronological order (starting with the earliest), followed by any undated documents. Sometimes it is helpful to subdivide the documents into categories and take each category in chronological order – for example, where there are separate claims and presenting all the documents relating to both claims in the same chronological sequence will confuse the story. Sometimes it will be clearer to include undated documents in with the chronological documents if, despite the fact that they do not have a date on their face, it is clear at what point in the sequence they occur.

8.16   Witness statements should not be included in the bundle because the witnesses will need to be able to be referred to different pages in the bundle while their statement is open in front of them.

8.17   Bundles should always be paginated throughout in numerical sequence: each page, rather than each document, should be given a number. If it is necessary to add documents after the bundle has been compiled, they should be inserted in their logical place and given a number and a letter – so, for example, a four page document inserted between pages 23 and 24 should be numbered 23a, 23b, 23c and 23d. The index should be altered to show the insertion.

P8.3 Index to bundle of documents – unfair dismissal

IN THE EMPLOYMENT TRIBUNAL   Case No 123456/2004
LONDON CENTRAL

BETWEEN

YASMIN KHAN

Claimant

and

FIRST CALL CLEANING SERVICES LIMITED

Respondent

---

draft /AGREED BUNDLE OF DOCUMENTS

Date   Description   Page

Statement of case

Documents

Bundles for specific purposes

8.18   Sometimes it will be necessary to prepare separate bundles for specific purposes. For example, there may be a preliminary hearing on a question about whether the claimant had sufficient continuous service to complain of unfair dismissal, or whether the complaint was presented in time. In that case, the tribunal will much prefer to have a bundle restricted to documents (sometimes very few documents) relevant to that issue only. It will often be more convenient to make a separate bundle of documents relevant to remedies, including mitigation of loss – especially if the mitigation bundle is extensive – and provide it to the tribunal only after there has been a decision in the claimant's favour on liability. Unless the tribunal has indicated before the hearing that it will consider remedies at a separate hearing, however, the remedy bundle should always be ready for the main hearing day in case it is needed. If there is to be a costs application, it is helpful to make a separate bundle of documents relevant to that – normally correspondence between the parties, and possibly attendance notes recording telephone conversations.

8.19   In the following example, because the costs application depended on a long course of unreasonable conduct by the respondent almost all of which took the form either of correspondence or failure to answer correspondence, it was convenient to draw up a document that doubled as a bundle index and a chronology. The detail of this is not interesting, so only a short sample of the documents is shown.

P8.4 Combined index and chronology for strike-out application

IN THE EMPLOYMENT TRIBUNAL   Case No 123456/2004
LONDON CENTRAL

BETWEEN

ANNE COOPER

Claimant

and

THE BIG OFFICE SUPPLIERS LTD

Respondent

BUNDLE OF DOCUMENTS

**COMBINED INDEX AND CHRONOLOGY
FOR STRIKE OUT APPLICATION**

Date	Description	Page
17 January 05	A's Claim Form (ET1)	1
18 Febuary 05	R's Response Form (ET3)	3
26 April 05	Directions hearing–	7

- order for additional information of ET1 by 24 May 2002
- order for amended ET3 by 14 June
- other directions, substantive hearing 29/30 August 05

Date	Description	Page
27 May 05	A's additional information	10
30 May 05	Letter R/A refusing to provide amended ET3 until more detailed particulars of ET1	11
30 May 05	Letter R/ET: requesting A's claim to be struck out for failure to comply adequately with order for further particulars	12

Skeleton arguments[9]

8.20　Skeleton arguments will be the exception rather than the rule. They are helpful where there is a difficult legal point for the tribunal to decide. More often the applicable law is well enough settled, and the main battleground between the parties will be the disputed facts – whether the respondent had grounds for its belief that the claimant was guilty of misconduct; what was the real reason for the dismissal; whether the claimant's colleagues subjected him to racial harassment; whether the employer did enough to implement its equal opportunities policy and so on.

8.21　　Where a skeleton argument is needed, it should be prepared and sent to the tribunal and the other side at least seven days before the hearing, in accordance with rule 14(5).[10] Where one party has submitted a skeleton argument, the other party may be prompted by this to decide that it wishes to submit a skeleton argument in reply. If the first skeleton argument was sent to the tribunal seven days before the hearing, any skeleton argument in reply will inevitably be late. Probably tribunals will routinely agree to consider skeleton arguments in reply even if they are late, but a claimant might[11] seek to head this off by writing a letter to the respondent warning that he or she intends to submit a skeleton argument but will oppose any late skeleton argument in reply.

9　See also paras 9.26–9.29 below on written submissions.

10　Employment Tribunals (Constitution and Rules of Procedure) Regulations 2004 SI No 1861 Sch 1.

11　It is not suggested that this is something that must always, or even should normally, be done: it is a tactic that could be employed if the claimant is particularly keen to prevent the respondent from producing a skeleton argument at the last minute.

P8.5 Notice to the respondent that the claimant intends to submit a skeleton argument

George Bean
Carrot & Marrow Solicitors
21 Lower Street
London N12 3AB

my ref NC/1234/04
your ref GB/dr.6789

28 January 2005

Dear Mr Bean

Rochdale v George Fable Ltd ET/123456/04

Please note that I intend to submit a skeleton argument to the tribunal dealing with the questions (i) whether the claimant's employment was terminated by dismissal or resignation; and (ii) whether, if the claimant was dismissed, the reason for her dismissal was redundancy.

As you will be aware, Employment Tribunal Rules of Procedure r14(5) requires written representations to be submitted at least seven days before the start of the hearing. Time is short, and I expect to present my skeleton argument on the last permissible day, that is on 9 February 2005. If you wish to present a skeleton argument dealing with the same (or any other) point, you should therefore do so on or before that date. I will rely on this letter in opposing any application to present a skeleton argument in reply to mine later than 9 February.

Yours sincerely

Natalie Cummings

P8.6 Skeleton argument–redundancy claim

IN THE EMPLOYMENT TRIBUNAL   Case No 123456/2004
LONDON CENTRAL

BETWEEN

MARGARET ROCHDALE

Claimant

and

GEORGE FABLE LIMITED

Respondent

SKELETON ARGUMENT

Introduction

1. George Fable Limited is an estate agents' business which until November 2004 was split between two offices, one at premises called Marchmont House in Camden Town, and the other in Kentish Town. Mrs Rochdale was employed by the respondent as a part-time book-keeper at its Camden office from 28 October 1997 until 12 November 2004. Her contract of employment provided by clause 7.3 that she could be required to work 'anywhere in England and Wales.' She lives less than five minutes' walk from Marchmont House.

2. The respondent owns Marchmont House, where until November 2004 it used the ground floor for its estate agents' business and let the first and second floors to a tenant. In April 2004, the respondent received an offer from its tenant at Marchmont House for a lease of the whole building. The respondent considered that the offer was advantageous, and decided to expand its Kentish Town office and relocate its Camden Town operations to Kentish Town in order to take advantage of the offer.

3. The respondent announced the proposed move to all the Marchmont House staff at a meeting on 5 May 2004. Trevor English, the respondent's Managing Director, told them that the move was not yet a certainty, but was likely to take effect in September or October 2004. He invited staff to contact him if they had any questions or concerns about the move.

4. It is common ground that it would have taken Mrs Rochdale about 25 minutes to walk to the new office from her home, and a comparable time (including waiting time) if she travelled by bus.

5. On 12 May 2004, Mrs Rochdale wrote to Mr English about the move. Her letter said:

> I am afraid that because of the situation with my Mother I will not be able to move to the new office. Please let me know what your intentions are in relation to my employment.

6. Mrs Rochdale's mother is in her late eighties and very frail, and it is common ground that Mr English was aware both of this, and of the fact that it was Mrs Rochdale's habit to go home every lunchtime to give her mother her lunch. He was also aware that her mother would also occasionally call her home during the working day to attend to minor domestic emergencies. He had always been tolerant of this as Mrs Rochdale was a conscientious worker and always made up the time lost.

7. Mr English's reply to Mrs Rochdale's letter of 12 May 2004 indicated that he was sorry that she had decided to resign, but that he understood her reasons. Mrs Rochdale wrote back to say that she was not proposing to resign but that she wanted to know if he was proposing to make her redundant. There were several further exchanges of correspondence in which Mr English insisted that he was not dismissing Mrs Rochdale, and therefore no question of redundancy arose, and Mrs Rochdale insisted that she had no wish to resign.

8. On 31 August, Mr English held a further meeting with staff at which he announced that the Camden Office would close on Friday 12 November 2004, and staff should report for duty at the Kentish Town office on Monday 15 November.

9. On Friday 12 November, Mr English gave Mrs Rochdale an envelope containing her P45, showing her leaving date as 12 November. She was paid up to that date.

The issues

10. Mrs Rochdale has complained to the tribunal of wrongful dismissal and failure to pay statutory redundancy pay. The respondent has contended that she was not dismissed, but that if she was she is not entitled to a redundancy payment because she has unreasonably refused an offer of suitable alternative employment.

11. The issues for the tribunal to decide are:

(i) Was Mrs Rochdale dismissed, or did she resign?
(ii) If she was dismissed,
  (a) on what date was she given notice of dismissal?
  (b) was her dismissal wholly or mainly attributable to the fact

that their employer had ceased or intended to cease to carry on the business for the purposes of which she was employed in the place where she was employed?

(iii) If she was dismissed for redundancy, did she receive an offer of suitable alternative employment?

(iv) If she received an offer of suitable alternative employment, did she unreasonably refuse it?

Argument for the claimant

(i) Resignation or dismissal

12. Mrs Rochdale expressly stated on several occasions that she did not intend to resign and that she was willing to continue working at Marchmont House. Her statement in her letter of 12 May that she would not be able to work at the new office was not capable of being a resignation because it was not certain or unequivocal. It did not state a definite intention to cease her employment, nor did it state a date on which her employment would terminate. It was clearly implicit that if the move did not take place, Mrs Rochdale would be content to continue to work at Marchmont House. For similar reasons, none of Mrs Rochdale's subsequent letters is capable of being construed as a resignation.

13. The first occasion on which either party took any step that unequivocally indicated that her employment was to terminate was the respondent's act in giving Mrs Rochdale her P45 on Friday 12 November.

14. Moreover, the termination of her employment was brought about by the respondent's closure of the claimant's workplace, which was determined on by the respondent for its own purposes. The claimant made it clear at an early stage, before the move was a certainty, that one of the consequences of the move would be the termination of her employment. The respondent went on to take the step that it knew would terminate Mrs Rochdale's employment.

(ii)(a) Date of dismissal

15. It is submitted that Mrs Rochdale was dismissed without notice on 12 November when she was given her P45. Until that date, the respondent continued to insist that it was not dismissing her. Dismissal must be unequivocal, and certain as to the date on which it takes effect. Despite Mrs Rochdale's repeated requests for clarification, the respondent had not previously told her on what date her employment would terminate.

(ii)(b) Reason for dismissal

16. It is submitted that it is clear that the reason for Mrs Rochdale's dismissal was the respondent's closure of her workplace. By section 139(1) of the Employment Rights Act 1996:

> ... an employee who is dismissed shall be taken to be dismissed by reason of redundancy if the dismissal is wholly or mainly attributable to –
>
> (a) the fact that his employer has ceased or intends to cease–
>
> > (i) to carry on the business for the purposes of which the employee was employed by him, or
> >
> > (ii) to carry on that business in the place where the employee was so employed.

17. The respondent intended to cease carrying on business from Marchmont House where Mrs Rochdale worked, and this was the reason for the termination of her employment. The fact that her contract of employment contained a mobility clause is neither here nor there: the *place* where she was in fact employed was the Camden office – see *High Table v Horst* [1997] IRLR 513 and *Bass Leisure v Thomas* [1994] IRLR 104.

(iii) Was Mrs Rochdale offered suitable alternative employment?

18. It is conceded that it was made clear to Mrs Rochdale that the same job was available for her at the new location if she was willing to relocate, and that this constituted an implicit offer of suitable alternative employment.

(iv) Did Mrs Rochdale unreasonably refuse the Respondent's offer of alternative employment?

19. It is well established that the question whether an employee's refusal of alternative employment was unreasonable is subjective and should take account of her relevant personal circumstances, and the burden is on the employer to show that the decision was unreasonable. Mrs Rochdale had compelling personal reasons for her decision not to go to work at the new office, and she cannot be said to have acted unreasonably in insisting that she needed to be available for her mother at very short notice. Moreover, her decision is conclusively demonstrated to have been reasonable by the fact that she succeeded in securing similar employment at a slightly higher salary five minutes' walk from her home only four weeks after her dismissal.

Conclusion

20. The Tribunal is invited to find that Mrs Rochdale was dismissed without notice on 12 November 2004, and to award her:

(i) damages for wrongful dismissal; and

(ii) redundancy pay.

Natalie Cummings

9 February 2005

Miscellaneous documents for hearings

8.22   It would be impossible to draw up an exhaustive list of the kinds of documents that it might be necessary or helpful to draft in a case: every case is different, and one of the aims of this book is to encourage users not to assume that case preparation will always follow the same course, and to be prepared to think flexibly about what might be needed in the particular circumstances.

8.23   With that reservation, there are some kinds of documents that are often but not always needed. Some will be ordered by the tribunal in some cases. In many cases it will be helpful to agree the contents with the respondent, but if that is impossible, the next best thing will be to go to the hearing armed with a draft. If the claimant is well prepared with a draft list of issues, for example, and the respondent has not given any clear thought to what the issues are, then the respondent is likely to come under pressure from the tribunal to agree the claimant's draft. The following is a list of some of the main possibilities.

List of issues

8.24   If the case is at all complicated, it is a good idea to have a written list of the main legal and factual questions that the tribunal will have to decide. However, this needs to be drafted with care, and can be a hostage to fortune: it will not be open to a claimant to complain on appeal that the tribunal has failed to make a decision on a certain key question if the claimant offered the tribunal a list of issues that did not include that particular question.

Chronology

8.25   The tribunal will almost certainly be helped by a chronology – that is, a list of the main events in the case in date order, showing their dates – if the parties have time to prepare it.

Cast list

8.26   If there are a lot of different individuals involved in the story, a list of them showing briefly how they fit into the picture will assist.

List of essential reading

8.27   If the case is particularly document-heavy, then it is a good idea to agree a list of the most important documents for the tribunal to read at the beginning of the hearing, and to invite them to set aside a day or half a day for this purpose.

Glossary

8.28   If the tribunal will have to understand technical terms, or if the story involves a large number of organisations or departments familiarly referred to by their initials, the tribunal will be helped by a glossary.

Organogram

8.29   If the employer's organisational structure is at all important, a diagram showing this structure (often called an 'organogram') will be useful.

The main or substantive hearing

The hearing room

9.1   Hearing rooms vary in size, but they are laid out in a conventional way. The tribunal members sit facing the rest of the room, usually on a slightly raised platform, behind a long desk. There will be desks facing them at the front of the room for the parties and/or their representatives, with room for at least two people to sit on each side. The claimant and his or her representative (if any) sit on the right hand side of the room facing the tribunal, and the respondents and their representative sit on the left. There are usually one or two rows of chairs behind the parties for members of the public and the Press, etc. Between the parties desks and the tribunal there is a table and chair for the witness who is giving evidence at any given time; opposite that on the other side of the room, there may be a table for a member of tribunal staff. If the parties are represented, it is usual for the representatives to sit on the inside of their respective desks, with their clients nearer the walls. This is because there may be occasions when the representatives need to speak to each other in the course of the hearing.

Formalities

9.2   The chairman and members of the tribunal are addressed 'Madam' or 'Sir' as appropriate.[1] Everyone remains seated, except witnesses while they are being sworn. While a witness is being sworn, everyone else in the room should remain still and silent: some tribunals will be very much annoyed if there is any fidgeting with papers or whispering during this solemnity. Barristers sometimes refer to their opponents as 'my learned friend' in the hearing. Traditionally, only barristers are allowed to have learned friends: anyone else using the expression may cause a slight wince. 'My colleague' or just 'Miss Fanshawe' is preferable in any event.

The shape of the hearing

9.3   Employment tribunals have a wide power to regulate their own procedure, but there is a conventional order in which hearings are usually taken.

---

1   It is a good idea to get this right.

As so often, this appears nowhere in the employment tribunal rules, but is a practice drawn from the ordinary courts. Tribunal chairmen are encouraged now to introduce themselves and their wing members and start either by stating what they consider the issues to be or by asking the parties to clarify what they think the issues are. Then, unless either party has any preliminary application to make (for an adjournment, for example, or for the other party's claim or response to be struck out), the hearing will normally proceed as follows:

either

Claimant calls his or her first witnesses
Respondent cross-examines

Claimant calls his or her second witness
Respondent cross-examines

... and so on until all the claimant's witnesses have given evidence

Respondent calls its first witnesses
Claimant cross-examines

Respondent calls its second witness
Claimant cross-examines

... and so on until all the respondent's witnesses have given evidence

Respondent makes closing submissions
Claimant makes closing submissions

or

Respondent calls its first witness
Claimant cross-examines

Respondent calls its second witness
Claimant cross-examines

...

Claimant calls his or her first witness
Respondent cross-examines

Claimant calls his or her second witness
Respondent cross-examines

...

Claimant makes closing submissions
Respondent makes closing submissions

9.4   The choice between these two possibilities usually – but not invariably – depends on which side has something to prove first. In a discrimination case, the claimant cannot succeed without showing discrimination, so the claimant calls his or her witnesses first. In an unfair dismissal case (if dismissal is admitted), the employer has to start by showing that it had an acceptable reason for the dismissal – if it fails, the dismissal was unfair without further argument. So in that case, the employer starts. In a constructive dismissal case, the claimant has to start by showing that he or she was dismissed, so the claimant starts.

9.5   Often there are cases where it is hard to say exactly how this rule should apply – for example, where the claimant is complaining of both unfair dismissal and discrimination. It is not worth getting bogged down in this question. It is worthwhile for the claimant to know the conventions, so that whoever starts, he or she knows what is likely to happen next and is not taken by surprise – but it almost never really matters who starts the case.

Opening statements

9.6   Occasionally one party or the other wishes to make an opening statement to the tribunal before the evidence begins. This is very much the exception rather than the rule, and some tribunals will be resistant to the suggestion: the claimant should certainly not feel that an opening statement is expected. The purpose of an opening statement, if it is made, will be to ensure that the tribunal knows what the issues are that it will have to decide, focus its attention on what it should be looking for in the evidence, and give it a framework for understanding what it hears. Long opening statements will normally be strongly discouraged.

Reading time for the tribunal

9.7   Tribunals do not routinely read bundles of documents and witness statements before the beginning of the hearing. In a complicated case involving a lot of documents, it will often be helpful to ask the tribunal to spend an hour or so – or longer if necessary – at the start of the hearing reading the witness statements and the most important documents, so that by the time the oral evidence begins they know what the case is about. If the case is long enough to justify it – probably six or seven days at least – the pre-reading may take a whole day. If that is likely, it is sensible to try to agree this with the other party and the tribunal at a directions hearing, or in correspondence before the hearing starts. Otherwise everyone will turn up on the first day of the hearing only to be sent away until the next day while the tribunal does its homework.

Observing a hearing

9.8 It is always a good idea for a claimant who has not taken part in a tribunal hearing previously to observe a case before their own comes on for hearing. Lawyers often speak of tribunal hearings as 'informal.' They might seem so to anyone accustomed to appearing in the Chancery Division of the High Court, but for many claimants, the tribunal hearing will be the most formal meeting they have ever taken part in. Being cross-examined, in particular, can be stressful and intimidating. Observing another case will at least take the edge off complete unfamiliarity of proceedings.

9.9 Tribunal hearings are normally public: anyone can go and sit at the back at (almost) any hearing for as much or as little of the hearing as they wish. Tribunal chairmen do occasionally quiz those present about who they are and what their role is. A claimant who wishes to observe a case should not be put off by this, and should not be made to feel that they have to identify, explain or justify themselves if they do not want to: it should be perfectly adequate to say 'I am a member of the public and I want to watch the tribunal doing its work,' or similar.

Claimants with special needs

9.10 The tribunal should be willing to adjust its practices to take account of the special needs of parties. If any adjustments are needed, a request should be made in writing, or at a case management discussion. The following is a list of the kinds of adjustments that might be requested, but claimants should be ready to ask for whatever meets their own specific needs:

- sign language interpreters;[2]
- rest breaks;[3]
- to be given extra time to take notes;

2 The tribunal service will pay the interpreters' reasonable fees.
3 For example, for a claimant who has difficulty concentrating for a long period.

- to have a friend or support worker sit by them when they give evidence;[4]
- opportunity to get up and move around;[5]
- additional hearing days (where other arrangements mean the hearing will be slower than usual);
- modified lighting;[6]
- to be allowed to use a Braille machine or laptop with speech output;
- to be accompanied by a guide dog or other assistance animal;
- a less formal physical environment – for example, to have the hearing with the tribunal members and parties sitting around a large table instead of in a normal hearing room;
- to have repetitive or hostile questioning strictly controlled, or questions relayed through the chairman.[7]

Taking notes at the hearing

9.11   It is important for claimants to take good notes of the employment tribunal proceedings for two reasons. The first is to assist with the conduct of the hearing itself: it may be necessary to put to a witness something that he or she has said earlier, or to refer to what a witness said under cross-examination in closing submissions. The impact of this may be damaged or destroyed if the claimant does not have a reasonably accurate note of what was said. The second is that the evidence that was given at first instance may be important when it comes to an appeal.

9.12   Taking good notes while conducting a case in the employment tribunal is difficult. If the respondent is represented by a barrister, there will probably be someone from the respondent's solicitors at the hearing to take notes. The claimant may not be so lucky: voluntary sector advice agencies, in particular, will almost never be able to spare two lawyers to attend a hearing. If there is a representative, he or she should aim to take notes of the most important things that are said, but

---

4 For example, where the claimant is particularly intimidated by the process by reason of mental health problems or learning difficulties.

5 For example, for a claimant with back pain.

6 For example, for a claimant with a visual impairment.

7 This will be difficult, as cross-examination is very much the traditional method of testing the truthfulness of a witness. However, the request itself may serve to restrain the respondent's representative significantly: advocates will have their own preference not to be seen to bully a vulnerable witness.

priority obviously has to be given to conducting the proceedings, not recording them. Taking good notes of your own cross-examination is almost impossible. The claimant herself may be able to take good notes, but is likely to be very preoccupied, so if possible it is better to have a friend, relative or colleague present for this purpose.

9.13   It is worthwhile giving some thought to this before the hearing. An adviser who is going to rely on someone who is not used to taking notes should make sure the note-taker has a suitable notebook and pens, and knows what it is most important for them to take notes of. The task is tiring, especially for someone who is not used to it, so it will often be sensible to ask the note-taker to take the best notes he or she possibly can of the claimant's cross-examination of the respondent's witnesses plus the answers to any additional questions from the tribunal, but otherwise only to write down anything he or she considers particularly important.

9.14   The respondent's legal team will sometimes turn up at the hearing with a laptop computer and ask for permission to take notes on that. This is the best way of getting a really accurate record of the course of the hearing, because a good typist can type considerably faster than most people can write longhand, and it is potentially in both parties' interests that full notes of the evidence should be made. If this arises, it is suggested that the claimant should propose that permission should be given on condition that the respondent undertakes (a) to take complete notes of the proceedings (that is, not merely taking notes of what they think is helpful to their side) and (b) to make their notes of the hearing available to the claimant, unedited, immediately after the end of each hearing day. This could be done by e-mailing or faxing each day's notes to the claimant on return to the office.

9.15   This way both sides will benefit from the convenience of full notes of the evidence, and if there is any appeal, both sides will be saved the expense and inconvenience of trying to agree the notes many weeks or even months after the hearing. It would be extremely unlikely for the respondent's representatives to attempt to doctor the notes in any way under these circumstances, but if the claimant did have any concern about the accuracy of notes made and provided in this way, he or she should be sure to raise that with the respondent immediately. Neither party's notes of the hearing are privileged.[8]

---

8 *Lambert v Home* [1914] 3KB 86; and for the meaning of privilege see glossary and paras 4.28–4.35 above.

Cross-examination

9.16   Cross-examination of the other side's witnesses is probably the most difficult job that the claimant or his or her adviser has to do. The point of cross-examination is to test the accuracy of the other side's witness statements and explore questions that they have not dealt with in their statements. Many tribunals and practitioners will say that a further – or the main – purpose of cross-examination is to *put your case to the other side's witnesses.*

9.17   This last is a throw-back to the days before witness statements, when witnesses for one side would only have the chance to comment on the other side's evidence if that evidence was put to them in cross-examination. Suppose Mr Sneath, the claimant, was going to say in his evidence that Mrs Blewitt, the personnel manager, gave him a thumbs down sign the day before the disciplinary hearing and said 'I hope you've got good lawyers because you're going to need them.' Mrs Blewitt gives her evidence first. If witness statements have not been exchanged before the hearing, Mrs Blewitt does not know what Mr Sneath is going to say. The tribunal will want to hear what she says to his allegation – does she admit it or deny it, and if she denies it does she do so convincingly? So if there have been no witness statements, Mrs Blewitt must be asked: 'You gave Mr Sneath a thumbs down sign the day before the hearing didn't you?' and 'and then you said "I hope you've got good lawyers, etc"?' Otherwise she will never get a chance to comment on Mr Sneath's evidence.

9.17   Lawyers are conservative by nature, and it is still conventional – even though witness statements are now almost universal in employment tribunal proceedings – to put the case to the opposing witnesses. Tribunals will still sometimes refuse to take account of evidence for one side that has not been put to the other side's witnesses.[9] Although there is no longer a practical need for this exercise, therefore, it is still advisable to ensure that every disputed allegation by the claimant is put to the relevant witness or witnesses on the other side. This can feel very artificial: the result is likely to be a series of questions of the form:

Q: 'You did ABC didn't you?'
A: 'No.'
Q: 'And then you said DEF?'
A: 'No.'

9   This must be wrong if a witness statement containing the evidence in question was given to the other party before the hearing. A claimant whose case has been severely impeded by the tribunal's refusal to take part of his or her evidence into account for this reason should consider appealing.

Q: 'The claimant did not do GHI as you say, did he?'
A: 'Yes he did.'
Q: 'The truth was you said JKL wasn't it?'
A: 'Nope.'

9.18 This is a wearying performance for everyone,[10] but until the Employment Appeal Tribunal rules that the practice is redundant it is necessary.

9.19 In any event, this should not be the character of the whole cross-examination. Often there will be deliberate ambiguities in a statement that need to be teased out. Sometimes there will be inconsistencies between one part of the statement and another, or between this witness's evidence and that of one of the respondent's other witnesses. Sometimes there will be documentary evidence that contradicts what the witness says. Sometimes the statement will have been drafted by a lawyer who has been too keen to put the 'right' words into the witness's mouth, and the witness when asked will simply contradict her own statement.

9.20 Some rules of thumb may be helpful. Leading questions are usually preferable: the aim is to take the witness where you want him or her to go by asking a series of questions to which there is only one possible answer. It is a good idea to start with easy, non-threatening questions. If the representative is going to give a witness a particularly hard time on one issue, it is better to save that to the end: otherwise the witness is likely to be defensive and unforthcoming from the start. The order in which questions on a particular issue are asked can be crucial. The key is often to predict what the witness will think is the 'right' answer, and then ask the questions in an order that makes use of that.

> **Example 1**
> Suppose the witness to be cross-examined is the manager who decided to dismiss the claimant. The reason given for the dismissal was that the claimant was believed to have been responsible (accidentally) for starting a damaging fire. The claimant believes that the fire was a convenient excuse, and the real reason for his dismissal was that he had been complaining about changes in the way he was paid. His representative has noticed that the date on the fire service report implicating the claimant is after the date of the dismissal letter. This is damaging for the respondent,

---

10 Unless of course the witness breaks down in tears, and admits he has told a pack of lies. This will be rare.

because it tends to support the claimant's belief that the fire was not the real reason for his dismissal – but it is not necessarily fatal and the manager may be able to explain it away.

What follows is a pair of demonstrations, with comments in italics, of how the cross-examination might go, one effective and the other very much less so:

Wrong
Q: Please turn to the fire report on page 24. What is the date on it? *The witness has no scope to hedge – the date is there in black and white.*

Q: Now turn to the dismissal letter on page 21. What is the date on that? *Again, there is only one possible answer, and already the witness will see the point that is about to be made and be starting to think about how she can deal with it.*

Q: Why didn't you wait until you had seen the fire service report before deciding to dismiss the claimant? *This is the witness's opportunity for damage limitation. She has not damaged her credibility by lying because she has been given no opportunity to do so.*

Right
Q: This was an important decision wasn't it? *The only possible answer to this is 'yes.'*

Q: Did you make sure you had all relevant information before you took it? *Here too there is an obvious 'right' answer and 99 in 100 witnesses will give it.*

Q: There was a fire service investigation into the cause of the fire wasn't there? *There is no point denying this: the witness will almost certainly know that the report is in the bundle.*

Q: The point of that was to establish the cause of the fire? *There is not much point denying that either.*

Q: Did you take the fire service report into account before you decided to dismiss? *Now the witness is in a tight place. She has just confirmed that she took into account all relevant information. She is now being asked about a piece of highly and obviously relevant information that she did not take into account. With luck, she may forget in the heat of the moment that the report post-dates the dismissal letter, and give the 'right' answer – 'Yes, of course I did.' If she does, the trap can be sprung:*

Q: Turn to the dismissal letter – what is the date on it?
Q: Turn to the fire report – what is the date on that?

Q: So your answer just now that you read the fire report before you decided to dismiss was not true, was it? *Even if the witness was too canny to lie, she is still much worse placed having claimed to have taken all relevant information into account and then being forced to admit that this was not the case that she would be if simply challenged directly about the sequence of events as in the first example.*

Example 2

The witness is a manager who claims to have been unaware that the claimant, whom she appointed, was disabled at the time she dismissed him for poor performance. In the papers there are two probationary appraisals, conducted by the manager, that say that the claimant was trying his best and was responsive to feedback. The job is not a difficult one, and on paper the claimant is over-qualified for it. The manager says that she knew the claimant was dyslexic, but did not think it was serious enough to amount to a disability for the purposes of the Disability Discrimination Act 1995.

Wrong

Q: You knew Derek was dyslexic didn't you? *This much is uncontroversial.*

Q: You knew he was intelligent enough to get a first class degree in history? *The witness is given the opportunity to wriggle with something like 'I interview a lot of new staff – I did not remember his exact qualifications.'*

Q: So if he was underachieving in this junior role it must have been because of his dyslexia? *This is an open invitation to the witness to think of some other plausible reason – 'No – I thought he was over-qualified for the role and not very well motivated.' She can be challenged on her own assessment in his probationary reviews that he was doing his best, but now she knows where the questioning is going she may say that this was an over-generous assessment in an attempt to motivate him.*

Right

Q: You appointed Derek? *There is no reason why she should deny this.*

Q: You read his CV? *Reading his CV before appointing him was obviously the right thing to do, so 9 out of 10 personnel managers will say 'yes' even if they have no specific memory of having done so.*

> **Q:** So you knew he had a first class degree? *This is hard to deny – the CV is there in the bundle, and she has just admitted to having read it.*
>
> **Q:** You did not require a graduate at all in this role? *She is unlikely to deny this – she knows that the person specification is in the bundle.*
>
> **Q:** You conducted the two probationary reviews? – *Again, she cannot sensibly deny this.*
>
> **Q:** Did you conduct them fairly and accurately to the best of your ability? *Again, there is only one answer to this.*
>
> **Q:** So you stand by your assessment that Derek was doing his best? *Now she is in a place where it is difficult for her to deny this too.*
>
> **Q:** And that he was responsive to feedback? *Similarly.*
>
> **Q:** But he was under-performing so badly that you had to dismiss him? *She has to say yes to this because it is at the heart of her case.*
>
> **Q:** You knew he was dyslexic? *In this context, the question is going somewhere.*
>
> **Q:** Given that you knew Derek was able and doing his best, that was the obvious explanation for his difficulties wasn't it? *All the likely alternative explanations have been ruled out, so it is difficult for the witness to deny this now.*

Preparing to cross-examine

9.21　Cross-examination needs to be carefully prepared. That is not to say that it is ever possible to stick to a rigid list of prepared questions, but the strategy needs to be thought out in advance and lists of probable questions and areas to cover are essential. It is a difficult skill that only improves with practice, but preparation can make up to some degree for inexperience.

9.22　The most important thing is to be thoroughly familiar with all the statements on both sides, and with all the relevant documents. In some ways preparing for a hearing is like revising for an exam: it is necessary to know the material well enough to realise at once in the course of the hearing when a witness has said something that is inconsistent with his or her own statement, or with the statement of another witness, or with one of the documents in the bundle. If you are going to want to take a witness to a particular document in the bundle, then it is sensible to put a sticky note on that page of the bundle, highlight the relevant passage, and cross-reference your cross-examination notes to the page number. Often it will be necessary to take each witness to a number of different pages in the bundle. It may be helpful to use colour-coded sticky notes: red for one witness, blue for another and so on.

9.23 Reasonably detailed cross-examination notes are useful, but in case you stray widely from these, it is also helpful to have a summary check-list of the key areas to cover with each witness and to remember to look at it before ending the cross-examination. In the heat of the moment – and especially if one part of the cross-examination went either particularly well or particularly badly – it is all too easy to forget to cover a whole topic. For an adviser, it is sensible to take a moment[11] to check with the claimant that there is nothing he or she thinks you should have asked that you did not. A claimant acting in person should similarly be allowed to confer briefly with a friend or relative accompanying them.

P9.1 Check-list for cross-examination

The witness to be cross-examined, P, is a manager who decided to dismiss the claimant, who is disabled, for poor performance. The claimant, N, was the highest-earning salesperson in his department before a spell of severe back pain. He complains of disability discrimination. A full set of cross-examination notes would be much more detailed; this is an outline of the main topics N wishes to cover in cross-examination.

P's knowledge of disability:

- knew of back problems on appointment
- knew it was serious at least by 7 October 2003

Performance during probationary period

Reason for performance issues – back pain[12]

---

11 A long conversation will be frowned on by the tribunal, but a brief exchange should certainly be permitted. It is worth emphasising the need to take a little time at this point: the process is stressful, and the tribunal may have been pressing for speed, but there is still nothing wrong with a couple of minutes' silence while the claimant checks through his or her notes before confirming that the cross-examination is finished.

12 N wishes to establish that he was dismissed for a reason relating to his disability.

Knowledge of prognosis[13]

Specific requests for adjustments:

- request for different working hours
- request to work part of the week at home
- request for ergonomic assessment of workplace
- request for 'Access to Work' assessment

Reasonableness of adjustments:

- size of department
- departmental sales figures – recent Group award
- claimant's performance before back problems
- cost of ergonomic assessment
- nil cost of 'Access to Work' assessment

Submissions

9.24   After the witnesses have given their evidence, each side has an opportunity to make submissions to the tribunal: in other words, to make a speech to the tribunal seeking to persuade it to find one way or the other.

9.25   Submissions, like cross-examination, should be carefully prepared. If time permits, a set of written submissions or a skeleton argument is almost always helpful.[14]

9.26   Rule 14(5) of the Employment Tribunals Rules of Procedure 2004[15] provides that:

> If a party wishes to submit written representations for consideration at a hearing ... he shall present them to the Employment Tribunal Office not less than 7 days before the hearing and shall at the same time send a copy to all other parties.

13 This is relevant because P says dismissal was justified even if discrimination. N wishes to make him admit that he had not bothered to find out what the prognosis was, and if he had, he would have learned that N's consultant believed that he would be back to full productivity within a short time.

14 The distinction between these two is not very important, but 'skeleton argument' is normally used to refer to a written argument on a point of law, whereas 'written submissions' may incorporate some legal argument, but will deal with the evidence and inferences to be drawn from the evidence as well.

15 Contained in Employment Tribunals (Constitution and Rules of Procedure) Regulations 2004 SI No 1861 Sch 1.

This rule is new, and ill-considered: a skeleton argument on a point of law can be provided before the hearing begins, but written submissions dealing with the evidence cannot usefully be drafted until after the evidence has been heard. Under the old rules, where all the evidence has been heard during the time allotted for the hearing but there is no time left for oral submissions, it was common for the tribunal to direct that submissions should be made in writing within, say, 14 or 21 days of the end of the hearing.

9.27   Fortunately rule 14(6) gives tribunals power to consider representations submitted later if they consider it appropriate – in other words, to ignore rule 14(5) whenever they like. It is to expected that tribunals will exercise this power freely. Written submissions tend to be helpful – at the very least because they save the tribunal the trouble of taking detailed notes of submissions – and tribunals will be slow to refuse what is in effect an offer of assistance from the parties' representatives.

9.28   It is suggested that claimants should continue, where appropriate, with the sensible practice of drafting written submissions during the course of the hearing,[16] and presenting them at the end either alongside or instead of oral submissions. It is prudent to have a first draft ready for the start of the hearing, but it is to be expected that much of the work will need to be done after the witnesses have given their evidence and been cross-examined: late nights between consecutive hearing days will often be unavoidable.

9.29   The likelihood is that the tribunal will accept written submissions offered on the last day of the hearing, but if not that does not mean that the work in preparing them has been wasted. They will still be very useful as a memory aid for the representative making oral submissions, and they may also prove useful if there is any subsequent dispute in relation to an appeal about whether a particular point was made at first instance.[17]

16   Obviously this is only possible for a hearing lasting 2 or more days.
17   See para 11.30 below.

P9.2 Written submissions in an unfair dismissal case

IN THE EMPLOYMENT TRIBUNAL   Case No 123456/04
STRATFORD

BETWEEN

PATRICK POOLE

Claimant

and

SAVEMORE PLC

Respondent

CLOSING SUBMISSIONS FOR CLAIMANT

*Numbers in bold are references
to pages of the agreed bundle*

Introduction: the agreed facts

1. Mr Poole worked for the respondent as a full time member of the 'night crew' from January 1989 at their supermarket in Tower Hamlets. His job involved replenishing shelves and stock-room duties. From June 1996, he reduced his hours to 30 a week over three 10 hour night shifts, normally between Monday and Thursday, although occasionally working other shifts when he was asked to. This agreement is set out in the exchange of correspondence at pages **19** and **20** of the bundle.

2. Most of the respondent's regular night crew at the relevant time were already flexible across the six nights, Sunday to Friday. Saturday nights were at the time covered by day staff or night crew members on a voluntary overtime basis.

3. In the autumn of 2003, the respondent commenced consultation with a view to the introduction of a requirement that all night crew staff must work fully flexible rotas across all seven nights. The additional compulsory shift was the Saturday night/Sunday morning shift.

4. Night shifts at the respondent's Tower Hamlets Store ran from 8pm until 7am apart from the 'Sunday' night shift which ran from midnight on Sunday until 7am on Monday. Thus the 'Saturday' shift was, when discussions about the change began, the only shift that included any time falling on a Sunday.

5. The new policy was first explained to the night crew, of which Mr Poole was a member, at a meeting on 27 November 2003 (**33**). Further meetings followed, including two individual meetings between Mr Poole and his line manager, Keith Harpar. It became clear that Mr Poole was not willing to accept the new rota arrangements, and because of this Mr Harpar decided to dismiss him.

6. Before the dismissal took effect, Mr Poole was given the opportunity to appeal against the changes that were being imposed upon him. He did so, and the appeal was heard by the store manager, Patricia Westlake, on 16 August 2004 (**61**). At this meeting Mr Poole was told for the first time of a proposal to change the Sunday shift so that it began at 8pm on Sunday.

7. The dismissal took effect on 30 September 2004. After the dismissal took effect, Mr Poole was given the opportunity to appeal against his dismissal. He did so, and the appeal was heard by Daniel Hewitt at a meeting on 15 December 2004 (**76**). This appeal too was rejected by Mr Hewitt's letter of 10 January 2005 (**84**).

The issues

8. Section 101(1) of the Employment Rights Act 1996 provides, so far as is material:

    (1) Where an employee who is–
        (a) a protected shop worker or an opted-out shop worker ...
        (b) ...
    is dismissed, he shall be regarded for the purposes of this Part as unfairly dismissed if the reason (or, if more than one, the principal reason) for the dismissal is that he refused (or proposed to refuse) to do shop work ... on Sunday or on a particular Sunday.

9. It is accepted by the respondent that Mr Poole was at all material times a protected shop worker, and that the work that he did was 'shop work.' It follows that if the reason or the principal reason for his dismissal was that he refused or proposed to refuse to work on Sundays, his dismissal was for an inadmissible reason and was unfair. The main issue for the tribunal is therefore the question of what was the reason for Mr Poole's dismissal.

10. Alternatively, if the respondent's contention that Mr Poole was dismissed for reasons relating to conduct or for some other substantial reason is accepted, the question for the tribunal is whether in all the circumstances the respondent acted reasonably or unreasonably in dismissing him.

Submissions for the claimant

11. In summary, it is submitted for Mr Poole:

    (i) that his dismissal was for refusing Sunday work and was therefore automatically unfair;

    (ii) alternatively, even if his dismissal was not for an automatically unfair reason, that the respondent cannot succeed in showing an admissible reason for his dismissal, and therefore that the dismissal is unfair;

    (iii) alternatively again, even if the tribunal is persuaded that the respondent has shown an admissible reason for the dismissal, that the decision to dismiss was unfair in all the circumstances.[18]

(i) Automatically unfair dismissal

12. The primary submission for Mr Poole is that the reason or the principal reason for his dismissal was his refusal to work the Saturday night shift, that is, his refusal to work on Sundays.

13. The greater part of the 'Saturday' night shift fell during the 24 hours of Sunday, and throughout most of the discussions between the parties prior to dismissal it was the only shift that contained any Sunday hours. If the reason or the principal reason for Mr Poole's dismissal was that he refused to work the Saturday shift, therefore, he was dismissed for an inadmissible reason and his dismissal was unfair.

14. If the respondent dismissed him for refusal to accept an additional compulsory shift most of which fell on a Sunday, it cannot be open to it to defend the unfair dismissal on the ground that a lesser part of the disputed shift did not fall on a Sunday. The respondent sought to impose a requirement which it had no right to impose, and it dismissed Mr Poole for refusing to accept that.

15. Staff affected by the changes made it clear from the outset that they objected and that they wished to place reliance on their statutory right not to be forced to work on Sundays: see in particular notes of the meeting on 27 November 2003 (**33**, **34**, **35**, **36**). The respondent made no answer to this, and failed to offer any of the staff an alternative that did not include any compulsory Sunday hours despite their repeated references to the right not to be compelled to work on a Sunday.

---

18 It is preferable, if possible, to set up a number of alternative arguments so that even if the claimant loses on his or her primary argument, there is still something to fall back on.

16. At the individual meeting between Mr Poole and Keith Harpar on 26 April 2004 (**42)** it is still abundantly clear that the only sticking point is the Saturday night shift: see in particular (**44**).

17. There was a further individual meeting between Mr Poole and Mr Harpar on 26 July 2004 (**49**) at which Mr Harpar read a prepared statement that as from 22 August Mr Poole would be required to be fully flexible over seven nights, and that if he refused to accept this he would be dismissed with effect 21 August 2004. Mr Poole was also offered the alternative at this meeting of accepting a reduction in his hours from 30 to 20 as the price of being exempted from the 'Saturday' shift.

18. Mr Poole accepts that the notes of both meetings prepared by Angela Chiles are accurate in all material respects.

19. It is not open to an employer to evade the restrictions on compulsory Sunday working by offering employees a choice between Sunday working and a drastic reduction in their working hours.

20. The position was confirmed by Mr Harpar in his letter of 2 August 2004 (**55**), which states: 'We require that your shifts become fully flexible between Sunday and Saturday inclusive and that Saturday becomes part of your working week.'

21. It is submitted that this documentary evidence is alone ample to establish beyond doubt that Mr Poole was dismissed for an inadmissible reason.

22. However, Mr Harpar, whose evidence was straightforward and credible,[19] made the position even clearer. He agreed that the new factor for discussion at the meeting on 27 November 2003 was the compulsory Saturday night shift. He explained that at the time he believed that the respondent had the right to compel Sunday working, and he agreed that he told staff they would have to work all through Saturday night. He was not aware that Mr Poole was a protected worker, and he said that if Mr Poole had offered to work the first 3 hours of the Saturday night shift (until midnight) but refused the rest, he would still have dismissed him. He agreed that there was no real issue about nights other than Saturday. He accepted that Mr Poole was prepared to work Friday and Sunday nights, albeit reluctantly, and he indicated that reluctant compliance was good enough. He was certain that he would have still dismissed him if he had been completely flexible about every night but Saturday.

19 Often winning the case depends on persuading the tribunal to disbelieve the other side's witnesses, but if a witness on the other side has given evidence that is positively helpful this should be emphasised strongly.

23. The respondent's own undisputed evidence, then, was that the Mr Poole's refusal to work Saturday nights was the whole reason for his dismissal.

24. Mr Poole's appeal against the changes being imposed on him was heard by Patricia Westlake on 16 August 2004 (**61**). It is clear from the notes of that meeting (which again Mr Poole agrees are accurate) that Saturday night is still the sticking point. Mrs Westlake had in mind the previous agreement that Mr Poole would be flexible over the other six nights, with a preference for Monday to Thursday nights, but he made the point that Saturday nights were now seen as essential (**62**).

25. At this meeting, Mrs Westlake told Mr Poole that she had now agreed with the night crew that the Sunday shift could start at 8pm instead of midnight. She went on to ask Mr Poole about Sunday night specifically (**64**). The Sunday shift that Mr Poole had previously been willing to do started at midnight. In response to Mrs Westlake's inquiry about Sunday, he pointed out that he did not get home on Sundays until about 4pm which would make a shift starting at 8pm considerably more awkward for him than the shift starting at midnight. His apparent reluctance to work Sunday nights on this basis was equivocal, however, and the point was not pursued to a final conclusion by Mrs Westlake, nor was it explored whether Mr Poole would be willing to work the old-style Sunday shift starting at midnight. In fact it is clear from a later passage in the notes that Mrs Westlake accepted for the purposes of this discussion that Mr Poole was willing to work Fridays and Sundays: see (**66**) where Mrs Westlake is recorded as saying: 'I have re-read your letter where it says you'd prefer to work Monday to Thursday where possible. I'm just looking at Saturday.'

26. The importance of Saturday was again emphasised in Mrs Westlake's letter of 17 August 2004 to Mr Poole (**68**).

27. In her oral evidence, Mrs Westlake insisted that Saturday night was not the whole or the main sticking point, and that Mr Poole's reluctance to work Friday and Sunday nights was also at issue. However, this is at odds with the overwhelming impression from the respondent's own documentation, and in particular the notes of the meeting of 16 August 2004. It is also at odds with the clear evidence of Mr Harpar, who made the initial decision to dismiss. The tribunal is invited to prefer the undisputed documentary evidence, and the oral evidence of Mr Harpar, both of which are consistent with Mr Poole's evidence. Even if Mrs Westlake's evidence that Fridays and Sundays were a real part of the problem is accepted, it is submitted that the evidence

is clear that the principal reason for Mr Poole's dismissal was his refusal to work the Saturday night shift.

28. Mr Poole's dismissal with effect 21 August 2004 was confirmed in Mr Harpar's letter of 14 September 2004. Mr Poole's appeal against dismissal to Mr Bateman, Area Operations Manager, was held on 15 December 2004 (**70**). Mr Poole spelled out his understanding of the situation at the outset: 'I had contract with Savemore working three nights over six nights. He wanted three over seven. Not prepared to do. Give reasons why wanted to stick to what doing. Work at weekends.' It is again clear from this that as far as Mr Poole is concerned, he has an understanding which he wishes to stick to that he will be flexible over six nights. As he understands it, the sole reason for his dismissal is his refusal to accept flexibility over seven nights. The seventh night was Saturday.

29. It emerged at the appeal hearing that there was some confusion over the nature of the appeal. It appeared that Mr Bateman believed that the respondent had intended to provide two separate lines of appeal, the first against the imposition of the changes and the second, after the decision to dismiss had been taken, against the decision to dismiss.

30. These two had been confused by Mrs Westlake who had, in her letter of 17 August confirming the decision to impose the changes, offered Mr Poole a further right of appeal but this time against *dismissal*. Mr Bateman offered to treat the hearing as a final appeal against both the decision to impose the changes, and the subsequent dismissal. However, it was clear throughout this meeting that in fact there was still no question of any concession from the respondent on the question of compulsory Saturday night shifts. Mr Bateman was advised at the hearing by Ms Roberta Blake, a personnel officer. Ms Blake took notes of the meeting (**76**) and gave oral evidence at the hearing in place of Mr Bateman.

31. Ms Blake admitted that she had not advised Mr Bateman that Mr Poole was a protected worker who could not be compelled to work Sundays, and she explained her belief that he would have had to opt out in order to get that protection. She said in her evidence: 'We had the right to change his contract. We are changing everyone's contract to include Saturday night working.' She appeared to maintain that belief before the tribunal, despite the concession by the respondent's solicitor at the outset that Mr Poole was a protected worker.

32. It follows that the reason or the principal reason for Mr Poole's dismissal was that he refused as a protected shop worker to work

on Sundays. This was an inadmissible reason and his dismissal was automatically unfair.

(ii) Failure of Respondent to show an admissible reason

33. If Mr Poole's assertion that he has been dismissed for a prohibited reason is rejected, the respondent must still show what was the reason for the dismissal and that it was an admissible reason.

34. The respondent says first that this was a dismissal for a reason relating to conduct, namely Mr Poole's refusal to obey a lawful order. However, the order which Mr Poole refused to obey was the requirement that he accept full flexibility across seven nights, including the Saturday and Sunday shifts, parts of each of which fell on Sunday. This cannot possibly be characterised as a lawful order because Mr Poole had a statutory right to refuse Sunday work.

35. It was put to Mr Poole in cross-examination that when he was asked to agree to be fully flexible across all seven nights, he should have offered to work any shift except that part of the Saturday and Sunday shifts that fell between midnight on Saturday and midnight on Sunday. This, with respect to the respondent, is absurd. The respondent's requirement for flexibility might have been put in terms that amounted to a lawful order, but it never was. The respondent's case amounts to the assertion that, faced with an order he could not lawfully be compelled to obey, it was for Mr Poole to think of a different order that he could have been compelled to obey and then to offer to obey that instead; and that his failure to do so somehow amounted to misconduct.

36. Similarly, it cannot sensibly be said that a refusal to accept a change in conditions of employment or a kind that an employee has a statutory right not to be compelled to accept amounts to a 'substantial reason' capable of justifying the dismissal of an employee. Again, the respondent could have offered a variant that preserved Mr Poole's 30-hour week without including any compulsory Sunday hours, but it did not.

(iii) Fairness in all the circumstances

37. If the tribunal is persuaded that the respondent has established that Mr Poole was dismissed for an admissible reason, it must then decide whether in all the circumstances the respondent acted reasonably or unreasonably in treating it as a sufficient reason to dismiss him.

38. It is submitted that the respondent's behaviour in dismissing Mr Poole was unreasonable in the following ways:

(i) The respondent proceeded in all the steps leading to dismissal on the erroneous basis that it had the right to compel Mr Poole to work on Sundays; at no time did it either acknowledge that right or offer him an alternative to the proposed changes (apart from a drastic reduction in his hours) that would not have infringed it.

(ii) The respondent admits that it made no effort to investigate whether Mr Poole could have been redeployed to another store.

(iii) The respondent admits that it gave no consideration to any alternative method of securing the Saturday night cover that it required apart from demanding seven-night rotas from night crew on pain of dismissal.

(iv) By offering Mr Poole an appeal against the proposed changes, which the respondent had no intention of reconsidering, and then by confusing the question whether any further appeal would be against the changes or the dismissal, it denied Mr Poole any effective right of appeal against his dismissal.

Conclusion

39. The tribunal is asked to find that Mr Poole was dismissed for refusing Sunday work, and therefore that his dismissal was unfair. If the tribunal finds that Mr Poole was dismissed for a reason relating to conduct or for some other substantial reason, it is asked to find that in all the circumstances, including the size and administrative resources of the respondent, the dismissal was unfair.

Natalie Cummings
North London Law Centre

I April 2005

What can go wrong at the hearing?

9.30   Hearings are unpredictable, and all kinds of things can go wrong on the day. What follows is a list of some of the most common problems that can crop up, with suggestions as to how they might be handled.

The respondent comes to the hearing with a large pile of new documents that the claimant has not seen before.

9.31   This is fairly common. The claimant will have to make a fairly swift decision about how important the new documents are. It may be sufficient to ask the tribunal for a short break of 20 minutes to half an hour to enable the claimant to read the new documents and consider them. If they are particularly important, or the claimant will have difficulty in analysing them in a short time, then it may be necessary to ask the tribunal to adjourn[20] the hearing to another day. If this is necessary, the claimant should consider making an application for a costs or preparation time order.[21]

9.32   Alternatively, the claimant may simply wish to ask the tribunal to exclude the new material from its consideration on the grounds that it should have been disclosed earlier. Either way, stress should be laid on the respondent's failure to comply properly with whatever order was previously made about disclosure of documents.

The respondent makes new allegations at the hearing that the claimant was not previously aware of but could refute given time.

9.33   This is a variation on the previous example. Again, if the new material is important enough, it may be necessary to request a postponement.

The chairman treats the claimant with evident hostility

9.34   If this happens, accurate and complete note-taking becomes extremely important. If the chairman (or a member) of the tribunal says something that indicates hostility to the claimant, the claimant should write it down at once and, if he or she has anyone with him or her, ensure that they write it down as well.[22] The claimant should consider whether to make an application for the chairman to remove him or herself

---

20 This is the usual term used for putting the hearing off to another day once the parties have attended the tribunal.

21 See paras 10.10–10.13 below.

22 There is nothing wrong with turning briefly to the accompanying person and whispering: 'Please write that down' if this happens.

from the case because of apparent bias. Obviously this is a tactic that has a high cost, and should not be used lightly. First and foremost, it will certainly antagonise the tribunal, so unless the tribunal grants the application it will make it more likely that the claimant loses the case. It is therefore a tactic that has more to do with laying the foundations for a subsequent appeal than with winning the case this time round. If granted, it will almost certainly – unless there happens to be another tribunal free to hear the case on the same day – necessitate an adjournment.

The chairman refuses to permit the claimant to cross-examine in an important area

9.35 The tribunal has a general power to control proceedings, and will sometimes restrain a particular line of cross-examination on the grounds that it is not relevant. It may be necessary to explain where the questions are heading or why they are relevant. Unfortunately this will sometimes lose what would have been a useful element of surprise. If the tribunal is determined to restrain a series of questions that the claimant regards as crucial, careful notes should be taken of this exchange in case it needs to form the basis of a subsequent appeal.

The chairman imposes strict time-limits on evidence or submissions

9.36 This is becoming more and more common with increasing pressure on tribunals to deal with cases quickly. Tribunals sometimes ask for estimates of how long each stage will take, and then hold parties to their estimates. This is particularly unfair in the case of an unrepresented claimant because it takes experience to estimate how long cross-examination will take. In any event, much depends on the manner in which the witness answers questions: a witness who gives terse one-or two-word answers will finish his or her evidence much faster than a witness who tells a long rambling story in answer to each question. If the claimant feels that he or she is being seriously disadvantaged by time limits, he or she should put up a fight at the time: outline briefly what remains to be covered and why it is important. It may be helpful to refer the tribunal to Employment Tribunals (Constitution and Rules of Procedure) Regulations 2004[23] reg 3 and point out that the need to deal with cases justly comes first, and trumps (if necessary) the aim of dealing with them 'expeditiously'.[24]

---

23 SI No 1861.
24 Legalese for 'quickly'.

The claimant forgets to ask one of the respondent's witness about a crucial topic

9.37   This is easily done. If the witness is still present, it should not be too difficult to remedy. The claimant should explain the omission to the tribunal, and ask for the witness to be recalled. Although the tribunal will not be best pleased, it should normally agree, especially if the claimant is a layperson representing him or herself. If the witness was released on a previous day and is no longer attending the hearing, the tribunal is likely to be more reluctant, but if the omitted topic is important enough it may be necessary to make the request anyway. Thought should be given to whether this will extend proceedings enough to necessitate an extra hearing day: if it does, there will be a real risk of a costs order.

Remedies hearings

9.38   In most cases the notice of the main hearing will indicate that the tribunal intends to deal with the question of remedy at the same time if the claim succeeds. It follows that as a rule claimants should make sure that they are ready to give evidence and argue about the correct remedy at the main hearing if necessary. The tribunal will rarely wish to hear evidence about this question before it has decided whether or not the claim succeeds,[25] but if the question whether or not the claim succeeds is decided in time, the tribunal may go straight on to hear evidence and argument about he correct level of award.

9.39   However, it is also very often the case that by the time the tribunal has made its decision on liability, there is insufficient time left to deal with remedies, and the case gets adjourned to a separate remedies hearing. Sometimes part of the reason for this is that the tribunal hopes that once it has settled the question of liability, it will be possible for the parties to agree on remedy. Tribunals, like the rest of us, tend to have a preference not to do sums if they can help it; they will also be aware of the potential impact of recoupment[26] on an award of compensation and may wish to give the parties the opportunity to reach a settlement that avoids this.

---

25 This tends to be referred to as the question of liability.
26 See ELAH paras 18.52–18.56.

9.40　　Remedies hearings proceed in very much the same way as liability hearings,[27] with oral evidence, cross-examination and submissions. The main difference, typically, is that only the claimant will need to give evidence. If expert evidence is needed on any question as to remedy (for instance, actuarial evidence about the value of pension loss, or medical evidence about the effect on the claimant's health of the treatment he or she was subjected to by the employer), this tends to be a very good reason to ask the tribunal to hold a separate remedies hearing. It makes no sense for a claimant (and if the claimant, often the respondent too) to instruct experts to give evidence as to remedy – probably at significant expense – before there is any certainty that there will be a remedies hearing at all.

27　That is, the main hearing to decide who has won and who has lost.

The decision and after

The decision

10.1   The decision may be given orally at the end of the hearing, or the tribunal may wish to take time to consider and write its decision,[1] in which case the parties may be sent away not knowing who has won and who has lost.

10.2   If the tribunal announces its decision and gives reasons at the hearing, it will send out a written judgment[2] afterwards. The judgment will simply state which party has won, who has to pay what in compensation or costs, and may include a declaration (for example, that one party has discriminated against the other). The tribunal will not send out written reasons unless one of the parties requests them. A party wishing to appeal must have written reasons. It is suggested that unrepresented claimants who have lost their cases should always request written reasons in order to be able to think about (and get advice on) whether or not to appeal. Even if there is no question of an appeal, written reasons will make it easier to understand the result. The request can be made either at the hearing or within 14 days after the written judgment is sent out. If the claimant requests written reasons at the hearing, he or she should make an immediate note of having made that request.

10.3   If the tribunal reserves its decision, it will always send out written reasons for the decision.[3] Reserved decisions are usually sent out within four to six weeks of the hearing. If a decision has not been received within about eight weeks of the hearing, it is worth making inquiries: occasionally the tribunal makes a mistake and sends reasons to one party but not the other, or to the wrong address, or records that it has sent out reasons when it has not; and of course there is always the possibility of a postal failure. Because of strict time limits for appealing,[4] if reasons have not been received it is important to find out promptly if the tribunal believes it has sent them. The Employment Appeal Tribunal has said in *Kwamin v Abbey National plc*[5] that delay of

---

1   This is called 'reserving' its decision.

2   See glossary.

3   Employment Tribunals Rules of Procedure 2004 rule 29(1), found at Sch 1 to Employment Tribunals (Constitution and Rules of Procedure) Regulations 2004 SI No 1861.

4   See para 11.30 below.

5   [2004] ICR 841, EAT.

more than $3^1/_2$ months between the last hearing day and sending out[6] of the decision will normally be culpable and can provide grounds for appeal.

Costs and preparation time orders

10.4   In certain limited circumstances the tribunal will order one party to reimburse the other's legal costs of fighting the case (this is a costs order) or to pay the other a sum of money to compensate for the time that they or their advisers have spent preparing the case (this is called a preparation time order).[7] Unlike the ordinary courts, employment tribunals do not as a matter of routine order the unsuccessful party to pay the successful party's costs. The tribunals' power to award costs is much more restricted.

10.5   The rules state[8] that if the tribunal is satisfied that a party has 'acted vexatiously, abusively, disruptively or otherwise unreasonably, or the bringing or conducting of the proceedings by the paying party has been misconceived',[9] then it *shall consider* making a costs or preparation time order. In practice tribunals almost never consider such an order unless an application is made.

10.6   Applications are usually made, if at all, after the decision is announced,[10] and are usually decided immediately. This means that a claimant who intends to make a costs application, or who fears that a costs application may be made by the respondent, should go to the substantive hearing equipped with all the information that he or she needs to support or, as the case may be, resist the application.

---

6   'Promulgation'; see glossary.

7   The term 'costs' will be used below for both costs orders and preparation time orders except where it is necessary to distinguish between them.

8   Employment Tribunals Rules of Procedure 2004 rule 40.

9   This formula will be shortened to 'unreasonably, etc' in what follows. For a discussion of what these terms mean, see ETP 3 at paras 18.14–18.19.

10   This should not be regarded as an absolute rule. Occasionally unexpected additional hearing days may prejudice the claimant's ability to go on paying for representation. If this is the case, and the delay is clearly the fault of the respondent, a costs application should be made straight away. The tribunal should be told that if a costs order is not made the claimant may not be able to afford to be represented at the resumed hearing. This of course must not be said unless it is true.

When to apply for costs or a preparation time order

10.7   Before the 2004 rules came into force, the costs regime was heavily weighted in favour of parties – more often than not respondents – who were paying for legal representation: only costs actually incurred could be recovered. The introduction of preparation time orders does not completely redress the balance, but it is likely to have the effect that successful costs applications by claimants become more common. It should be noted that a claimant can apply for a preparation time order in respect of time spent by legal advisers who have not charged any fees.

10.8   A costs application can be made by the claimant whenever the respondent has acted unreasonably, etc,[11] or where the respondent has caused a postponement or adjournment of the hearing. In general, the application will have a greater chance of success if the claimant has previously warned the respondent that he or she considers its conduct unreasonable and is contemplating a costs application,[12] but sometimes there will be unreasonable conduct at the hearing which the claimant has not foreseen.

10.9   Typical grounds on which a costs application might be made against a respondent include:

- insistence on running a misconceived defence, for example, that the claimant was not an employee when she very clearly was, or that there had not been a TUPE transfer[13] when it was clear that the undertaking in which the claimant was employed had retained its identity in the hands of the transferee, or that a claimant with a prosthetic leg did not have a disability for the purposes of the Disability Discrimination Act 1995;
- refusal to agree a realistic settlement proposal;[14]
- failure to provide documents or information ordered by the tribunal, or to exchange witness statements when ordered;
- production of a large volume of new documentation on the day of the hearing;
- excessive requests for disclosure, further information or written answers;[15]

---

11   See fn 9 above.
12   See, eg, P6.8.
13   See glossary and ELAH 5.
14   But see paras 6.60–6.63 above.
15   See paras 4.6–4.8 above for discussion of the difference between legitimate and excessive requests.

- making new allegations against the claimant on the day of the hearing;
- late amendment of its response;
- abusive letters or telephone calls or attempts to intimidate the claimant into dropping the claim;
- attempts to interfere with the claimant's witnesses;
- unfounded allegations against the claimant, his or her advisers or the tribunal.[16]

Arguing for a costs or preparation time order

10.10   Sometimes the conduct in question will be a single unreasonable act, but often it will be necessary to take the tribunal through a history of the communications between the parties in order to demonstrate that the respondent has been unreasonable. If that is the case it is prudent to collate a separate bundle of documents relevant to the costs application so that the tribunal can quickly and conveniently be shown the sequence of events. This is where a history of conspicuously patient and forbearing letters on the part of the claimant comes into its own: the unreasonableness of the respondent will be displayed to much better advantage against a background of consistent courtesy on the part of the claimant.

10.11   The fact of unreasonable, etc, conduct by one party gives the tribunal power to make a costs order in favour of the other party. Once that fact is established, however, it does not follow that the tribunal *must* make a costs order. Tribunals quite often make this mistake, and as this is a basis on which a costs order could be challenged on appeal it is sensible for the party seeking costs to remind the tribunal that it has a discretion once it is persuaded that it has power to award costs.

10.12   Factors that can influence the tribunal in its exercise of discretion include:

- the seriousness of the unreasonable conduct relied on;
- the degree of inconvenience and/or expense caused to the claimant;
- warnings that the claimant has given the respondent about the possibility of a costs application;

---

16 It is particularly helpful if the respondent makes wild accusations of bias or unfair dealing against the tribunal, or otherwise shows a disrespectful attitude to the proceedings.

- the conduct of the party seeking costs;[17]
- the means of either party.

10.13   When it comes to an argument that the respondent's defence was misconceived, the tribunal may suggest that unless it was clear on the papers that the defence was doomed, it cannot be said to have been misconceived. This is a mistake: the point is what the respondent knew or should have known. If the employer's response to the claim and witness statements look convincing, but its witnesses when they give evidence simply do not back what has been put in their statements, then the defence may still have been misconceived: the employer after all had access to its own witnesses before the tribunal did, and should have made sure their statements reflected what they believed to be the truth.

Preparation time orders

10.14   Although the discretion whether to make a preparation time order is expressed in the same terms and can be expected to be exercised in the same way as the discretion to make a costs order, there are some features of this power that are quite distinct.

10.15   First, it should be noted that unlike a costs order, a preparation time order cannot be made in respect of the time spent by a party or his or her adviser at the hearing itself. It is difficult to understand the policy behind this: often the consequence of unreasonable conduct is that a hearing is extended. A party who is paying for legal representation may be able to recover the cost of the additional day(s) in tribunal; but a party who is representing him or herself, or is represented by an unqualified adviser (whether or not for free) will not.

10.16   Secondly, preparation time orders do not reimburse the receiving party for money spent on the preparation of a case, but for the time spent at a fixed hourly rate.[18] This has two odd effects. The first is that a party who is paying for an unqualified representative at more than £25 per hour will recover less than he or she has spent. The second is that a party who is represented for free by an unqualified adviser will recover £25 per hour for his or her adviser's preparation time. The latter will be something of a windfall for the claimant.[19]

---

17 The tribunal will be reluctant to award costs if it feels that there is significant blame on both sides.

18 £25, rising to £26 on 6 April 2006 and by a further £1 on each subsequent 6 April.

19 Who may well think it appropriate to pay any money received as a result of a preparation time order in respect of time spent by an adviser acting for free to the Citizens' Advice Bureau, law centre or other advice charity in question.

10.17   Free advice and representation can bring a further complication. A claimant represented by an unqualified adviser will in a suitable case be able to claim for that adviser's preparation time. A claimant represented for free by a qualified lawyer will, ironically, be in a weaker position. A preparation time order is only available to a party who has *not* been legally represented at the hearing (or at the time the case was determined, if it was determined without a hearing). So a claimant who has been legally represented for free throughout cannot claim a preparation time order. However, having been represented for free, he or she has incurred no costs – so there can be no costs order either.[20] Some examples may help.

Example 1
Claimant A pays a considerable sum of money for advice and assistance by a solicitor with the preparation of the case, but decides that the cost of representation at the hearing is prohibitive. She will not be legally represented at the hearing, so she will be limited to a preparation time order at £25 per hour. She will be able to be awarded this in respect of the time her solicitor has spent, but at an hourly rate much lower than any solicitor is likely to charge.

Example 2
Claimant B is represented for free by a solicitor from his local law centre. She appears for him at the hearing. Claimant B cannot claim for preparation time because he has been legally represented at the time the case was determined; he cannot claim for costs because he has not incurred any: his solicitor has acted for free.

---

20 One possible way around this is by way of conditional fee agreement (CFA), under which the claimant becomes liable to pay for the services of the advice agency if, but only if, a costs order is made. It is arguable that this does not really give the tribunal jurisdiction to make a costs order, but some tribunals have made costs orders on this basis and since the sums involved have been modest the question has not yet been made the subject of an appeal. See further the Department of Constitutional Affairs (DCA) consultation paper 'Making Simple CFAs a Reality' at http://www.dca.gov.uk/consult/simplecfa.htm.

> **Example 3**
> Claimant C is also represented for free by the same law centre
> solicitor. Because his case is listed on the same day as Claimant
> B's case, she refers him to the Free Representation Unit[21] for
> representation. He is represented at the hearing by a law student.
> Claimant C, not having had legal representation at the hearing,
> will be able to claim preparation time. He can claim £25 per hour
> for all the time spent by his solicitor and his FRU representative
> in preparing the case, even though he has not had to pay anything
> for the services of either.

The amount of a costs or preparation time order

10.18   A claimant seeking a costs or preparation time order should be ready
to give the tribunal clear and credible information about the costs he
or she has incurred or about the time that has been spent in preparing
for the hearing. This should not present any particular difficulties for
claimants who are paying for legal representation and have incurred
actual legal costs, but claimants who are either representing themselves
or being represented for free are likely to have difficulty quantifying the
time spent unless they and/or their advisers have kept a running note
of this.[22]

Resisting a costs or preparation time order

Misconceived ground

10.19   If the respondent applies for costs on the basis that the claim was misconceived, this will normally rely on the definition of misconceived
as including 'having no reasonable prospect of success.' The claimant
should argue that her claim was not misconceived unless at some
point before the hearing she knew or should have known that her case
had no reasonable prospect of success. The fact that the claim has
failed is not enough: it needs to have been doomed to failure, and
evidently so, before the tribunal should find that it was misconceived.
It may be helpful to remind the tribunal that it would have been open

---

21   See para 1.11 above.
22   See P1.2 above.

to the respondent to invite the tribunal to list the case for a pre-hearing review and order the claimant to pay a deposit under rule 20[23] if it considered that the case was self-evidently hopeless. If the respondent did not do this, then its assertion now that the case was misconceived may be opportunistic.

Refusal of a settlement offer

10.20   If the respondent applies for costs on the strength of a previous offer of settlement headed 'without prejudice save as to costs,' the claimant may be assisted by *Kopel v Safeway Stores plc*[24] which makes it clear that claimants in the employment tribunal will not be penalised in costs merely for failing to do better after a hearing than they could have done by accepting an offer of settlement. Failing to predict the tribunal's award accurately should not be regarded as unreasonable in itself; refusing an offer of the maximum the tribunal could reasonably be expected to award may well be.

Postponement or adjournment

10.21   The power to award costs of a postponement or adjournment is confined to the cost of the additional work required by reason of the postponement or adjournment. A party resisting a costs order should take a sceptical view of the *additional* costs caused by a postponement: the obvious consequence of a postponement is that preparation for the hearing has been done early, but not necessarily that additional preparation has to be done. It is different of course if the case is adjourned after parties and lawyers have arrived at the hearing: then, inevitably, there will be additional costs.

The claimant's means

10.22   Tribunals have power to take the paying party's means into account when deciding whether and if so at what level to make a costs order.[25] It follows that claimants who think there is a significant risk of a costs order against them should go to the tribunal with evidence about their income and expenses.

23   Employment Tribunals Rules of Procedure 2004. See also ETP 3 paras 11.9–11.12.
24   [2003] IRLR 753.
25   Employment Tribunals Rules of Procedure 2004 rr41(2) and 45(3).

The respondent's choice of representation

10.23   If the respondent argues before the hearing that the applicant's case is misconceived, and/or the applicant's total award cannot exceed a certain modest sum that is being offered by way of settlement, then a real question may arise whether it made sense for them to instruct solicitors at all. If the respondent has chosen to instruct City solicitors at £200 or £300 an hour and specialist counsel at £800 or £1,000 per hearing day on a case which, it says, never had any real chance of success, it can quite sensibly and properly be suggested by the claimant that the respondent's choice of legal adviser is disproportionate. The employment tribunals are after all designed to be accessible to lay people. If the respondent takes the view that a case had no reasonable prospect of success or was incapable of resulting in an award of more than £1,000 or so,[26] then a fair question is: 'Why do you need a team of highly paid specialist lawyers? Why could a personnel officer not deal with this?'

Changing the judgment

10.24   There are three ways that a judgment can be changed or altered after it has been sent out to the parties.

10.25   For minor clerical or uncontroversial arithmetic errors, a certificate of correction should be requested from the chairman who heard the case.[27] There is no time limit for applying for a certificate of correction.

10.26   Where there is reason to ask the tribunal that decided the case to look again at its decision – because new evidence has become available, for example, or because one party was unaware of the date of the hearing – then an application should be made to the same tribunal to review its decision. Where the tribunal has made an error of law in coming to its decision, there is a right of appeal to the Employment Appeal Tribunal: see chapters 11 and 12 below.

Applying for a certificate of correction

10.27   All that is required is a letter to the tribunal explaining the error and making the request.

---

26   And if it took highly paid legal advisers to tell them that, the next question is, 'why did your lawyers not advise you to dispense with their services at an early stage?'

27   See Employment Tribunals Rules of Procedure 2004 r37.

P10.1 Letter applying for a certificate of correction

The Regional Secretary
London Central Employment Tribunal
19–29 Woburn Place
London WC1H 0LU

11 August 2004

Dear Madam

Rajiv Menon v Saint Julian's Hospital NHS Trust

I should be grateful if you would put before Mr Ruby, who heard this case on 10–15 January 2005, my request for a certificate of correction. The judgment reads at paragraph 2 'the respondent is ordered to pay the claimant £57.65.' It is clear from the rest of the judgment and the reasons that the correct sum is £57,653.34. £10,000 is awarded for injury to feelings (see paragraph 46 of the written reasons) and £47,653.34 for lost earnings (see paragraph 49 of the written reasons).

Yours faithfully

Natalie Cummings

Applying for a review of a decision[28]

10.28   There are limited grounds on which it is possible to ask the tribunal to review[29] certain kinds of decision[30] – that is, to look again at the decision and decide whether to revoke or vary it. The grounds are set out at rule 34(3),[31] and they are:

(a) the decision was wrongly made as a result of an administrative error;

(b) a party did not receive notice of the proceedings leading to the decision;

---

28   See also ETP 3 paras 19.9–19.41.

29   See glossary.

30   That is, a judgment (the final outcome of the case or part of the case) or a decision not to accept a claim or a response. Case management orders are not subject to review.

31   Of the Employment Tribunals Rules of Procedure 2004.

(c) the decision was made in the absence of a party;

(d) new evidence has become available since the conclusion of the hearing to which the decision relates, provided that its existence could not have been reasonably known of or foreseen at the time;

(e) the interests of justice require such a review.

10.29   When an application for review is received by the tribunal, the chairman who heard the case will decide whether or not to hold a review hearing. There will be no hearing if the chairman considers that there are no grounds for the decision to be reviewed, or that there is no reasonable prospect of the decision being varied or revoked.

10.30   If the chairman decides to grant a review hearing, the review will, if practicable, be heard by the original tribunal. It can be seen from this that a review is essentially a request *to the same tribunal* to think again about the case, so it will rarely be useful to apply for a review unless there is a real possibility that the tribunal might change its mind. Some examples of situations in which it might be sensible to apply for review are:

- *The claimant did not receive notice of the hearing, and the case was dismissed in her absence.* At a review application she would need to satisfy the tribunal that she genuinely did not receive the notice of hearing. That will be easiest if the tribunal's file shows that it was wrongly addressed, but a claimant in this position should not assume that she will be disbelieved if the problem is simply that some of her post went astray. If she does persuade the tribunal that she genuinely did not receive the notice of hearing, the tribunal should revoke its decision and list the case for a new hearing date.

- *The claimant failed to attend the hearing, although he knew when it was, for urgent and compelling reasons.* If the claimant did not explain his absence at the time, his reasons for that failure would have to be very compelling indeed. A serious accident on the way to the tribunal should be sufficient, for example, or a call to attend hospital to be with a critically ill spouse or child.

- *The claimant was dismissed for redundancy. She argued at the hearing that there was no genuine redundancy situation, but her employer had not replaced her and the tribunal accepted that her post was redundant. A few days after the hearing she heard saw her old job advertised in the local paper.* Here there is new evidence – which was not available at the time of the hearing – which gives the tribunal reason to reassess its conclusion that the redundancy was genuine.

- *The claimant, who was unrepresented at the time, received a letter from the respondent's solicitors saying that his claim was misconceived and they would apply for costs of up to £10,000 against him. He withdrew his claim and it was subsequently dismissed by the tribunal on the respondent's application. A week or two later, the claimant was advised that his case had been strong and there were no grounds on which the respondent could have realistically applied for costs.* This would be an application on the grounds that 'the interests of justice require such a review.' If the tribunal refused a review, that decision could be appealed. It is important to note here that the review application is a necessary first step, even if an appeal then follows. This is because the original decision dismissing the case on withdrawal cannot be said to be in any way in error: at the time it was made, it was the only sensible thing the tribunal could do. The only decision of the tribunal's that is open to attack by way of appeal is the refusal to review their original decision in light of new information.

10.31　An application for review must be made within 14 days of the date when the decision[32] was sent to the parties. The application for review should spell out which of the grounds listed at rule 34 are relied upon.

P10.2 Application for review of a decision

The Regional Secretary
London Central Employment Tribunal
19–29 Woburn Place
London WC1H 0LU

18 November 2004

Dear Madam

Mike Hardwick v ADAL Ltd[33]

I should be grateful if you would put before Mr Colt, who heard this case, my application for a review of the tribunal's decision of 8 October 2004 under rule 34 of the tribunal Rules of Procedure on the grounds that:

32　See glossary.
33　See P4.2 above.

(i) new evidence has become available since the hearing which was not available, and could not have been foreseen, at the time of the hearing; and

(ii) the interests of justice require a review.

The claim was of unfair dismissal. The respondent had dismissed Mr Hardwick, giving redundancy as the reason and alleging a downturn in business that forced them to reduce their staff costs. Mr Hardwick alleged that his post was not genuinely redundant, and that the real reason for his dismissal was that there had been personal friction between him and his manager.

The tribunal's decision recorded that the evidence of a downturn in business was equivocal, but (at paragraph 24) that it was clear that the respondent had reduced its management team by one with a cost saving of some £57,000 per year. On the basis of this the tribunal accepted that there had been a genuine redundancy situation, and proceeded to find that Mr Hardwick's selection for redundancy had been fair.

On 12 November Mr Hardwick received anonymously in the post a copy of an advertisement in the Sutton Echo for an 'Engineering Process Manager.' I enclose a copy. The post appears to be Mr Hardwick's old job.

I suggest that in light of this new evidence there are grounds for a concern that the tribunal may have been materially misled by the respondent as to the reason for Mr Hardwick's dismissal.

Yours faithfully

Natalie Cummings

Review and appeal

10.32   An appeal is a complaint that the tribunal has made an error of law.[34] This will rarely if ever be something that it is appropriate to raise by way of application for review. However, there will sometimes be borderline cases where it is difficult to decide whether to ask the tribunal to review

---

34 See paras 11.15– 11.19 below.

its own decision, or to appeal the decision to the Employment Appeal Tribunal. In these cases, the best course is probably to do both, but to inform the EAT of the review application and ask it not to take any action on the appeal until the review has been determined. Alternatively a review application can be made at once and a decision on appeal postponed in the hope that the review application will be decided by the time the time for appealing expires. If this course is chosen, however, great care must be taken to ensure that the appeal deadline does not slip by before the review application is decided.

CHAPTER 11

Appealing to the EAT: preliminary matters and the notice of appeal

Terminology

11.1   The party who appeals to the Employment Appeal Tribunal (EAT) is technically known as the appellant, and the other party is the respondent (that is, the party who responds) to the appeal. This can get confusing, because the respondent to the appeal is not necessarily the same person as the respondent to the original claim: if the employer (who was the respondent at the employment tribunal) appeals to the EAT, the former employer is now the appellant and the employee becomes the respondent.[1] For this reason, the EAT usually prefers that in argument the parties should stick to the terms used before the employment tribunal and refer to the employee as the claimant and the employer as the respondent, even if the appeal is brought by the employer.

11.2   In a book of this nature (as opposed to in a particular case) it is sometimes necessary to generalise about what is required of those who are challenging the decision of the tribunal, and those who are seeking to uphold it, so that approach is not followed here. In this chapter, the term 'appellant' is used to refer to the party who is challenging the employment tribunal's decision, and the term 'respondent' to refer to the party (even if the employee) who is seeking to uphold the tribunal's decision. In the precedents, the parties are either referred to by name, or as 'the employee' and 'the employer' or 'the company', 'the hospital', etc.

Public funding

11.3   It is important to note as a preliminary that public funding is available in theory for representation at appeals to the EAT. Claimants who are thinking of appealing and are not earning or are on a low wage may wish to consult a law centre or solicitors with a Legal Services Commission contract for employment work to find out whether they are eligible. However, the sums of money involved in employment cases are often too small to justify public funding even where the claimant is financially eligible, so many claimants will be on their own at this stage too. The Employment Appeal Tribunal is, like employment tribunals, very used to dealing with non-lawyers.

---

1   The plot thickens again if the appeal is allowed, and the respondent to the appeal – that is, the claimant as was – appeals to the Court of Appeal. Then the claimant, who was the respondent at the EAT is now the appellant, and the respondent, who was the appellant at the EAT, is now the respondent again.

Free representation before the Employment Appeal Tribunal

11.4   The factors governing the availability of free representation operate slightly differently at the level of the EAT than at first instance, and claimants who cannot afford to pay for representation will have a better chance of finding someone to act for free if they understand a certain amount about how this works. There are two significant factors.

11.5   The first is that appeals are normally much shorter than employment tribunal hearings. This is because, except in very unusual cases, no witnesses will be heard, and because the questions on which the EAT will hear an appeal are narrowly defined. Appeals only rarely last more than a day, and a large number will be completed in half a day or less. This also means that preparation for an EAT case is normally much lighter than for a first instance case: witnesses do not have to be interviewed, statements do not have to be prepared, documents do not have to be requested and disclosed, the hearing bundle will be much shorter and so on. This means that offering free representation on an appeal is less daunting in terms of work for the lawyer who makes the offer.[2]

11.6   The other factor is double-edged. This is that appearances before the EAT, which is the next step up the legal hierarchy, tends to be regarded by representatives both as more interesting and more intimidating than appearing in the employment tribunals. Hearings are often presided over by High Court judges, and proceedings are superficially more formal. Some advisers who conduct cases routinely and skilfully in the employment tribunals simply lack the confidence to appear at the EAT and may be unwilling to take cases to appeal because they feel (although unqualified advisers are allowed to appear there and often do) that the EAT is the preserve of barristers and solicitors. The other side to this, however, is that some advocates will be more willing to take on appeals for free because they provide valuable – and comparatively rare – experience.

---

2   Especially for someone who is acting for free in the sense that *they themselves* are doing the work for no pay – this is a distinction that may be lost on the client, who does not pay in either event, but it can be useful to be aware of it. A lawyer working full time for a legal charity that provides free representation is normally paid a salary. A lay adviser at a Citizens' Advice Bureau (CAB), a Free Representation Unit (FRU) volunteer or a barrister acting for no fee ('pro bono' as barristers and solicitors still call it) is giving his or her time for nothing, so the longer the case takes the more time he or she loses from paid work.

11.7   Both of these factors mean that a claimant who has failed to secure free representation at first instance from a local legal charity or other body should not assume for that reason that he or she will be refused help with an appeal. It is worth asking again at this stage, especially if the appeal raises a question that could be of general importance to other claimants in the future.

11.8   It is worth mentioning two specific sources of free representation at the EAT, both of which tend to find it easier to help at this stage than at first instance. One is the Free Representation Unit (FRU), and the other is the Bar Pro Bono Unit. Both organisations are London-based, and part of the reason they are more likely to be able to help with appeals is the simple geographical fact that the EAT for the whole of England and Wales has its hearings in London.

11.9   Claimants who live or work(ed) in greater London will often be able to be referred direct from their local Citizens Advice Bureau (CAB) or law centre. Claimants from outside London will have a harder task, but as the EAT in London deals with appeals from the whole of England and Wales, FRU will accept referrals on appeal[3] for claimants from elsewhere in the country provided the referral comes from a registered FRU referral agency. The best bet for claimants outside London is to ask their local CAB to refer the case first to the Citizens Advice Specialist Support Unit in Wolverhampton. The Specialist Support Unit is registered with FRU and will, if it thinks the case is appropriate, refer it on.

11.10   The Bar Pro Bono Unit (BPBU) does not at the time of writing require a referral from another advice agency, and claimants who do not have the assistance of an advice agency can simply download an application form from their website,[4] complete it and send it in. It is possible that this will change in the course of 2005, however, so potential applicants should read the guidance on the Unit's website carefully before making an application for assistance.

11.11   The Bar Pro Bono Unit applies more stringent tests than FRU on the question whether a client is able to afford to pay for representation, and on the merits of the case, so to maximise chances of an offer of representation it is sensible to make parallel applications to both organisations. Once an offer of representation from one has been accepted, the other should be informed immediately. Although FRU volunteers are mostly still in training and BPBU refers cases only

---

3   But not for first instance cases.
4   www.barprobono.org.uk.

to qualified barristers, FRU volunteers have the benefit of specialisation (and specialist support) whereas most junior barristers are generalists. Because of this, there is, as a rule, nothing to choose between the two organisations in the quality of the representation they can provide. Neither FRU nor the BPBU can ever guarantee to provide representation for every case they accept: both are dependent on the availability of a suitable volunteer on the particular day.

11.12   A third source of free representation is called the Employment Lawyers Appeals Advice Scheme (ELAAS). This cannot be directly accessed by claimants and is not guaranteed, and for that reason should probably – although the quality of the representation is usually very high – be treated as a last resort. Where there is a preliminary hearing (as to which, see paras 12.3–12.16 below), litigants who have no representative on record with the EAT as acting for them may be offered the assistance of an ELAAS adviser. The ELAAS adviser will be at the EAT on the day to advise and represent if appropriate. He or she will have had the papers a few days in advance, but will not be able to meet the client before the day of the hearing and will not be able to take on conduct of the case. If the case then goes forward to a full hearing, there should be an opportunity to be referred to FRU and/or the Bar Pro Bono Unit at this point also.

The Employment Appeal Tribunal's composition and powers

11.13   The EAT is governed by the Employment Appeal Tribunal Rules 1993[5] as amended in 2001 and 2004. An updated version of the rules should be available on the EAT website,[6] also the rules are reproduced in full in *Employment Tribunal Procedure*.[7] A practice direction – giving more detailed instructions on how to run an appeal – was issued in December 2004.[8] Again, it is a good idea for anyone embarking on an appeal to the EAT to take twenty minutes or so to read through the current rules and practice direction so as to have an idea, in broad outline, of how the process works and where to find specific powers.

---

5   SI No 2854.

6   At the time of writing the EAT website (www.employmentappeals.gov.uk) had not been updated to show the latest amendments.

7   McMullen, Tuck and Criddle (3rd edn, Legal Action Group, 2004). Abbreviated to ETP 3 throughout this book.

8   This is also available from the EAT website and in ETP 3.

11.14   The EAT is composed in a similar way to an employment tribunal, with a judge supported by two lay members, one with a background in the trade union movement and the other having management experience. The presiding judge will be either a circuit judge or a High Court judge.

What kind of appeal will the EAT hear?

11.15   It is usually said that the EAT will hear appeals only on questions of law. Unfortunately it is far from obvious what this means. To understand what the EAT will and will not do, it is more helpful to understand why the EAT is confident that it knows best on certain kinds of questions, and why on others it has a strong inclination to defer to the employment tribunal. The point that disappointed claimants often find difficult to understand is that there is built in to the system an acceptance that tribunals will sometimes get the wrong answer, and this will not always be able to be corrected. Justice is not always done in the employment tribunals, any more than in any other court.

11.16   If there is a disagreement between the EAT and the employment tribunal about what the law is – what a certain provision in the legislation means, for example, or what is the effect of previous decisions of the EAT or higher courts, then the EAT will impose its own view. The law is to be found in legislation and law reports, and the EAT has equal access to these materials and, as the senior judicial body, can interpret them more authoritatively.

11.17   When it comes to deciding which witnesses are telling the truth, deciding whether one party or another has acted fairly or reasonably, or exercising a discretion about what it is just to do in all the circumstances, however, the EAT is at a striking disadvantage. The employment tribunal has heard the witnesses give their evidence: it has observed their demeanour when they were questioned, it has heard their hesitations and their tone of voice, it has had various opportunities to judge their character. It also has access to a great wealth of nuance in the case that the EAT – which, except in very rare cases, does not hear witnesses at all, and will certainly not have heard all the evidence that the tribunal has heard – lacks. It will have built up, from hearing the evidence of countless employees, managers, personnel officers, etc, in other cases, a broad experience and 'feel' for how employers and employees behave and how it is reasonable to expect them to behave. It is altogether closer to the 'coal face' than the EAT.

11.18   For these reasons, the EAT approaches decisions of the employment tribunal in the latter category with great deference, and will not interfere unless they are very clearly wrong. Thus, to attack a finding of fact it will be necessary to show that there was no evidence[9] at all to support the finding, or that the evidence was so thin and implausible that no reasonable tribunal could have accepted it. To attack an inference[10] or an exercise of discretion,[11] it will need to be shown that no reasonable tribunal could have drawn that inference or exercised the discretion in that way: in other words, that the decision was 'perverse'.

11.19   This is often hard for claimants to accept: the outcome that tends to make a claimant feel most aggrieved is having been disbelieved when he or she has told the truth. Losing on a legal technicality may well be less painful. Unfortunately it is the legal technicality that is likely to be appealable, and the tribunal's wrong assessment of the truthfulness of the witnesses that will not. Perversity appeals are unpopular with the EAT and very few of them succeed.

Bias appeals

11.20   The only ground of appeal less popular with the EAT than perversity is bias. This places two demands on the claimant or adviser. The first is to approach the question whether to appeal on grounds of bias with caution. Bias should never be inferred simply from the result. If the claimant's reasoning amounts to 'They found against me when I was clearly right so they must have been biased,' then an appeal on grounds of bias should not be attempted. More often, the claimant's perception that the tribunal was biased will be based on the tribunal's manner in conducting the hearing, subtle differences in the way the tribunal addressed counsel for the respondent and the claimant or his or her representative, hostile body language, signs of boredom or exasperation when the claimant was speaking and so on. These impressions may be extremely compelling at the time, and they may well be justified. They are also an extremely difficult basis for an appeal: there will be no record of them, the tribunal and the respondent will almost certainly deny that anything was amiss, and a detailed analysis of the tribunal's body language will be more likely to convince the EAT that the claimant

---

9 It must be remembered that evidence includes what witnesses have said. A common error among non-lawyers is to say: 'So-and-so *said* such-and-such, but there was no evidence.' That a witness has said it is in itself evidence.

10 See glossary.

11 See glossary.

is paranoid rather than that the tribunal was biased. It will almost never be advisable to pursue an appeal on grounds such as this.

11.21   On the other hand, there will sometimes be real – and demonstrable – grounds to complain of bias, and here it will be necessary to face down the EAT's reluctance to entertain or allow an appeal on this basis. If the bias allegation is based on what a member of the tribunal said in the course of the hearing, then it will be very difficult to proceed unless either the other party or the tribunal, or both, agree what was said. This places an emphasis on note-taking at the hearing. If something is said that appears to indicate bias,[12] the best course is to write it down and then immediately read back the note of what was said and ask the tribunal to confirm that the note is accurate; and to make a note too that that confirmation was received. This will make it very difficult for the tribunal or the other party to deny subsequently that the offending remark was made.

11.22   It will very rarely be possible to deduce bias from the decision itself, but tribunals do occasionally betray a fixed unwillingness to contemplate the possibility that a respondent witness could have lied simply because of his or her status or importance in the employer organisation. In these cases it may well be possible – and if it is possible, it will normally be preferable – to put the appeal on grounds of perversity, or failure adequately to explain the decision.

11.23   There are specific rules at paragraph 11 of the EAT Practice Direction 2004 as to the procedures that will be followed if an allegation of bias or other improper conduct of a hearing is to be made. Any claimant basing an appeal on such grounds must take care to follow these. There is a warning at paragraph 11.6.3 that unsuccessful pursuit of such an appeal may put the appellant at risk of an order for costs, but it should be remembered that the EAT's power to award costs is limited. By rule 34A of the Employment Appeal Tribunal Rules 1993,[13] the EAT may only make a costs order where it appears that 'any proceedings brought by the paying party were unnecessary, improper or vexatious or misconceived or that there has been unreasonable delay or other unreasonable conduct in the bringing or conducting of proceedings by the paying party.'[14] It is not unreasonable or improper, without something more, to bring an ultimately unsuccessful bias

---

12 See example 6 at para 11.42 below.

13 SI No 2854 as amended by the Employment Appeal Tribunal (Amendment) Rules 2001 SI No 1128 and 2004 SI No 2526.

14 EAT Rules 1993 r34A(1).

appeal. Any appellant who has been permitted to pursue his or her appeal to a full hearing despite the availability of a rejection on the papers under rule 3(7)[15] or a preliminary hearing should be able to point to the fact that the EAT itself thought that there was enough in the allegation to justify a full hearing.

Appeals on preliminary or procedural matters

11.24   It is not just final decisions of the employment tribunal that are open to appeal: sometimes the claimant may wish to appeal a decision of the tribunal on a preliminary point, or on procedural matters. The latter are often referred to as 'interlocutory'[16] decisions, and an 'interlocutory appeal' is an appeal on this kind of matter. The following are lists of some examples of each kind of decisions that a claimant might wish to appeal.[17]

Preliminary substantive[18] decisions

- a decision that the claimant was not an employee and the tribunal therefore lacks jurisdiction;
- a decision that a complaint was not presented in time;
- a refusal to extend time for a complaint;
- a decision that the claimant does not have sufficient continuous service to complain of unfair dismissal;
- a decision that the claimant was not disabled within the meaning of the Disability Discrimination Act 1995.

11.25   These are all substantive decisions that can be appealed in the same way as final decisions after a full hearing. No special considerations apply to them, except that it is important that if any of these preliminary issues is heard first, and full hearing of some part of the claim follows some weeks or months later, any appeal on the preliminary matter must be started within 42 days *of that decision.*

---

15   See paras 11.49–11.51 below.
16   See glossary.
17   As usual with such lists, it is not exhaustive.
18   See glossary: the opposite of 'procedural'.

Interlocutory decisions

- a refusal to permit the claimant to amend the claim;
- a decision to permit the respondent to present a late response;
- a decision to permit the respondent to amend the response;
- a refusal to postpone a hearing;[19]
- a refusal to order the respondent to provide written answers, further information or disclosure of particular documents;
- a refusal to make adjustments to arrangements for the hearing for the benefit of a disabled claimant;
- a refusal to order the attendance of a witness;
- a refusal to strike out the employer's response;
- a refusal to give a direction for expert evidence;
- a refusal to hear argument on a procedural application on a particular occasion;
- a decision to conduct a hearing in private, or not to.

11.26   These kinds of decisions are difficult to appeal because of the broad discretion that the tribunal has to manage the procedural aspects of the case. The EAT will not interfere just because it considers that it would have exercised any discretion differently: again, it will have to be persuaded that the tribunal's approach demonstrates an error of law.

11.27   There are three typical directions of attack on a decision of this nature. The first is that the tribunal did not accept that it had power to do what it was asked to do at all: here the ground of appeal is not that the tribunal exercised its discretion wrongly, but that it did not exercise it at all because it did not believe that it had a discretion to exercise. Suppose, for example, the claimant points out that there is a witness employed by the respondent who has highly relevant evidence and from whom the tribunal may wish to hear, and invites the tribunal to call the witness and make him or her available for cross-examination by either side. If the tribunal's response is that it considers that this will extend proceedings considerably and it does not believe it is necessary or proportionate, it will be extremely difficult to attack that decision on appeal. If, on the other hand, the tribunal's response is to say that it is for the parties to call witnesses and the tribunal has no power to do what

---

19 It will almost never be practicable to appeal a decision to postpone, partly because by the time the appeal is heard the original hearing date will be lost, and partly because a decision to postpone can be annoying for a claimant but will very rarely significantly damage his or her prospects of success; a refusal to postpone, on the other hand, may deprive a party of representation or of the evidence of a particular witness.

has been asked, then this is a clear error of law and the tribunal has not exercised the discretion that it undoubtedly had.

12.28   The second and third kinds of attack are closely related. One is that the tribunal has exercised its discretion without taking account of all relevant considerations, and the other is that the tribunal's decision has been influenced by some irrelevant consideration. Suppose, for example, the claimant has requested a postponement because her law centre adviser is unable to attend on the day fixed for the hearing, and the tribunal explains its refusal to postpone on the basis that it is not usual to list cases to suit the availability of professional legal representatives. The claimant may found an appeal on the fact that the tribunal has failed to take into account the relevant consideration that she is not paying for her representation and therefore cannot necessarily substitute a different professional representative.[20]

11.29   For an example of a procedural decision based on an irrelevant consideration, suppose the tribunal decides to conduct a hearing in private because one of the respondent's witnesses is a high-ranking public servant who will be cross-examined about allegations of serious misconduct against him. The status of the respondent's witnesses and the gravity of any allegations against them are both irrelevant to the question whether the hearing should take place in public,[21] so the claimant will be able to attack this decision on the basis that an irrelevant matter has been taken into consideration by the tribunal.

Points not argued below

11.30   The EAT will not as a rule entertain arguments that were not put to the employment tribunal.[22] In situations where the new point would require additional findings of fact which the tribunal could have made if the point had been raised at first instance, the justice of this is apparent. If, for example, a complaint of constructive unfair dismissal succeeds, but on appeal the employer seeks to raise for the first time an allegation that the claimant had affirmed his contract[23] by waiting several weeks after the breach before resigning, the EAT will rightly refuse to hear the appeal. If the employer had said earlier that the claimant had affirmed, the tribunal could have made findings on

20 See para 8.8 above.
21 See ETP3 paras 16.22–16.23.
22 See *Kumchyk v Derby City Council* [1978] ICR 1116, EAT.
23 See ELAH 5.

whether the delay amounted to affirmation in the circumstances. An appeal is not intended to give either party the chance to reformulate their case in the light of experience and then have a second and better-informed bite at the cherry. If on the other hand the tribunal simply makes a spontaneous error of law in the course of its decision against which the losing party did not think to give it specific warning, it is much harder to see why the decision should be immune from appeal. The EAT's practice in this kind of situation is inconsistent. If the error is clear enough and does not arise from the appellant's failure to formulate his or her case properly, the question 'was this argued below?' may well be overlooked. The result is that it is often difficult even for experienced lawyers to predict in advance which appeals will fall foul of this rule and which will not.[24] This underlines, however, the usefulness of presenting the tribunal that hears the case at first instance with written submissions so that there can be no subsequent doubt about what points were taken then.

Starting an appeal

11.31   The document that starts an appeal to the EAT is the notice of appeal. This must be received by the EAT within 42 days of the date when the written record of the decision, direction or order which is appealed was sent to the parties, together with the written record of the decision and written reasons for it and the original claim and response. It is essential that all of these documents are included with the notice of appeal: the EAT takes an extremely rigorous approach to incomplete appeals, and an appeal from which one of the required documents has been omitted will not be accepted. If the missing document is provided even one day late the appeal will be deemed out of time.[25] If any documents are unavoidably missing, it is necessary to explain why.

11.32   It is preferable, if possible, to draft and send the skeleton argument at this stage. The reason for this is that the process of writing a skeleton argument will very often help the appellant to clarify the issues and the arguments in his or her own mind. The best way to find out whether an argument is convincing is to write it all down in order. If the appellant

---

24 A cynic might say that the rule is most accurately stated thus: the EAT does not entertain arguments that have not been put to the employment tribunal *unless it feels like it.*

25 See *Gdynia America Shipping Lines Ltd v Chelminski* [2004] IRLR 725 and *Kanapathiar v Harrow LBC* [2003] IRLR 571.

finds that by the time she has finished writing her skeleton, she has not even persuaded herself of the merit of a particular ground of appeal, there is probably not much in that ground and it will be best to drop it. On the other hand, in the process of writing down the argument for another ground, the appellant may realise that it is better put as two separate errors rather than one. Often the best way of approaching the task will be to start with the skeleton argument, and then edit the same document to create the (much shorter) notice of appeal. This covering letter enclosing a notice of appeal is intended to double as a check-list for the documents that need to be included.

P11.1 Covering letter enclosing an appeal to the EAT

The Registrar
Employment Appeal Tribunal
Audit House
58 Victoria Embankment
London EC4Y 0DS

Fax 020 7273 1045

13 September 2004

Dear Madam

Yasmin Creasey v Bristol Advocacy Project

I enclose the following:

☑ Notice of appeal

☑ Judgment of the employment tribunal

☑ Written reasons for the decision of the employment tribunal

☑ Claim form (ET1)

☑ Response (ET3)

Yours faithfully

Natalie Cummings

Drafting the notice of appeal

11.33 The standard form for an appeal to the EAT is to be found at the schedule to the EAT Rules or on the EAT website.[26] Unlike form ET1, it is a simple form that can easily be typed out. It looks like this:

> 1. The appellant is (*name and address of appellant*).
> 2. Any communication relating to this appeal may be sent to the appellant at (*appellant's address for service, including telephone number if any*).
> 3. The appellant appeals from (*give particulars of the decision of the [employment tribunal] from which the appeal is brought including the date*)
> 4. The parties to the proceedings before the employment tribunal, other than the appellant, were (*names and addresses of other parties to the proceedings resulting in decision appealed from*).
> 5. A copy of the employment tribunal's decision or order and of the written reasons for the judgment, direction or order are attached to this notice.
> 6. The grounds upon which this appeal is brought are that the employment tribunal erred in law in that (*here set out in paragraphs the various grounds of appeal*).

11.34 Item 6 above is the difficult part to complete. The grounds of appeal should be carefully drafted: they will often be the first thing that the EAT judges will read, and the basis on which they decide whether or not the case can go ahead to a hearing. Sometimes it will be sufficient simply to put the error of law complained of in two or three concise sentences; in more complex cases it may be necessary to outline the factual background and summarise the tribunal's decision in order to put the errors alleged in context. Both approaches are illustrated here.

11.35 The most important single piece of advice that can be offered on drafting a notice of appeal is to keep it as simple as possible. Tribunals are far from perfect and they often make mistakes, but they rarely make a very large number of different mistakes in a single decision. Any temptation to 'pad' the notice of appeal by expressing what is essentially the same ground of appeal in several different ways should be resisted. There is nothing wrong with a notice of appeal that complains of one error only: the word 'various' in the italicised instruction at

26 www.employmentappeals.gov.uk.

item 6 should not be taken as indicating that multiple grounds are compulsory. A rambling 10 page notice of appeal that complains of 14 separate counts of perversity will make an EAT judge feel tired from the outset: appeals are not won by boring the judge into submission.

11.36　　The notice of appeal should normally be a self-contained document that is sufficient, read on its own, to tell the EAT what the case was about, what the employment tribunal decided, and why it is said that that is wrong. The EAT judges may sometimes skim or even skip the claimant's account of the facts because they have started by reading the employment tribunal's decision which also sets out the facts. Nevertheless it is suggested that it is best to include it. Employment tribunal decisions vary greatly in quality, and sometimes the account of the facts will be unclear, inadequate or misleading.

11.37　　Where the appellant sets out the factual background in the notice of appeal (or for that matter the skeleton argument), he or she should make it clear which assertions are uncontroversial and which are or were matters of dispute between the parties. If the notice of appeal is at all long, it is helpful to divide it into sections under different headings. However short it is, it should be divided into numbered paragraphs. Here as in any other kind of writing 'a paragraph per idea' is a good rule to follow. Long paragraphs that deal with several different subjects are very difficult to read.

The choice of order disposing of the appeal

11.39　　The grounds of appeal should also specify what the claimant is asking the EAT to do.[27] This is something that requires careful thought at the outset.

11.40　　An appeal will rarely be a simple matter of win or lose: there will be various different ways in which the EAT could deal with the case. Sometimes the decision below will simply be reversed. Sometimes the EAT will hold that, contrary to the tribunal's decision, the complaint was justified – there has been discrimination, or an unauthorised deduction from pay, or unfair dismissal or whatever was the subject of the complaint – but will send the case back ('remit' it) to the tribunal for an assessment of the remedy. Sometimes the EAT will hold that the

---

27　See EAT Practice Direction 2004 para 2.4 which is set out in full at appendix B of ETP 3 or see the EAT website at www.employmentappeals.gov.uk.

tribunal has approached one of its factual findings in the wrong way, or failed to make findings of fact that it needed to make. In that case it will almost always be necessary to remit the case to the same tribunal or a different one[28] to make more findings of fact.

11.41 Losing an appeal outright is simpler of course: the EAT dismisses the appeal and the employment tribunal's decision or order stands.

11.42 The range of options, and the kinds of factors that influence the EAT in deciding how to dispose of the appeal and whether to remit to the same or a different tribunal, are probably best understood in the context of some concrete examples.

Example 1

The claimant complains that she has been dismissed for using inappropriate language in the workplace. She says that male colleagues have spoken in the same way without being disciplined and she has suffered sex discrimination. Her employer's defence is that conventional standards of conduct are different for men and women, so what it has done is impose the same rule on both men and women, namely that they observe conventional standards of conduct. The tribunal accepts this argument and dismisses the claim. The claimant appeals.

The EAT has no difficulty with this.[29] It holds that imposing different standards on men and women is sex discrimination and allows the appeal. However, the EAT does not hear witnesses, and the employment tribunal has made no findings about the losses that the claimant has suffered because it dismissed her claim. The EAT is not in a position to decide how much compensation to award, so it remits the case to a different tribunal to hear evidence on this and decide on the appropriate remedy.

Comment
The EAT could, here, have remitted the question of remedy to the same tribunal. The attack, superficially anyway, was only on the tribunal's understanding of how to apply the law rather than on the fairness of the hearing. The appellant may well fear that if the tribunal did not decide in her favour in the first place, its assessment of compensation may be adversely affected by its belief that she has not suffered a real injustice. In light of the

---

28   See paras 11.44–11.46 below for the choice between these options.
29   'Of course,' it might be said; but see *Schmidt v Austicks Bookshops Ltd* [1978] ICR 85 for a closely analogous case.

decision in *Sinclair Roche & Temperley v Heard*,[30] the EAT is unlikely to be willing to accommodate this fear expressly, but it may reach the same result by deciding that the original tribunal's handling of the case was 'wholly flawed' or 'completely mishandled'. As the factual considerations affecting the remedy have probably not previously been explored, there is no duplication of effort in sending that question to a new tribunal.

Example 2

The claimant complains that he has been dismissed for refusing to work on Sundays. His employer says that the reason for the dismissal was his inflexibility. The tribunal accepts this, and the claimant appeals.

The EAT examines the tribunal's decision and holds that it is impossible to tell from the tribunal's decision whether the tribunal considered that the claimant was inflexible in any way other than in refusing, as was his right, to work on Sundays. The EAT holds that if this was the only respect in which the claimant was inflexible, then his complaint must succeed, and remits the case to a different tribunal for consideration of whether, in light of this guidance, his dismissal was unfair.

Comment

The earlier decision contains within it the suggestion that the tribunal felt that the employee had been unreasonable, and had fundamentally misunderstood how the protection against compulsory Sunday working operates. Sending it back to the same tribunal is likely to leave the claimant with a doubt that he has had a fair hearing if the tribunal reaches the same result again. The claimant will have had to persuade the EAT that this outweighs the saving of costs and time that would be achieved by sending the case back to the same tribunal.

Example 3

The claimant complains of sexual harassment. The tribunal does not believe her complaint, and finds that none of the incidents she complains of actually took place. The respondent applies for costs on the grounds that bringing a claim to the tribunal that was based on lies was unreasonable. The tribunal agrees, and says in

30 [2004] IRLR 763, EAT.

its decision: 'In the circumstances we consider we have no option but to award costs to the respondent.'

The claimant appeals, saying that even if the tribunal was persuaded that her conduct in bringing the case was unreasonable, it still had a discretion to exercise whether or not to award costs. The EAT agrees, and remits the case to the same tribunal so that it can exercise its discretion whether or not to award costs.

Comment
Here the claimant has won a very hollow victory. The question whether to award costs depends heavily on what happened in the course of the hearing, so it is very difficult to ask a different tribunal to exercise the discretion: it would not have any better access to the factual background than the EAT. The likely outcome is that the tribunal will make the same decision again, but this time it will tick all the right boxes on the way.

Example 4
The claimant is dismissed for fighting at work. She says it was a very lively workplace and the fight was a play-fight that got out of hand, and she complains of unfair dismissal. The tribunal says that the claimant's conduct was very reprehensible but that taking all the other factors into account it considers that a final warning would have been more appropriate.

The employer appeals, saying that the employment tribunal erred in substituting its own judgment for the employer's[31] as to what penalty should have been imposed. The EAT allows the appeal, and remits the case to a different tribunal for a complete rehearing.

Comment
Here the first tribunal took completely the wrong approach to the question of fairness: the employer's complaint that it substituted its judgment for the employer's is clearly well-founded. For similar reasons to examples 1 and 2 it is preferable to send the case back to a different tribunal.

---

31 See *Foley v Post Office* [2000] ICR 1283.

Example 5

The claimant is dismissed within a few weeks of starting work for a new employer when she insists on being paid the £25,000 per annum at which the job was advertised. She brings complaints under the Sex Discrimination Act 1975 and the Equal Pay Act 1970, the latter because the employer employs a man in an identical role and does pay him £25,000 per annum.

The tribunal finds the employer's evidence unsatisfactory[32] and holds that the claimant was entitled to be paid the same as her male colleague. It dismisses her sex discrimination complaint on the grounds that this simply duplicates her equal pay claim.

The claimant appeals, and the EAT finds that the tribunal has failed to deal with the question whether or not the claimant's dismissal was an act of sex discrimination. It remits the case to the original tribunal for findings on this.

Comment

Here it is clear that the original tribunal took a dislike to the claimant's employer and disbelieved his evidence, and the error was more a matter of oversight or misunderstanding of the claimant's case than a positive finding against her. The attack on the decision is not an attack on the fairness of the process and the claimant is probably very happy for the remaining question to go back to the same tribunal.

Example 6

When the claimant walks into the hearing room, the Chairman rolls his eyes heavenwards and says 'You again! You had better watch your step.' The claimant's previous complaint had been heard by the same chairman, who had disbelieved his evidence and awarded substantial costs against him. The claimant is again unsuccessful, and appeals to the EAT on grounds of bias.

The EAT finds that there was an appearance of bias and remits the case to a different tribunal for rehearing.

Comment

For obvious reasons, it would be impossible to remit a case to the same tribunal after a successful bias appeal.

32 This is the standard judicial code for 'a pack of lies.'

Example 7

The claimant has complained of sex discrimination. Four weeks before the hearing, she seeks permission to amend her complaint to clarify that she is relying on both direct and indirect discrimination. The tribunal refuses permission on the grounds that a new claim is now out of time and there are no grounds on which it can properly extend time. The claimant appeals this decision to the EAT, which manages to hear the appeal within 10 days.[33]

The EAT considers the claimant's formal claim, as originally presented, and takes the view that the allegations she has made there are sufficient to support an indirect discrimination claim. It holds that for this reason the question about time limits did not arise, so the tribunal approached the exercise of its discretion on a mistaken basis. The EAT considers that it has sufficient knowledge of all the relevant factors to allow it to exercise the discretion itself. It does so, and permits the amendment.

Comment

Often where the complaint on appeal is that the tribunal exercised a discretion wrongly, the appellant may prefer that the EAT should exercise the discretion itself rather than remit the case either to the same or a different tribunal. The EAT is likely to be willing to do this – particularly if there is a reason for urgency – if it feels that it has all the relevant facts at its disposal. Quite often both parties will prefer that the EAT should exercise the discretion itself, especially if neither has any way of predicting how the EAT is likely to exercise it.

11.43   It can be seen from these examples that there is a great variety of ways of disposing of a successful appeal, and the claimant should think carefully about what order he or she would wish the EAT to make if he or she wins his or her appeal. If it is the employer's appeal, the claimant will obviously prefer that it is dismissed, but he or she should still think about whether there is scope for limiting the damage if the employer wins by influencing the terms of the order the EAT makes.

---

33 This is not unrealistic: if there are real grounds for urgency – for instance on an interlocutory (see glossary) appeal where a hearing date is imminent – the EAT can move with startling speed. If you ask the EAT to expedite a hearing, you should be ready to work fast yourself: otherwise there is a danger of getting more than you bargained for.

11.44   Often an important consideration is whether the case goes back to the same, or a different, tribunal. For detailed guidance on this, see *Sinclair Roche & Temperley v Heard*.[34] If there has been a successful challenge to the fundamental fairness of the employment tribunal's process and the case is to be re-heard in its entirety, remission will almost always be to a different tribunal. If there has been some fairly technical failure by the tribunal in exercising a discretion that is liable to be influenced by the factual context, with which the original tribunal is already familiar, then the EAT may be more inclined to remit the case to the same tribunal. If there is a decision that fails by an oversight to deal with one of the claimant's heads of claim, again the EAT will probably remit that matter to the same tribunal.

11.45   The claimant's tactical decision whether she wants the case remitted to the same or a different tribunal will probably depend in part at least on whether she feels that the original tribunal was fundamentally well-disposed to her case or not. The EAT's decision whether to remit the case to the same or a different tribunal may depend in part – although this will not be acknowledged – on whether it feels that the tribunal got the wrong answer, or got the right answer by the wrong route.

11.46   Often, but not always, the party appealing the decision will prefer that remission should be to a different tribunal, and the party resisting the appeal will prefer remission to the same tribunal. Example 5 is an exception to this.

Remission to the same tribunal for expanded reasons

11.47   One of the basic requirements of an employment tribunal's decision is that it must contain sufficient factual findings and reasoning to allow the parties to understand why they have won or lost.[35] The EAT has recently adopted the troubling practice of adjourning the appeal in cases of this sort and remitting the case to the same tribunal before the appeal is heard so that it can rewrite its decision: see *Burns v Consignia plc (No 2)*.[36] The problem with this is that inadequate reasons tend to indicate *inadequate reasoning* by the tribunal: a tribunal that has not given sufficient reasons for its decision is unlikely to have gone through the necessary mental processes to justify the result it arrived at.

---

34 [2004] IRLR 763, EAT.

35 *Meek v City of Birmingham District Council* [1987] IRLR 250, CA.

36 [2004] IRLR0 425, EAT.

Unfortunately a remission to enable the tribunal to improve on its reasons *after* it has arrived at its decision will not mean that the tribunal reconsiders the case – in other words it will not revisit the mental processes by which it arrived at the result – but will instead simply act as an invitation to the tribunal to explain a process of reasoning by which it could properly have arrived at the result it did arrive at.

11.48   This means that, for the moment,[37] appeals based on inadequate reasoning by the tribunal will very often be futile.

P11.2 Short notice of appeal

IN THE EMPLOYMENT APPEAL TRIBUNAL   Case No EAT/
BETWEEN

MRS YASMIN CREASEY

Appellant

and

BRISTOL ADVOCACY PROJECT

Respondent

NOTICE OF APPEAL
---

1. The appellant is Mrs Yasmin Creasey.

2. Any communication relating to this appeal may be sent to the appellant at the North London Law Centre, 14 Border Street. Shoreditch, London EC2A 1AB, tel: 020 7123 1234.

3. The appellant appeals from the decision of the employment tribunal sitting at Bristol on 9 August 2004 to dismiss her complaint of sex discrimination.

4. The other party to the proceedings before the employment tribunal was the Bristol Advocacy Project, 14 Tavistock Rd, Clifton, Bristol.

5. A copy of the employment tribunal's judgment ~~or order~~[38] and of the written reasons for it, and of the claim and response, ~~direction or order~~ are attached to this notice.

---

37 The practice is likely to be referred to the Court of Appeal before too long for an authoritative ruling on whether it is permissible in this context.

38 See glossary.

6. The grounds upon which this appeal is brought are that the employment tribunal erred in law in that:

    (a) It failed to address the question of whether the abbreviation of the appellant's probationary period by reason of her absence on maternity leave constituted a detriment, and if so, whether this was a detriment to which the appellant was subjected on grounds of her sex.

    (b) The appellant asks the Appeal Tribunal to find that the abbreviation of the appellant's probationary period by reason of her absence on maternity leave was a detriment to which she was subjected on grounds of her sex, and to remit the case to the same tribunal for a further remedy hearing on that element of her complaint.

Natalie Cummings
NORTH LONDON LAW CENTRE
13 September 2004

DO11.1 Long notice of appeal

Paragraphs 1 to 5

grounds of appeal

outline of the facts (including, if relevant, what took place at the hearing)

summary of the employment tribunal's decision, indicating which parts are challenged

explanation of error(s) of law by the tribunal

account of the order the claimant wants the EAT to make

P11.3 Long notice of appeal

IN THE EMPLOYMENT APPEAL TRIBUNAL   Case No EAT/
BETWEEN

CLAUDIA CHAMPION

Appellant

and

MINISTRY OF TRUTH

Respondent

GROUNDS OF APPEAL

THE FACTS

1. The appellant, Miss Champion, started work in the Information Service in 1976, aged 16. Between 1976 and her resignation in 2003, she worked at various Information Units and Information Service offices in London and the South East. On 1 May 1997 she was appointed to a higher executive officer (HEO) role at the Guildford Area Managers Office (AMO), which was housed in the same building as the Joint Information Unit's Office at Adshead Way, Guildford. The Joint Information Unit's Office employed an HEO, as did the separate AMO at Croydon. Information Service rules defined HEO as a 'mobile grade' with the result that Miss Champion could under her contract of employment be transferred to any suitable civil service post in the UK.

2. In June 2003, a reorganisation was announced in which the Croydon and Guildford AMOs would be merged at the Adshead Way site, and the Croydon AMO would close. The effect at HEO level was that three HEO posts (two at Adshead Way and one at Croydon) would be replaced by two HEOs at Adshead Way.

3. An Information Service manager, Mr James Petrie, was in general control of the reorganisation. Mr Petrie consulted affected staff about their preferred outcomes to the reorganisation, and Miss Champion reiterated her wish, which had previously been discussed with managers as a realistic medium-term career goal, to be appointed Manager of the Central London Information Unit. Because of this, Miss Champion was not appointed to either of the HEO posts in the new structure. By September 2003 Miss Champion's existing post had disappeared without any decision having been taken about her future.

4. The question of Miss Champion's redeployment became the subject of dispute between her and the respondent, and the cause of distress to her, and on 13 September 2003 her General Practitioner signed her off work for 28 days with stress and depression. She did not return to work full time after that date.

5. Miss Champion met with Mr Petrie in October 2003. The parties are in dispute as to the content of this meeting, which is referred to below as 'the disputed meeting.' Specifically, Miss Champion says that by the end of the meeting, she had been offered no certainty of any substantive posts at any fixed time in the future. Mr Petrie says that she had been offered, and had refused, a vacant HEO post at the Guildford Strategic Information Centre.

6. Miss Champion raised a formal grievance about the manner in which the reorganisation had been handled, and resigned in April 2004 after the rejection of her appeal against the outcome of that grievance.

THE HEARING BEFORE THE EMPLOYMENT TRIBUNAL

7. Miss Champion's complaint to the tribunal focused on the respondent's treatment of her in failing to provide her with any certainty about her future when her job ceased to exist; and more specifically the respondent's failure to declare a redundancy and follow its own redundancy procedure. These same facts founded a complaint of constructive dismissal claims for damages for breach of contract and disability discrimination.

8. This appeal hinges on the treatment by the tribunal of the evidence given by Mr Petrie relating to the disputed meeting. Mr Petrie described the meeting in his witness statement, and referred to notes he had made. In his oral evidence given during the first three days of the hearing he was emphatic that he had made these notes on the same day shortly after the end of the meeting.

9. Between the third day of the hearing on 6 February and the fourth day on 29 April 2005, Miss Champion obtained an order for the disclosure of the statistics files associated with Mr Petrie's typed file-notes of the meeting. These appeared to show that the computer file in question had been created not on 19 October 2003, but at 10.17 am on 3 January 2004, not long after the first letter from Miss Champion's solicitors to the respondent.

10. Miss Champion's representative asked for Mr Petrie to be recalled to explain the discrepancy between this and his previous sworn evidence. However, when the chairman warned that there might be costs implications and the Respondent's counsel said that costs

would be sought vigorously, he did not feel able to pursue the application.

THE DECISION

11. The tribunal made the following findings:

(i) Miss Champion's post had ceased to exist (page 12, para 3, [12]);

(ii) there was a vacant post at the Guildford Strategic Information Centre available for Miss Champion and (implicitly – page 11, para 8, [11]) she was aware of that;

(iii) the respondent had done its utmost to resolve Miss Champion's position despite her refusal to consider any possibility other than the Central London Information Unit Manager's post, so there was no breach of the trust and confidence term in the way they had handled the reorganisation (page 12, paras (10),(11), [12]);

(iv) Miss Champion had a disability for the purposes of the Disability Discrimination Act 1995 (page 9, para 18(2) [9]);

(v) but there was no discrimination because the failure to appoint her to a substantive post was attributable to 'the fixed attitude that she had adopted' (para 18(3), page 9, [9])

12. The decision did not address the conflict of evidence between Miss Champion and Mr Petrie as to the disputed meeting, nor did it allude to the doubt that had been cast on Mr Petrie's evidence or record any finding as to which account was accurate.

GROUNDS OF APPEAL

13. The tribunal erred in law in that:

(i) It failed to make a finding as to the content of the disputed meeting or to deal with the doubt cast on James Petrie's evidence as to the meeting. The appellant relies on *Anya v University of Oxford* [2001] EWCA Civ 405. The respondent's notice of appearance places the disputed meeting of October 2002 at the centre of its case and clearly identifies Mr Petrie as its key witness. The dispute as to the content of this meeting was central to the resolution of the case, and it was something on which the tribunal would have been obliged to express a view even if Miss Champion had not been able to produce the statistics file associated with Mr Petrie's alleged contemporaneous notes. The statistics file merely go to make the necessity for a finding on this point the more acute.

(ii) It failed to consider recalling Mr Petrie to explain his previous evidence in light of the statistics file. Rule 11(1) of the Employment Tribunals Rules of Procedure (Schedule 1 to the Employment Tribunals (Constitution and Rules of Procedure) Regulations 2001 SI No 1171) then in force provided, so far as is material:

> 'The tribunal shall make such enquiries of persons appearing before it and witnesses as it considers appropriate and shall otherwise conduct the hearing in such manner as it considers most appropriate for the clarification of the issues before it and generally to the just handling of the proceedings.'

14. When invited by Miss Champion's representative to recall Mr Petrie, the Chairman of the tribunal indicated that it was for the parties and not for the tribunal to call witnesses, and warned of possible costs consequences in insisting on recalling him. The appellant contends that the employment tribunal erred in failing to apprehend the tribunal's duty under rule 11(1) of the Rules of Procedure to make such inquiries as it considers appropriate *for the clarification of the issues before it.* Since the disputed evidence went to the heart of the case as put by both parties, and since serious doubt had been cast on Mr Petrie's evidence, it was incumbent on the tribunal at least to consider whether it should recall Mr Petrie of its own motion. Its insistence that it was for the parties to make an application to recall him if they wished to was a refusal to exercise a discretion that it undoubtedly had.

THE ORDER SOUGHT

15. The Appeal Tribunal will be respectfully invited to set aside the decision of the employment tribunal and remit the case for re-hearing by a differently constituted tribunal.

NATALIE CUMMINGS
NORTH LONDON LAW CENTRE
7 June 2005

Rejection of an appeal on the papers

11.49   Sometimes a judge at the EAT will read the notice of appeal and accompanying documents and form the view that the appeal discloses no reasonable grounds for bringing the appeal. In these cases, rule 3(7) of the EAT Rules of Procedure permits the EAT to reject the appeal without a hearing. It is important to be aware that this decision is not final: there is a right either to redraft and resubmit the notice of appeal within 28 days from the rejection, or (in effect) to request an oral hearing before a judge.

11.50   A claimant should only be deterred by rejection at this stage if she recognises that the appeal was really just an attack on legitimate findings of fact or an exercise of discretion. Claimants who believe that what they are complaining of is an error of law should persist: the EAT is rather too much inclined to seek to reduce its workload by rejecting appeals at this stage, and the decisions are not always well-founded. A significant factor for unrepresented claimants is that if they request an oral hearing, they may be able to benefit from free representation at that hearing under the Employment Lawyers' Appeals Advice Scheme (ELAAS).[39] This can be extremely valuable: the ELAAS advisers are experienced employment lawyers who may be able to focus the appeal on its one or two best points and dramatically improve its chances of success.

11.51   An oral hearing on a decision to reject an appeal on the papers is requested by writing to the Registrar to 'express dissatisfaction' with the reasons given by the judge or Registrar for rejecting the appeal. This letter can be very brief. It will do unrepresented appellants no harm to request ELAAS representation in the same letter.

---

39 See para 11.12 above.

P11.4 Letter expressing dissatisfaction with decision to reject the appeal on the papers

The Registrar
Employment Appeal Tribunal
Audit House
58 Victoria Embankment
London
EC4Y 0DS

3 November 2004

Dear Madam

Croke v Little Sprigs Nursery PA/123/05

Thank you for your letter of 18 October 2004. I am dissatisfied with the decision to reject my appeal at this stage, and I request an oral hearing.

I should be grateful for representation at the oral hearing under the ELAAS scheme if a representative is available.

Yours faithfully

Sharon Croke

Notes of oral evidence given at the original hearing

11.52   Sometimes it will be necessary for the purposes of an appeal to draw the EAT's attention to oral evidence that was given to the employment tribunal. Employment tribunal hearings are not tape-recorded or recorded by a shorthand writer, but the chairman has a duty to take notes of the evidence. These notes – written in longhand – are of widely variable quality and completeness. Some chairmen take nearly verbatim notes of the hearing (some slow proceedings right down to dictation speed for the purpose), some write down only what they consider important; some are accurate and others less so.

11.53   When it comes to a remitted hearing, it can be useful to get hold of the whole of the other side's notes of the previous hearing, particularly if there is any risk that their evidence may change. Very often the respondent, having a full legal team, will have taken very good notes of the hearing: these can be useful on a remitted hearing. Notes of a hearing are not privileged and must be disclosed if relevant.[40]

When are notes of evidence needed?

11.54   Notes of evidence will normally be needed if the appeal is on grounds of perversity: if it is said that the tribunal made findings of fact for which there was no evidence at all, or made findings against the overwhelming weight of the evidence, the EAT will not be able to decide whether this is so unless it knows what evidence was given. If it is said that the tribunal has failed to resolve one of the key factual issues between the parties, notes of evidence may not be necessary if the relevant difference between what the claimant says and what the respondent says is clear from the witness statements. There may, however, have been an important factual issue that only emerged clearly in cross-examination. If that is so, then notes of those parts of the cross-examination will be needed.

11.55   Again, this will make more sense in the context of concrete examples. The examples used are those that appear at para 11.42 above.

> In example 1, there is no relevant dispute of fact between the parties: the employer says that the rule it applied was not discriminatory, the claimant says it was, but both sides agree what happened. This appeal can clearly be resolved without notes of evidence.
>
> In example 2, the respondent would probably have wanted the EAT to see notes of any evidence given about how the claimant was said to have been inflexible, in the hope of persuading the EAT that the tribunal had a legitimate basis for finding that the claimant had been inflexible in some way other than merely refusing to work on Sundays.
>
> In examples 3 and 4, both appeals concern the complaint that the tribunal applied the wrong legal test. The test applied by the tribunal appears from its decision, so notes of evidence will not help the EAT decide this.

---

40   See *Lambert v Home* [1914] 3 KB 86 and see para 4.35 above.

> In example 5, whether or not notes of evidence are needed depends on how the respondent approaches the appeal. If the respondent says that the reason the tribunal did not deal with the sex discrimination issue is that the claimant did not give any evidence about it, the EAT may require notes of evidence in order to establish whether or not that is the case. If the respondent simply argues that as a matter of law the claimant cannot run an equal pay case and a sex discrimination case on the same facts, then notes of evidence will not be needed.
>
> In example 6, notes of evidence will not be needed unless the claimant says that there is something in the way the tribunal has analysed the evidence that amplifies the impression of bias.

Getting hold of notes of evidence

11.56   The EAT Practice Direction 2004[41] directs, at para 7.1:

> 7.1 An Appellant who considers that a point of law raised in the Notice of Appeal cannot be argued without reference to evidence given (or not given) at the Employment Tribunal, the nature and substance of which does not, or does not sufficiently appear from the Written Reasons, must ordinarily submit an application with the Notice of Appeal. The application is for the nature of such evidence (or lack of it) to be admitted, or if necessary for the relevant parts of the Chairman's notes of evidence to be produced. If such application is not so made, then it should be made:
>
> 7.1.1   if a PH is ordered, in the skeleton or written submissions lodged prior to such PH; or
>
> 7.1.2   if the case is listed for FH without a PH, then within 14 days of the seal date of the order so providing.

11.57   This is far from user-friendly. What it seems to mean is that if the appellant thinks that the notes of evidence will be needed, he or she should ask the EAT to give directions about them. The subsequent sub-paragraphs of paragraph 7 set out the procedure that the EAT will follow. The gist is that the EAT will ask the parties to try to agree a note of what evidence was given in the relevant respects. If they cannot agree then, provided the EAT considers that notes of evidence are necessary it will send a request for the chairman's notes to the tribunal.

---

41   See para 11.13 above.

There is a warning about possible costs penalties if parties unreasonably request notes of evidence or unreasonably fail to co-operate in agreeing what evidence was given.

11.58   Before the 2002 practice direction,[42] the EAT would routinely request the chairman's notes of evidence without first attempting to persuade the parties to agree their own notes. The thinking behind the change is evidently to shift the burden of producing notes of evidence from the Employment Tribunal Service to the parties. This is fair enough where each party has the benefit of a full legal team, but it is capable of putting claimants at a serious disadvantage if they have acted for themselves or been represented by one adviser who has been too busy conducting the hearing to take comprehensive notes.

11.59   The procedure set out in the practice direction is cumbersome. It is not obvious why the EAT needs to get involved at all in negotiations between the parties with a view to agreeing notes of evidence until and unless they have broken down. However, the practice direction had better be followed, so it is suggested that a party who thinks that notes of evidence will be needed should add at the end of his or her notice of appeal an application for directions as to notes of evidence. The following example could follow on from paragraph 15 of P11.3 above.

P11.5 Application for directions as to notes of evidence

APPLICATION FOR DIRECTIONS
AS TO NOTES OF EVIDENCE

16. The claimant believes that it will be necessary for the just resolution of the appeal for the Appeal Tribunal to have sight of notes of the evidence given by Mr Petrie and Miss Champion as to the dates and content of the disputed meeting, and by Mr Petrie as to when and how his notes of the meeting were created.

17. This evidence is relevant to the central question in the appeal, namely whether the tribunal failed to resolve a key factual issue between the parties.

18. The witnesses whose evidence is relevant are Mr Petrie and Miss Champion.

19. The relevant evidence is any evidence relating to the content of the disputed meeting, or as to the time or manner of creation of Mr Petrie's notes of that meeting.

20. The claimant's notes of the relevant evidence are incomplete, but they are attached.

42 The predecessor to the 2004 Practice Direction.

21. The claimant accordingly asks the Appeal Tribunal to direct that the parties should seek to agree notes of the relevant parts of the evidence, and, in default of such agreement, that the Chairman's notes should be requested.

Affidavits[43]

11.60 Where there is a challenge to the way the hearing was conducted, and particularly if there is a complaint of bias, it will often be necessary for the claimant and/or her adviser to make a sworn statement about what took place at the hearing. The statement can be drafted by anyone, but it has to be sworn in the presence of a solicitor. Any high street firm of solicitors or law centre is likely to be able to provide a solicitor to administer an oath at short notice, usually for a fee of around £10. Once the statement is drafted, it should be taken by the person making it to a solicitor and sworn.

---

43 This is the term for a formal sworn statement used in court proceedings.

P11.6 Affidavit in support of a bias appeal

> Sworn by José Corujo on 4 November 2004
> This is the 1st affidavit
> filed on behalf of the claimant by this deponent
> on .... November 2004

IN THE EMPLOYMENT APPEAL TRIBUNAL   Case No EAT/1234/04
BETWEEN

JOSÉ CORUJO

Appellant

and

SOUTHERN TRAINS PLC

Respondent

I, José Corujo, of 14 Marlborough Court, Mitcham Lane, Croydon, Surrey CR0 4BZ make oath and say as follows:

1. My complaint of unfair dismissal was heard at the London South employment tribunal on 3 and 4 April 2004. The presiding Chairman was Mr Marks.

2. When I walked in to the hearing room, Mr Marks raised his eyes heavenwards and said, 'You again! You had better watch your step this time.'

3. Mr Marks was the Chairman who heard a previous complaint I had made against Southern Trains in July 2003. He had not believed my evidence, and he had awarded £4,000 costs against me because he said that I had made up all my evidence.

4. I was very shaken when Mr Marks said this. I thought I had no chance of a fair hearing before him. I told him that I did not think it was fair that he was hearing this case because he was biased against me. He said 'You had a very fair hearing from me last time. Let's get on with the case.'

5. The hearing went very badly for me. When I was speaking Mr Marks glared at me, sighed heavily and interrupted me constantly. When I was giving my evidence he asked a lot of very hostile questions. He did not ask the respondent's witnesses any questions at all, and he listened and took notes without interrupting when their counsel was speaking.

Sworn at   in the   )
County of   )
this   day of   2004   )

Before me

Officer of a Court, appointed by the Judge to take Affidavits

Responding to an appeal

11.61 If the claimant is successful – wholly or in part – before the employment tribunal, the employer may appeal.

11.62   In a case that is listed for a preliminary hearing, the respondent to the appeal is sent the notice of appeal before the preliminary hearing and invited to make 'concise written submissions' on the notice of appeal with a view to showing that the appeal has no reasonable prospect of success. These submissions can follow a very similar format to a skeleton argument, but it is important that they should be concise: the point is to demonstrate that there is really nothing to argue about, so long and detailed argument is likely to demonstrate the exact opposite.

The respondent's answer

11.63 The form for this, like the form for a notice of appeal, is very straight-forward, and can be downloaded from the EAT website.[44]

11.64   Drafting the respondent's answer is often very easy, requiring nothing more than a statement that the respondent intends to resist the appeal on the grounds given in the tribunal's decision. There is need for some thought at this stage, however. Two decisions need to be made. The first is whether, if the employment tribunal's reasoning is defective, there is any alternative basis on which the *result* can be sup-ported. The second is whether the respondent should put forward a cross-appeal.

11.65   To decide whether to put forward an alternative argument in support of the tribunal's decision, the question the respondent to the appeal should ask is this: supposing the attack made by the appellant on the

44 www.employmentappeals.gov.uk.

decision is well-founded, can I say that given the tribunal's findings of fact (or the facts that are agreed to be common ground), this result was inevitable anyway? If the answer to this is yes, then an alternative basis can be put forward for the tribunal's decision.

11.66   However, there is a tactical aspect to this decision. Putting forward an alternative basis for the tribunal's decision does make it look as if the respondent to the appeal fears that that the decision as it stands is weak and needs bolstering. For this reason, additional grounds for the tribunal's decision should be used where the tribunal has missed the point, or set out a weak basis for its decision when there was a much stronger basis available to it. Additional grounds weaker than those relied on by the tribunal should never be thrown in as a make-weight if what is set out in the decision is the best argument for result reached by the tribunal.

P11.7 Respondent's notice

The facts of this appeal are taken from example 4 at para 11.42 above: Ms Loop was dismissed for fighting at work. The tribunal's decision that 'taking all the other factors into account a final warning would have been more appropriate' flies in the face of established authority and is indefensible. However, elsewhere in its decision the tribunal has accepted Ms Loop's evidence that play fights at this workplace were common, sometimes involving senior management and always condoned by them. In the circumstances, she says, in this workplace it was impossible to characterise such behaviour as gross misconduct and therefore unfair to dismiss her summarily for a first offence.

IN THE EMPLOYMENT APPEAL TRIBUNAL   EAT/1234/04

BETWEEN

PAMELA LOOP

Appellant

and

ADSARUS CREATIVE LTD

Respondent

_____
RESPONDENT'S ANSWER
_____

1. The respondent is Pamela Loop.

2. Any communication relating to this appeal may be sent to the respondent at the North London Law Centre, 43 Holloway Lane, London N19 5BQ

3. The respondent intends to resist the appeal of ADSARUS Creative Limited.

4. The grounds on which the respondent will rely are ~~the grounds relied upon by the Employment Tribunal for making the decision or order appealed from and~~[45] the following grounds:

   (i) The employment tribunal found (at paragraphs 13 and 14) that the respondent's conduct was indistinguishable from conduct that was regularly engaged in by colleagues working at the appellant's London Road premises and condoned by senior management. It follows from this that it was not open to the appellant to characterise what she had done as misconduct, and still less so to characterise it as gross misconduct.

   (ii) In the circumstances, the tribunal's decision that the appellant's decision to dismiss the respondent was unfair was an inevitable consequence of the findings of fact it had made (and which are not challenged by the appellant)[46] at paragraphs 13 and 14 and should stand.

5. ~~The Respondent cross-appeals from~~

6. ~~The Respondent's grounds of appeal are~~

NATALIE CUMMINGS
NORTH LONDON LAW CENTRE

Cross-appeals

11.67   A cross-appeal is an appeal – in reply to the main appeal – by the respondent to the main appeal. If both parties are aggrieved by the decision, it may simply be a matter of timing who is the appellant and who is the respondent.

---

45 This is an extreme case, where there is simply nothing to be said in defence of the grounds given by the tribunal. Normally the respondent will rely on the reasons given by the tribunal *plus* additional grounds if necessary.

46 This is important: except where the appeal challenges the fairness or propriety of the whole hearing, an appellant is normally stuck with any findings of fact the tribunal has made except where it has specifically challenged them.

11.68   A respondent who wishes to cross-appeal must decide whether he or she wishes to cross-appeal in any event, or only if the main appeal is successful. Sometimes the cross-appeal simply will not arise unless the main appeal is successful. This too will make much more sense in the context of some examples.

Example 1

Suppose Saifur Rahman of P3.2 and P5.5 wins his case. The tribunal finds that he has been unfairly dismissed and awards him compensation. However, by the time of the hearing he has decided to study full-time for a nursing degree, and the tribunal decides that he has not done enough to mitigate his loss and awards him no compensation past the point at which his nursing course started.

Mr Rahman and the Hospital are both aggrieved by this outcome. Mr Rahman says that his decision to study to be a nurse was entirely reasonable in the circumstances, and the tribunal wrongly approached the question of mitigation as if he had to prove that he had done enough.[47] The Hospital says that having found that Sister Winston had invented her allegation against Mr Rahman, the tribunal wrongly inferred that he had been dismissed for making a protected disclosure without making any findings of fact about what motivated the disciplinary panel to dismiss him.

Alternative (a)

The Hospital asks its lawyers to advise on appeal, but decides against as Mr Rahman's compensation is less than the amount it would cost to do so. Mr Rahman appeals the decision on mitigation, at which point the Hospital realises that if he wins his appeal, it may face a much larger compensation award. It therefore decides to cross-appeal the finding of liability. Here Mr Rahman is the appellant, the Hospital is the respondent, and the Hospital's appeal is a cross-appeal. The Hospital decides to make its cross-appeal conditional: it is not worthwhile going through a rehearing on liability just to escape paying Mr Rahman the modest compensation awarded by the original tribunal, but if Mr Rahman wins his appeal and opens up the possibility of much larger award, then it wants to have the chance of defeating the claim outright.

47   This is wrong but it is a mistake tribunals often make. See *Wilding v British Telecom* [2002] IRLR 524, CA.

Alternative (b)
Mr Rahman is disappointed with the amount of compensation he is awarded, but he decides that he does not have time, now he is studying, to conduct an appeal himself and he cannot afford to pay for representation. He decides not to appeal. Meanwhile the Hospital has decided that this is a matter of principle, and it lodges its notice of appeal. When Mr Rahman realises that he will have to argue a case in the EAT anyway in order to hold onto his award of compensation, he thinks he might as well appeal the decision on mitigation while he is about it, so he cross-appeals on the mitigation point. This time the Hospital is the appellant and it is Mr Rahman, respondent to the main appeal, who has cross-appealed. Mr Rahman decides to make his cross-appeal unconditional: if the Hospital loses its appeal, he would prefer to avoid a further hearing before the employment tribunal to reassess his compensation, but he thinks that if he wins his cross-appeal the Hospital will probably offer him some more money to settle the case.

Example 2
Suppose that on Mrs Rochdale's claim for redundancy pay[48] the tribunal finds that Mrs Rochdale has been dismissed for redundancy but has unreasonably refused an offer of suitable alternative employment so she is not entitled to redundancy pay. Mrs Rochdale appeals the finding that her refusal of alternative employment was unreasonable. The employer does not agree that it dismissed Mrs Rochdale at all, or that, if it did, the reason was redundancy, but neither finding matters to the employer if the tribunal's decision on the last point stands. The employer therefore makes its cross-appeal conditional: it only wants the EAT to decide it if Mrs Rochdale wins her appeal.

48 See P8.6.

P11.8 Respondent's answer and cross-appeal

This is Mr Rahman's cross appeal in example 1, alternative (b) above.

IN THE EMPLOYMENT APPEAL TRIBUNAL   EAT/ 1234/2004

BETWEEN

SAINT JULIAN'S HOSPITAL NHS TRUST

Appellant

and

SAIFUR RAHMAN

Respondent

RESPONDENT'S ANSWER

---

1. The respondent is Saifur Rahman.
2. Any communication relating to this appeal may be sent to the respondent at the North London Law Centre, 43 Holloway Lane, London N19 5BQ.
3. The respondent intends to resist the appeal of Saint Julian's Hospital NHS Trust.
4. The grounds on which the respondent will rely are the grounds relied upon by the Employment Tribunal for making the decision or order appealed from ~~and the following grounds:~~
5. The respondent cross-appeals from the tribunal's decision of 10 September 2004 that he should not be compensated for any financial loss after the commencement of his full-time nursing course in October 2003.
6. The respondent's grounds of appeal are:

    (i) That the tribunal erred in imposing on the respondent the burden of showing that he has sufficiently mitigated his loss. The correct test is to inquire whether the employer has demonstrated on the balance of probabilities that the employee has failed to mitigate his loss: see *Wilding v British Telecom* [2002] IRLR 524.

    (ii) In light of the tribunal's finding at paragraph 27 that the respondent has been unfortunate in failing to find alternative work despite vigorous efforts to mitigate his loss up to September 2004, its finding that he was unreasonable in deciding to enter full-time education as a student nurse from October 2004 was perverse in the sense that it was a finding that no reasonable tribunal properly directing itself on the facts already found could have reached.

Order sought

(iii) The respondent respectfully invites the Appeal Tribunal to allow the cross-appeal and remit the case for a re-hearing limited to the question of what further compensation he should be awarded for the period from 1 October 2003.

Natalie Cummings
NORTH LONDON LAW CENTRE
4 November 2004

The EAT hearing and after

The appeal bundle

12.1 Collating the appeal bundles is the appellant's job. The task is likely to be less onerous than putting together the bundle for the original hearing as the EAT's task is restricted compared to the employment tribunal's. The documents required for an appeal are listed in the EAT Practice Direction 2004 at para 6.2, and they are as follows:

1. Judgment or order appealed from and written reasons.
2. Sealed Notice of appeal.[1]
3. Respondent's answer or submissions for a preliminary hearing.
4. Formal claim (plus any additional information or written answers, that is, any information provided in response to the respondent's requests, but not including documentary evidence).
5. Response (plus any additional information or written answers).
6. Questionnaire and replies (if the case is a discrimination case).
7. Relevant decisions and orders of the employment tribunal (that is, any decisions or orders other than the one appealed that are necessary to allow the EAT to understand the background to the appeal).
8. Relevant orders of the EAT (and here it is probably wise to flatter the EAT that all its orders in the same case are relevant).
9. Affidavits[2] and employment tribunal comments (if any).
10. Any other relevant documents (including extracts from the bundle before the employment tribunal, and any necessary notes of the oral evidence that the tribunal heard, either as agreed by the parties or as recorded by the chairman).

12.2 The bundle should be compiled in this order. Like a bundle for the employment tribunal, it should be page-numbered throughout, and it should have an 'index' page at the front listing what is in it and where it is to be found.[3] If there are more than a hundred pages in all, the appellant should speak to the EAT clerk[4] to discuss whether two bundles are necessary. It is helpful (but not essential) to add 10 numbered tabs, so that the bundle is divided into the sections shown above.

---

1 See P11.2 and P11.3 above.
2 See glossary, P11.6 and para 11.60 above.
3 See P8.3 above.
4 This will be a specific member of staff at the EAT who is normally assigned to the case throughout. He or she is identified by the initials shown at the end of the EAT case number: for example if the clerk is Paula Clark, the case number will be along the lines EAT/1234/04/PC. The EAT clerks are mostly friendly and helpful. They cannot give advice on the law, but they are a useful source of guidance on administrative matters.

The skeleton argument

12.3   Judges of the EAT periodically complain that 'skeletons' are too inclined to turn into fleshy corpses. It is understandable that busy judges wanting to get to the heart of a lot of appeals in a short time should have a strong preference for concise documents. It is certainly inadvisable to submit a rambling or repetitive skeleton argument, but at the same time it should be remembered that the parties to the appeal have a slightly different agenda from the judge's. They want to win the case more than they want to help the judge deal with it quickly.

12.4   Unlike the employment tribunals, the EAT judges do read the documents in the case before the hearing starts. Often they will have a formidable command of the detail of the case by the time of the hearing. Some judges will listen patiently to advocates, and will genuinely not make up their minds until they have heard oral argument from both sides. Others will be very difficult to shift once they have read the papers and formed a preliminary view. Some simply take in information and argument better through their eyes than their ears.

12.5   These factors mean that parties to appeals do well to take warnings against long skeleton arguments with a pinch of salt. The skeleton argument should make all the main points that the party wishes to make, and should refer to any case law that the claimant wishes to refer to in argument. It should be a self-contained document that, read alone, is capable of persuading a judge that he or she knows what the case is about and what the right answer is. It is helpful to set out in the body of the skeleton argument any legislation relied on, and to indicate (and often quote) the relevant paragraphs of any case law. The standard advice on skeleton arguments is that the advocate should aim to write the judgment for the judge. This can be taken too literally, but it is a useful guide to the right style and tone, which should be calm and measured.

12.6   The skeleton argument should be sent to the EAT at least three weeks before a full hearing, or 10 days before a preliminary hearing.[5] These deadlines should be met if at all possible, but if a late skeleton argument is presented with an apology and a reasonable excuse the consequence will rarely be worse than a growl from the judge. The most important thing is to give the judge and members of the EAT a chance to read the skeleton argument in advance, so if all else fails a

---

5 See EAT PD para 13.9.

skeleton argument lodged three or four working days before the hearing will normally be enough to head off a postponement and costs.[6] The appellant's skeleton should be accompanied by a chronology.[7]

12.7   Skeleton arguments will vary widely with the needs of the particular case, so the following document outline is just a suggestion for one way that the skeleton could be laid out.

DO12.1 Skeleton argument

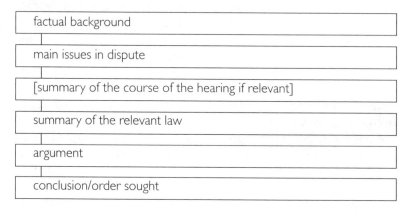

factual background

main issues in dispute

[summary of the course of the hearing if relevant]

summary of the relevant law

argument

conclusion/order sought

---

6 These comments are not intended to encourage parties to be relaxed about the deadlines in the EAT Practice Direction and the EAT rules: they are intended to be observed, and judges can be expected to be irritated if they are not. Irritating the judge is invariably a bad start. On the other hand, a party who is unavoidably late with a skeleton argument can be reassured that provided the excuse is reasonable the sky is unlikely to fall.

7 See EAT PD 13.4 and para 8.25.

P12.1 Skeleton argument

IN THE EMPLOYMENT APPEAL TRIBUNAL   EAT/1234/04
BETWEEN

CANDICE THOMAS

Appellant

and

THE SOUTHWEST ECHO LIMITED

Respondent

_____
SKELETON ARGUMENT
_____

INTRODUCTION

1. The appellant, Mrs Thomas, was employed by the respondent's predecessor from 15 July 1992 as area controller for the distribution of newspapers in the area of Exeter. Initially she worked mainly from home, visiting her employer's office once a week.

2. In September 2001, the respondent took over the undertaking in which Mrs Thomas worked. The respondent reorganised its business in November 2002. After the reorganisation, Mrs Thomas was required to attend the respondent's office every weekday afternoon. She accepted this variation in her conditions of employment.

3. By a letter dated 4 September 2003, the respondent informed Mrs Thomas of further changes to her work. From 15 September 2003, she was to spend most of her working time on visits to newsagents and others. Mrs Thomas was extremely unhappy with this proposed change, but agreed to co-operate while she tried to resolve the situation.

4. Mrs Thomas invoked the respondent's grievance procedure in relation her new working conditions. The procedure ran its course, and her appeal to the respondent's managing director was finally rejected by his letter of 12 February 2004. She had a further meeting with her line manager on 2 March 2004, but after discussing the financial implications with her husband, resigned by a letter dated 4 March 2004.

THE TRIBUNAL'S DECISION

5. The tribunal held that in imposing the changes of September 2003 on Mrs Thomas, the respondent had committed a fundamental

breach of her contract of employment, and that having made her dissatisfaction with the changes clear, invoked the grievance procedure and waited until its conclusion, she had not affirmed her contract. This finding has not been made the subject of any cross-appeal by the respondent.[8]

6.　However, the tribunal held (at paragraphs 19 and 20 of its decision) that Mrs Thomas had affirmed her contract by continuing to work for the three weeks between her receipt of the respondent's letter of 12 February 2004 rejecting her grievance and her resignation on 4 March 2004.

ARGUMENT FOR THE APPELLANT

(i)　Requirement to act reasonably

7.　The relevant portions of paragraphs 19 and 20 of the tribunal's decision read as follows:

> 'Although the period of three weeks between say 13 February and 4 March 2004 is not by itself very long, the Tribunal took into account the fact that the claimant had had several months to consider the effect on her of the new working arrangements imposed in September 2003. It would be *unreasonable* for her not to have contemplated, during this period, the situation she would be in were her grievance to be dismissed in the end ...
>
> The Tribunal accepted the claimant's evidence that the decision to resign was a big decision for her and that she needed to discuss the matter with her husband. But again, this could *reasonably* have been done over the previous months.' [*emphasis added*]

8.　There is no requirement for an employee faced with a fundamental breach of her contract of employment to act reasonably. She may resign and complain of constructive dismissal provided only that she is at the time of her resignation entitled to accept the repudiation. She retains this entitlement unless she has meanwhile affirmed her contract.

9.　Affirmation of a contract is not to be inferred from delay alone, and the innocent party is not bound to accept the repudiation within a reasonable or any other time: see *WE Cox Toner (International) Ltd v*

8　This is important: it may have been a tactical error on the part of the respondent not to cross-appeal this finding, but if it is not the subject of the cross-appeal then Mrs Thomas should ensure that she holds onto it – that is, that any remission of the case for a further hearing does not re-open this question.

Crook [1981] ICR 823, 828E-829A. It follows that the tribunal's view that Mrs Thomas could reasonably have made a provisional decision as to how to respond to her employer's rejection of her grievance during the period that the grievance was under consideration was not a relevant factor or one that the tribunal was entitled to take into account. In doing so, the tribunal in effect imposed on Mrs Thomas a duty to act reasonably in response to her employer's fundamental breach of contract, and then imposed a harsh standard when judging whether or not she had acted reasonably.

(ii) Failure to consider what was communicated by conduct

10. The facts of Mrs Thomas's case are superficially similar to the facts of *WE Cox Toner v Crook*, and it is submitted that the tribunal was led by the similarity into the error of failing to give independent consideration to the question of what Mrs Thomas's actions between receipt of the managing director's letter of 12 February and her resignation on 4 March would have communicated to her employer.

11. In *WE Cox Toner v Crook*, the employee was a senior employee who had demanded a retraction of certain allegations against him by way of a letter from his solicitors indicating that he regarded the allegations as a fundamental breach of his contract and would treat himself as constructively dismissed if they were not withdrawn. The Employment Appeal Tribunal considered that the employee's delay of a month, during which he continued to work, after the employer's reply refusing to retract the allegations amounted to an affirmation of the contract. It is clear from the judgment that the EAT considered the critical factor to be the question of what the employee's action would have communicated to the employer:

> 'When ... despite their refusal to withdraw the allegation, he continues to work ... for a month thereafter, viewed from the angle of the employers, *it must have appeared that he had decided not to resign but to continue in the employment.' [emphasis added]*

12. The tribunal proceeded as if bound by this to find that a similar period of delay after the final rejection of her grievance must in Mrs Thomas's case also be read as constituting affirmation. The tribunal's failure to direct itself to the question of what her conduct between 13 or 14 February and 4 March 2004 would have communicated to her employer is a fundamental error in their approach. Mrs Thomas had not, as Mr Crook had, previously threatened through solicitors

to resign if her grievance was not resolved, and had not therefore laid the foundation for the respondent to draw the conclusion that she must have changed her mind from so short a delay as three weeks.

13. In the absence of any finding as to what Mrs Thomas's actions between 13 February and 4 March 2004 would have communicated to her employer, it is submitted that the employment tribunal's decision cannot stand.

ORDER SOUGHT

14. The appellant respectfully asks the Appeal Tribunal to set aside the decision of the tribunal and remit the case to the same tribunal[9] for re-hearing on the correct basis of the question whether by her silence between 13 or 14 February and 3 March 2004 the appellant had affirmed her contract of employment on the correct basis, and if she did not, whether she was unfairly dismissed.

Natalie Cummings
NORTH LONDON LAW CENTRE
24 September 2004

Bundles of authorities

12.8   'Authorities' in this sense means the material used by the parties to persuade the EAT that their statement of the law is correct. The main appeal bundle[10] will be composed of material that is specific to the particular case: the decision in that case, the claim form and response, extracts from the hearing bundle before the employment tribunal, etc. The authorities bundle will normally contain reports of other decided cases of the EAT or higher courts and may also include extracts from the relevant legislation, extracts from textbooks or legal journal articles, etc.

12.9   Paragraph 14 of the EAT Practice Direction 2004[11] gives instructions for the citation of authorities.

12.10   The EAT should be sent three copies of a complete bundle of all authorities relied on. The bundle of authorities should be agreed with

---

9   This tactical decision could have been taken the other way: much will depend on the atmosphere of the original hearing. Here the rest of the tribunal's decision suggests that it had not taken a dislike to Mrs Thomas and had found her evidence credible, and only found against her because it felt bound to do so.

10   See paras 12.1–12.2.

11   See para 11.13 above.

the other party if possible so that all the authorities that either side is relying on are contained in a single bundle. Strictly speaking this is the appellant's job, but if the appellant is unrepresented or represented by a small organisation that does not have easy access to all the necessary materials it is worth trying to charm the respondent's representative into taking on the task. Ideally, the specific passages relied upon in the authorities should be sidelined (that is, a vertical line should be added in the margin beside the passages relied on) so that the EAT can quickly and easily find the relevant parts.

12.11 Cases should be listed first in date order, then any legislation, and finally any other materials. Extensive reference to authority is not encouraged. It will be fairly rare that a case can be argued in the EAT with no reference at all to authority, but if there is only one relevant previous case then the authorities bundle should contain only that case. There are certain cases that are so fundamental and therefore so well known to EAT judges that it will rarely be necessary to take the EAT to them in argument:[12] most of the cases listed at para 1.25 above are in this category.

12.12 Lawyers specialising in employment law are a fairly small sub-group of the legal profession. Because of this, there is always a real chance that the presiding judge at the EAT took part either as judge or as advocate in one or more of the cases on which the parties rely as authorities. It is a good idea to check whether this is so once the hearing list has appeared on the EAT website[13] (this will normally be by the Friday afternoon of the week before the hearing), in order to pick up any available clues as to the judge's likely direction of approach. If the judge today was on the losing side in the case that you rely on, it will be prudent to tread carefully. Assertions that the result in that case was 'obvious' or 'inevitable,' for instance, are unlikely to go down well. Even more tact will be called for if today's judge presided in the case you say was wrongly decided or seek to distinguish.[14] If the other party is in that position, being aware of it in advance may provide opportunities to increase their discomfort.

---

12 That is, a reference in oral argument or in the skeleton argument to the name of the case will be enough, and the EAT will not expect the advocate to provide a copy of the report and read out passages from it.

13 www.employmentappeals.gov.uk.

14 See para 1.22 above and glossary.

P12.2 Index to bundle of authorities

This example is of a substantial authorities bundle that was required for a complex argument, but it should not be regarded as typical. More often only two or three cases will be needed, and no other authorities. The EAT will have a copy of Butterworths Employment Law Handbook, so there is no need to include legislation unless it is not contained in that book.

IN THE EMPLOYMENT APPEAL TRIBUNAL   Case No EAT/1234/04
BETWEEN

THE STATE OF RURITANIA

Appellant

and

MR STEVEN NEWTON

Respondent

INDEX TO JOINT BUNDLE OF AUTHORITIES

CASES

LEGISLATION

OTHER MATERIAL

Preliminary hearings

12.13 If the EAT cannot decide on the papers whether there is enough in the appeal to justify a full hearing, it will list the case for a preliminary hearing. Preliminary hearings take place before a full EAT, and skeleton arguments are required as for full hearings. Employment Lawyers Appeals Advice Scheme (ELAAS) representation[15] may be available for an unrepresented appellant. Preliminary hearings can take anything from a few minutes to an hour or so. The purpose, from the appellant's point of view, is to persuade the EAT that there is a reasonably arguable case.

12.14 As so often, the theory is one thing and the practice is another. Some EAT judges have a tendency to hear the whole appeal at the preliminary hearing, and may dismiss it not because it is not reasonably arguable but because, having heard it fully argued, they do not think it is well-founded. For this reason an appellant whose case is listed for a preliminary hearing should be as well prepared for the preliminary hearing as he or she would be for the full hearing, and ready, in effect, to argue the case in full at this stage if necessary.

12.15 When it comes to authorities for a preliminary hearing, appellants are in something of a quandary. If the preliminary hearing is properly conducted only as an inquiry into whether the case is reasonably arguable, authorities will rarely be necessary, and many judges will be irritated by a full skeleton argument making extensive reference to authority at this stage. On the other hand, an appellant appearing before a different variety of judge may find him or herself faced with a series of pointed questions about the effect of such-and-such a case on the appeal. The best advice is probably not to cite authorities extensively in the skeleton argument for a preliminary hearing, but to go to the hearing equipped with copies of all the relevant authorities (and having read them carefully) in case it turns out that the judge wishes to discuss them.

12.16 Skeleton arguments for preliminary hearings should be lodged at the EAT not less than 10 days before the hearing. The appellant's skeleton argument should be accompanied by a chronology listing the main relevant events in date order.[16]

---

15 See para 11.22 above.
16 See EAT Practice Direction 2004 para 13.4.

The hearing

12.17   At the EAT, like the employment tribunal, the form of address for the members of the tribunal is 'Madam' or 'Sir' as appropriate.[17] Unlike in employment tribunal hearings, parties or advocates stand to address the court. It is conventional to pause at the door and bow[18] in the general direction of the presiding judge if leaving or entering the room while the court is sitting. Everyone in the hearing room stands when the judge and members enter or leave the room: this will be difficult to forget because an usher will say loudly 'Court rise!' at this point.

12.18   Often there will be several cases listed in each court for a 10.30 start: they will not all start at 10.30 of course, but the EAT may not always take them in the order in which they appear on the list, so it is necessary to attend promptly at the time given. An usher (curiously, ushers at the EAT wear a black robe, though no-one else does) will tell the parties when they need to go into court for their case, but this does not mean that the other parties and/or their representatives are not allowed in until called. It is a good idea for parties who are not called on first to sit at the back of the court for the hearing or hearings before theirs (or at least for part of them) to get an idea how this judge runs things. Hearings are normally public, and it is perfectly acceptable to enter or leave quietly while the hearing is going on. An usher will come to the waiting-room to call the parties to the hearing room in time for their hearing.

12.19   In the EAT, there will almost never be witnesses, so the hearing follows a simpler pattern than hearings in the employment tribunals. Almost always the appellant will be expected to make his or her submissions first, followed by the respondent. The appellant will then have the opportunity to reply to any points made by the respondent with which he or she has not already dealt. The EAT will then either adjourn to consider its decision, to be given the same day; or it may reserve its judgment, which means that it will not finalise the decision that day but will take some time over it (typically a few weeks) and hand it down on a date to be announced.

---

17   Barristers appearing at the EAT sometimes get this wrong and address the judge 'my lord' or 'my lady.' This is probably because the same judge was sitting a week or so previously in the High Court, where this is the correct form of address. When they sit in the EAT, however, 'Madam' or 'Sir' is correct.

18   A nod will do; anyone who finds this either embarrassing or objectionable can omit it without adverse consequences.

12.20   Occasionally the EAT will decide not to call on one side or the other to make any submissions at all. If this happens, it should not be taken as a slight or resisted: it is unequivocal good news. If the respondent to the appeal is not called upon, it means that the EAT has listened to the appellant's arguments and is not persuaded by them; the respondent need not add anything to persuade the court to dismiss the appeal. If, contrary to the usual rule, the respondent is asked to speak first, it almost certainly means that the EAT thinks that the appeal is strong and wishes to hear first from the party it considers has the harder task. If it happens this way around, then the decision not to call upon the appellant is bound to be provisional: if the respondent makes more headway than the EAT had expected, and having heard the respondent's arguments the court is inclined after all to dismiss the appeal, the appellant will certainly be called upon before a final decision is made.

Advocacy before the EAT

12.21   Presenting a case before the EAT feels very different from advocacy at the employment tribunal. In many ways it is easier. The issues are clearly defined in advance, each side has read the other's skeleton argument, and witnesses – the biggest wild-card in any hearing – are mercifully absent. Law students will be comfortably reminded of 'mooting.'[19] On the other hand, the legal argument itself is likely to be more focused and more difficult.

12.22   A representative who has submitted a fully reasoned skeleton argument may be at a loss to know what exactly to say on the day of the hearing. The judge and wing members will not want to hear the skeleton read aloud: they will almost certainly have read it themselves before the hearing begins. Much will depend on the style of the presiding judge. Some will say 'Yes, Miss Campbell?' and then wait in silence until you have finished speaking, giving no clue what is going on in their minds. Others will go straight to what they think is your weakest point and ask hard and pointed questions about it. The representative needs to be ready for either approach, or anything in between. It is helpful to have a prepared speech that picks up and develops the points made in the skeleton argument – adding illustrations or analogies, for example, or going into a more detailed analysis of the cases cited – but it is also

---

19 A game of formal legal argument, in a mock appeal court setting, that law students play.

essential to be ready to abandon the script and simply deal with what the judge or wing member indicates is troubling him or her.

12.23   The judge's task is to understand the submissions made by the parties or their advocates, and then to decide whether to accept or reject them. The advocate's task is to make his or her submissions as lucidly and persuasively as possible. Often the result is a lively debate between the presiding judge and an advocate. This is useful insofar as it helps the judge to understand exactly what points the advocate is making in order to be able to adjudicate on them. Sometimes, however, it becomes an attempt by the judge to persuade the advocate to see – and admit – the flaw in his or her case. Judges, after all, have almost always been advocates themselves for many years, and many still like to win arguments.

12.24   This can place the advocate in a difficult position. Occasionally it is prudent to give ground and admit that part of the argument originally put forward is not well-founded, but as a rule the advocate should resist making important concessions even under significant pressure from the judge since any concession made before the EAT will be very difficult to withdraw for the purposes of a further appeal.

12.25   This is easy advice to give, less so to follow. Judges are, as a rule, clever and determined individuals who are used to calling the shots, and they are authority figures in an environment where the people around them are more than averagely respectful of authority. Judges – like everyone else – should be treated with respect in the sense of courtesy, and the additional formality that is conventional in court is not in itself objectionable. At the same time, they should not be allowed to muscle in on the advocate's own decisions about how to run the case in the interests of his or her client. If an extended wrangle is developing[20] after it is clear that the judge has understood the submission and is not persuaded by it, a formula along these lines can be useful: 'You have had my submissions on that question and I have nothing to add them. The next point I wish to make is ...'

12.26   The point to remember – even if the judge has forgotten it – is that the judge's task is to decide the case, not to persuade one side or the other to concede it.

---

20   It is easiest if the judge heads this off. All the judge has to say, on hearing a submission by which she is not persuaded, but which she is content that she has fully understood, is 'I understand' or something to similar effect. This gives the advocate a clear signal to move on to the next point without forcing a concession or loss of face, and can shorten proceedings dramatically.

Judgments

12.27 In most cases the EAT will retire for a time after submissions have been completed to consider their decision, and will then announce it orally, with reasons, on the same day. The judgment is tape-recorded, but a transcript will not be made unless requested by one of the parties or ordered by the EAT.[21] It is usually prudent to request a transcript as it is difficult to take a full note if the judge gives oral judgment at normal speaking speed, and it is at the least unsatisfactory for parties to realise after it is too late that they did not properly understand the reasons for the decision. A transcript will be needed if there is to be any further appeal. A transcript can be requested once the judge has finished giving judgment, or in writing within 14 days of the hearing.

12.28 If the EAT thinks that the case is difficult, or it does not have time to finalise its decision on the same day, it will reserve its judgment. In that case the parties will be given a few days' notice of the date when the judgment will be handed down. Sometimes they will get a draft judgment – which is strictly confidential – to check for minor factual or drafting errors a day or so before it is handed down.

12.29 Whether or not a written judgment is provided, the EAT will always issue an order: this is a short document, normally only one page long, that says very briefly how the appeal is disposed of without giving reasons.

Costs

12.30 If judgment is given on the day, either party may wish to make an application for costs. The relevant rules are at 34A–D of the EAT Rules 1993[22] and at paragraph 19 of the EAT Practice Direction. If an application for costs at the hearing is contemplated, it is usually a good idea to notify the other party of the fact before the hearing. The EAT's power to award costs is similar to that of the employment tribunal, and costs are still very rare. The application should only be made if there are strong grounds for it. A party applying for costs should go to the hearing

---

21 The EAT will normally only do this if it considers that the judgment contains guidance that could be important for other cases, or if the appeal is allowed and the case is remitted to an employment tribunal. In the latter case, the employment tribunal will need a transcript of the judgment so that it understands what it is required to decide.

22 SI No 2854 as amended.

with several copies of a schedule showing what costs have been incurred and how.

12.31   Parties who have paid for legal representation can claim the costs they have incurred. Parties acting for themselves can claim payment for the time they have reasonably spent preparing the case in one of two ways. The detailed provisions are at EAT Rules para 34D, but broadly parties can claim either a fixed rate of £25 per hour, or for the amount that they can prove they have lost 'for the time reasonably spent on doing the work.' In other words, parties can claim for the loss of money they would have earned[23] in the time they have reasonably spent preparing the case, or if they cannot prove any such loss, then they can claim £25 per hour. It would seem to be open to a party representing him or herself who earns less than £25 per hour to choose not to prove his or her actual loss, but to claim the £25 hourly rate instead.

---

23 On the face of it there is no limit on this.

P12.3 Letter to the respondent warning of an intention to apply for costs

This is a letter written on behalf of the appellant in example 1 at para 11.42 above. She says that her appeal is so strong that the respondent should concede it.

Mr G Marrow
Carrot & Marrow Solicitors
21 Lower St
Islington
London N12 3AB

5 November 2004

Dear Mr Marrow

Fiona Cameron v The Old Fashioned Tailor Ltd EAT/1234/04/PC

Your client's evidence was clear, as recorded in the employment tribunal's decision in this case, that the company believed that it was entitled to impose different standards of workplace behaviour on men and women, and that it did so. Specifically, the tribunal found (at paragraph 14) that Ms Cameron was dismissed for using language that the company would have and did tolerate in male employees.

Ms Cameron's appeal is bound to succeed, as your client has admitted discriminating against her on grounds of her sex. Please consider urgently with your client whether they should agree that the appeal should be allowed and the case be remitted to a different tribunal to consider remedy.

If the appeal is not conceded, I have instructions to make an application for costs at the hearing.

Yours sincerely

Natalie Cummings

Withdrawing or settling an appeal

12.32   Appeal cases are settled more rarely than first instance cases, but it can be fruitful to negotiate at this stage. It is slightly more complicated withdrawing or settling a case that has been appealed to the EAT than a case that is pending before an employment tribunal: the permission of the EAT is required to withdraw an appeal, and it is not sufficient simply to write to the EAT indicating the wish to withdraw.[24]

12.33   If the appellant wishes to withdraw, then, a letter must be written to the EAT signed by both parties asking for permission to withdraw the appeal and enclosing a draft order also signed by both parties. It is difficult to imagine circumstances in which this application would be refused.

P12.4 Letter to the EAT seeking permission to withdraw an appeal

The Registrar
Employment Appeal Tribunal
Audit House
58 Victoria Embankment
London EC4Y 0DS

FAX ONLY 020 7273 1045

5 November 2004

Dear Madam

Harriet Sharpe v Fencemarket plc EAT/1234/04/PC

The parties having agreed terms of settlement in this case, both parties request that the appeal should be dismissed on withdrawal.

We attach a draft order to that effect.

Yours faithfully

Natalie Cummings   George Marrow
for the claimant/appellant   for the respondent

---

24 See EAT Practice Direction para 15. It is not self-evident why this should be so.

P12.5 Draft order of the EAT dismissing an appeal by consent

EMPLOYMENT APPEAL TRIBUNAL

BEFORE   Appeal No EAT/1234/04/PC

[   ]^{25}

IN THE MATTER of an Appeal under section 21(1) of the Employment Tribunals Act 1996 from the decision of an Employment Tribunal sitting at Reading and entered in the Register on the 30th day of July 2004

BETWEEN

HARRIET SHARPE
Appellant

and

FENCEMARKET PLC
Respondent

DRAFT ORDER

UPON THE APPLICATION of the appellant and the respondent by letter dated 5 November 2004

AND BY CONSENT

AND UPON consideration of the aforesaid application

IT IS HEREBY ORDERED that leave be granted for the appeal to be withdrawn and the said appeal is thereby dismissed.

DATED _____

To: North London Law Centre for the appellant
Carrot & Marrow Solicitors for the respondent
The Secretary, Central Office of Employment Tribunals, England and Wales
(Case No 123456/04)^{26}

---

25 This should be left blank. The order will almost certainly be made by a Registrar, but it could go to a judge.

26 This case number should be the original employment tribunal case number, not the EAT case number.

Getting an appeal allowed by consent

12.34 This is less straightforward, because even if the parties are unanimous that the employment tribunal's decision is wrong,[27] that is no guarantee that the EAT will agree. Of course the parties themselves cannot set aside the employment tribunal's order or remit the case to the tribunal for a rehearing: only the EAT can do that.

12.35 However, if the parties are agreed as to the order the tribunal should make, they should write a letter to the EAT attaching a draft order and either explaining in the body of the letter or in a skeleton argument signed by both sides why the appeal should be allowed on the terms suggested. The EAT may list the case for a hearing at which one or both parties can seek to persuade them to dispose of the case as requested, but if the employment tribunal's error of law is clear, a persuasive skeleton argument submitted with the letter and draft order may be sufficient to head off a hearing.

27 This is unusual, but it can happen.

P12.6 Letter to the EAT requesting that an appeal be allowed by consent

Natalie Cummings' letter[28] to the respondent threatening a costs application if the appeal is not conceded has had the desired effect, and the parties are now agreed that sex discrimination did occur and the only live question is how much compensation Ms Cameron should receive.

The Registrar
Employment Appeal Tribunal
Audit House
58 Victoria Embankment
London EC4Y 0DS

FAX ONLY 020 7273 1045

5 November 2004

Dear Madam

Fiona Cameron v The Old Fashioned Tailor Ltd EAT/1234/04/PC

The parties are agreed that the tribunal erred in failing to find, in light of the respondent's own clear evidence that it dismissed Ms Cameron for conduct that it would have tolerated in a male employee (as to which see in particular paragraph 14 of the tribunal's decision) that the respondent discriminated against Ms Cameron by dismissing her.

Both parties request that the appeal should be allowed and the case remitted to a fresh tribunal for a hearing as to remedy. We attach a draft order to that effect.

Yours faithfully

Natalie Cummings   George Marrow
for the claimant/appellant   for the respondent

---

28 At P12.3 above.

P12.7 Draft order of the EAT dismissing an appeal by consent

EMPLOYMENT APPEAL TRIBUNAL

BEFORE   Appeal No EAT/1234/04/PC

[   ]²⁹

IN THE MATTER of an Appeal under section 21(1) of the Employment Tribunals Act 1996 from the decision of an Employment Tribunal sitting at Reading and entered in the Register on the 30th day of July 2004

BETWEEN

FIONA CAMERON

Appellant

and

THE OLD FASHIONED TAILOR LTD

Respondent

DRAFT ORDER

UPON THE APPLICATION of the Appellant and the Respondent by letter dated 5 November 2004

AND BY CONSENT

AND UPON consideration of the aforesaid application

IT IS HEREBY ORDERED that the appeal is allowed and the case is remitted to a fresh tribunal for consideration of remedy only.

DATED _____

To: North London Law Centre for the appellant
Carrot & Marrow Solicitors for the respondent
The Secretary, Central Office of Employment Tribunals, England and Wales
(Case no. 123456/04)³⁰

---

29 This should be left blank as a decision to allow the appeal will have to be made by a judge, and it is impossible to predict which judge it will be.
30 This case number should be the original employment tribunal case number, not the EAT case number.

Further appeals

12.36 Appeal from the EAT is to the Court of Appeal (or in Scotland to the Court of Session). Permission must be sought from the EAT when the decision is handed down, or from the Court of Appeal within 14 days of that date. Note that the EAT Practice Direction is misleading on this point. The PD says, at paragraph 21.1, that an application to the Court of Appeal for permission must be made 'within 14 days of the sealed order.' However, the Civil Procedure Rules (Part 52.4) require an application to be made within 14 days after 'the date of the decision' unless the lower court (in this context, the EAT) directs otherwise. The order may be sealed a day or so after the decision is made, but time runs from the date when the decision was made – that is, the day of the hearing, or where judgment is reserved, the day judgment is handed down. It could be argued that 'such period as may be directed by the lower court' in CPR 52.4 gives the EAT power to give a direction by way of a PD that overrides the period set out in CPR 52.4 in relation to all appeals from the EAT, but there is no certainty that that argument would be accepted. If it is important for the appellant to have an extra day or two in which to apply to the Court of Appeal for permission (and it often will be), the safer course is to ask the judge at the hearing for a specific direction that time run from the date on which the order was sealed, or to make the same request in writing to the Registrar as soon as the order is received. It will probably be necessary to point to the apparent conflict between the CPR and the PD, and to ask for a specific direction for the avoidance of any doubt.

12.37 Making an application to the Court of Appeal for permission to appeal is a cumbersome and time-consuming process[31] and the time in which it must be done is short. Parties should therefore give some thought, before the hearing at the EAT, to the question whether or not they will want to appeal further if unsuccessful. Funding is likely to be difficult (see below), but parties should not delay an application for permission until the funding problem has been solved: this is unlikely to be an acceptable excuse for a late application.

---

31 Guidance on this is beyond the scope of this book: see CPR 52 and the accompanying Practice Direction.

Funding an appeal to the Court of Appeal

12.38   Appeals to the Court of Appeal raise difficult – and often insuperable – practical problems for parties without much money. If there has been public funding for the first appeal, it may be worth an application for public funding for a further appeal, but this will normally be much more difficult. Only a solicitor or law centre that has a contract with the Legal Services Commission can help.

12.39   If public funding is not available, then if the would-be appellant either has an offer of free representation, or is considering representing him or herself at the Court of Appeal, the main obstacle will be the risk of having to pay the other side's costs if the appeal fails. Costs orders in the employment tribunal and the EAT are rare, and are generally only made against a party who has in some way behaved badly. The situation is very different in the Court of Appeal, where the normal rule – subject to fairly rare exceptions – is that costs are ordered against the losing party. Costs for even a short hearing in the Court of Appeal can run into many thousands of pounds, and the risk of losing the case and having to pay this will very often be prohibitive. If the employer loses the case at the EAT but then decides to appeal to the Court of Appeal, this fear can even force the 'successful' claimant not to oppose an appeal.

12.40   There are various approaches to this problem that can be tried, and sometimes one of them will work. None has much chance unless the case is in some sense a test case: that is, a case that is likely to determine the rights of a significant number of other people as well as the claimant him or herself.

12.41   The simplest of the available techniques is to persuade the other party to promise not to make an application for costs. This sounds optimistic, but if it is the employer who wishes to appeal further because the decision at the EAT sets what the employer regards as a dangerous precedent, it can work: in this event, the employer wants the case properly argued on both sides so that the precedent set by the Court of Appeal is final and authoritative. If the other party will not agree this voluntarily, then if there are reasons why it is clear that a costs order against the employee would be unfair whatever the outcome, the EAT or the Court of Appeal may be persuaded to grant permission only on condition that there will be no costs against the employee in any event. If, for example, the employer's appeal only arises because the employer behaved badly and got its response struck out at first instance, it might be said that – even if there is reason to ask whether the striking out order was excessive – there would be no question of an appeal at all if the employer had conducted its case properly. Even if it is the claimant's appeal, if the employer is treating the proceedings as a test case and has already spent a lot of money on them, it may be willing to co-operate in this way in order to have the point resolved finally by the Court of Appeal. Otherwise, the employer may have to fight the whole battle again against a different claimant.

12.42   If it is not possible to head off any threat of a costs application from the outset, the other approach is to look for backing from a body that will underwrite the risk of a costs order and/or fund the appeal in its entirety. If the case is one of discrimination, the first port of call should be one of the statutory Commissions – the Equal Opportunities Commission (EOC), the Disability Rights Commission (DRC) or the Commission for Racial Equality (CRE). However these bodies will only support a case that they think has a wide public significance. For non-discrimination cases, the claimant's trade union might be approached, but a trade union that has not supported a case at first instance will rarely be willing to back an appeal to the Court of Appeal: persuading it to do so will probably depend on getting it to agree – tacitly if not explicitly – that its previous decision not to back the case was a mistake. This will call for tact.

12.43   If no single body is willing to underwrite the risk, then it may conceivably be possible to put together a consortium of bodies each of which will agree to pay a proportion of the costs if the appeal is unsuccessful: trade unions, pressure groups, charities, advice umbrella organisations. If the case is important enough, this may be worth a try, but it will take luck, good contacts, strong powers of persuasion and a great deal of telephone time.

APPENDICES

Yearwood v Royal Mail

YEARWOOD

Appellant

V

ROYAL MAIL AND OTHERS

Respondents

EAT/843/97
Morison P, Messrs Jackson and Warman
11 July 1997

MR JUSTICE MORISON (PRESIDENT):

This is an interlocutory appeal, that is, it is an appeal against a refusal of an Industrial Tribunal Chairman to adjourn a case which is due to take place on 14 July 1997. It is a case in which there are allegations of race discrimination involving Royal Mail and three named individuals.

The circumstances in which the application for an adjournment came to be made are that the Applicant in this case, Mr Yearwood, presented his IT1 dated 3 February 1997, naming in paragraph 3, a Jenny Sabastion of the Wellingborough District Racial Equality Council as a representative. That organisation is a charity and is not in receipt of substantial funds. They provide legal assistance in race discrimination cases in their area. They are engaged on behalf of another applicant in a case in the Leicester Industrial Tribunal. The case has gone part-heard and was adjourned and re-listed for hearing on 14 July.

On 6 June, after the part-heard case had been listed for hearing, the organisation received formal notification from the Bedford Industrial Tribunal that Mr Yearwood's case was listed for hearing on 14 July. Promptly they wrote to the Bedford Industrial Tribunal requesting a postponement. The request was refused. They also wrote to the Leicester Industrial Tribunal on 12 June asking for the part-heard case to be re-listed. Not surprisingly, the Leicester Tribunal told the organisation that it would be better if they renewed their application to Bedford, because 'priority is given to part-heard claims'. Accordingly, further applications were made to the Bedford Industrial

Tribunal who have refused them subject to any decision, of course, that we make in this matter.

These questions, that is, whether cases should be adjourned or not in the interests of justice, are very difficult to determine and we have considerable sympathy with the attitude which has been taken by the distinguished Chairman in this case.

There are many good reasons for holding parties to a commitment which has been made. When the date was originally fixed for this case I think it was at a time when the organisation thought that they would be available.

Furthermore, the Respondents to the complaint have an interest in having their case heard and determined, particularly where individuals have been named as Respondent, as has happened in this case. Justice delayed is, as we know, justice denied, and we can understand the learned Chairman taking the attitude he did. But that said, this seems to us to be a listing crisis of the sort which is capable of causing injustice.

Had the organisation to which I have referred been a professional firm of Solicitors, there could be no doubt that it would have been the right decision to have refused an adjournment and to require Mr Yearwood to obtain alternative legal services, or the services of a different partner within the same firm. But organisations such as the one in question do, in our experience, provide useful assistance to the community which they serve, and we are mindful of the difficulties which listing problems can genuinely cause them. They have in our judgment, acted properly and promptly in this matter.

There is no particular prejudice which the Respondents are able to identify if the appeal were to be allowed, although they do point out that the three individuals do not work in the same place and have been organised to attend on 14 July, but that said, there is no further particular injustice which they can legitimately point to, if we were to accede to the appeal.

Not without some difficulty, we have arrived at the conclusions that the interests of justice require that this case should be adjourned. If it is not, Mr Yearwood would have to appear on 14 July without representation to ask for an adjournment; we imagine that, in those circumstances, the Tribunal would be likely to accede to his request. If that were to happen, then the inconvenience to the witnesses would be much greater than if we were to accede to the appeal. If, on the other hand, he turned up unrepresented on 14 July, and an application for adjournment was refused, we can well understand how he might feel at a disadvantage in proceeding with complaints of unlawful discrimination, which are serious complaints to make and to have tried. It seems to us, in general, that it is important that this type of case in particular should be heard after the parties have had a fair opportunity to prepare for the hearing before the Industrial Tribunal.

Therefore, with difficulty, we have on balance been prepared to accede to this appeal. Although for technical reasons we are forced to say that the refusal of the adjournment was, in our judgment, so unreasonable as to be worthy of our interfering with it, we would like to make it quite clear that we are not unappreciative of the reasons which must have lain behind the attitude which has been taken by the Chairman in this case.

For these reasons we feel obliged to allow this appeal and to order that the case be adjourned from 14 July.

APPENDIX B

Sex Discrimination Act 1975 s74 questionnaire

dti
Department of Trade and Industry

Sex Discrimination Act 1975: The Questions Procedure

This booklet is in four parts:

Part 1:   Introduction *(SD74)*.

Part 2:   Questionnaire of the person aggrieved: The Complainant *(SD74(1)(a))*.

Part 3:   Reply: The Respondent *(SD74(1)(b))*.

Appendix: Notes on the scope of the Sex Discrimination Act 1975.

Part 1: Introduction

General

- The purpose of this introduction is to explain the questions procedure under Section 74 of the Sex Discrimination Act 1975 *(the prescribed forms, time limits for serving questions and manner of service of questions and replies under section 74 are specified in the Sex Discrimination (Questions and Replies) Order 1975 No. 2048)*.

- The procedure is intended to help a person *(referred to in this booklet as the complainant)* who thinks he/she has been discriminated against by another *(the respondent)* to obtain information from that person about the treatment in question in order to:
  - decide whether or not to bring legal proceedings; and
  - if proceedings are brought, to present his/her complaint in the most effective way.

- We have devised a questionnaire which the complainant can send to the respondent. There is also a matching reply form for use by the respondent – both are included in this booklet. The questionnaire and reply form are designed to assist both the complainant and respondent to identify information which is relevant to the complaint. It is not obligatory for the questionnaire and reply form to be used: the exchange of questions and replies may be conducted, for example, by letter.

- The complainant and respondent should read this booklet thoroughly before completion and retain a copy of the information supplied.

- Guidance for the complainant on the preparation of the questionnaire is set out in Part 2.

- Guidance for the respondent on the use of the reply form is set out in Part 3.

- The Appendix explains the main provisions of the Sex Discrimination Act 1975. If you require further information about this Act or your rights and responsibilities, you can obtain it from the Equal Opportunities Commission *(EOC)* or from the detailed Guide to the Sex Discrimination Act 1975.

- If you require help or advice about completing or responding to this booklet, please contact the EOC.

- You can also obtain copies of this booklet *("Form SD74")*, as well as copies of the Guide to the Sex Discrimination Act 1975, free of charge from the Women and Equality Unit. See reverse of booklet for details.

Part I: Introduction *(continued)*

How the questions procedure can benefit both parties

The procedure can benefit both the complainant and the respondent in the following ways:

- If the respondent's answers satisfy the complainant and the treatment was not unlawful discrimination, there will be no need for legal proceedings;
- If the respondent's answers do not satisfy the complainant, they should help to identify what is agreed and what is in dispute between the parties. For example, the answers, should reveal whether the parties disagree on the facts of the case, or, if they agree on the facts whether they disagree on how the Act applies. In some cases, this may lead to a settlement of the grievance, making legal proceedings against unnecessary.
- If the complainant institutes proceedings against the respondent, the proceedings should be that much simpler because the matters in dispute will have been identified in advance.

What happens if the respondent does not reply or replies evasively

The respondent cannot be compelled to reply to the complainant's questions. However, if the respondent deliberately, and without reasonable excuse, does not reply within a reasonable period, or replies in an evasive or ambiguous way, the respondent's position may be adversely affected should the complainant bring proceedings against him/her. The respondent's attention is drawn to these possible consequences in the note at the end of the questionnaire.

Period within which the questionnaire must be served on the respondent

There are different time limits within which a questionnaire must be served in order to be admissible under the questions procedure in any ensuing legal proceedings. Which time limit applies depends on whether the complaint would be under the employment, training and related provisions of the Act *(in which case the proceedings would be before an employment tribunal)* or whether it would be under the education, goods, facilities and services or premises provisions *(in which case proceedings would be before a county court or, in Scotland, sheriff court).*

Employment tribunal proceedings

In order to be admissible under the questions procedure in any ensuing employment tribunal proceedings, the complainant's questionnaire must be served on the respondent either:

- before a complaint about the treatment concerned is made to an employment tribunal, but not more than 3 months after the treatment in question; or
- if a complaint has already been made to a tribunal, within 21 days beginning when the complaint was received by the tribunal.

However, where the complainant has made a complaint to the tribunal and the period of 21 days has expired, a questionnaire may still be served provided the leave of the tribunal is obtained. This may be done by sending a written application to the Secretary of the Tribunal, stating the names of the complainant and the respondent and setting out the grounds of the application. However, every effort should be made to serve the questionnaire within the period of 21 days as the leave of the tribunal to serve the questionnaire after expiry of the period will not necessarily be obtained.

Use of the questions and replies in employment tribunal proceedings

If you decide to make *(or have already made)* a complaint to an employment tribunal about the treatment concerned and if you intend to use your questions and the reply *(if any)* as evidence in the proceedings, you are advised to send copies of your questions and any reply to the Secretary of the Tribunals before the date of the hearing. This should be done as soon as the documents are available. If they are available at the time you submit your complaint to a tribunal, send the copies with your complaint to the Secretary of the Tribunal.

County or sheriff court proceedings

In order to be admissible under the questions procedure in any ensuing county or sheriff court proceedings, the complainant's questionnaire must be served on the respondent before proceedings in respect of the treatment concerned is brought, but not more than 6 months after the treatment[1]. However, where proceedings have been brought, a questionnaire may still be served provided the leave of the court has been obtained. In the case of county court proceedings, this may be done by obtaining form Ex23 from the county court office, completing it and sending it to the Registrar and the respondent, or, by applying to the Registrar at the pre-trial review. In the cases of sheriff court proceedings, this may be done by making an application to a sheriff.

---

[1] *Where the respondent is a body in charge of a public sector educational establishment, the 6 month period begins when the complaint has been referred to the appropriate Education Minister and 2 months have elapsed or, if this is earlier, the Minister has informed the complainant that he/she requires no more time to consider the matter.*

Part 2

Questionnaire of person aggrieved: The Complainant

Note:

- Before filling in this questionnaire, we advise you to prepare what you want to say on a separate piece of paper.
- If you have insufficient room on the questionnaire for what you want to say, continue on an additional piece of paper, which should be sent with the questionnaire to the respondent.

Enter the name of the person to be questioned (the respondent)

To

Enter the respondent's address

of

Enter your name (you are the complainant)

1. I

Enter your address

of

Please give as much relevant information as you can about the treatment you think may have been unlawful discrimination. You should mention the circumstances leading up to that treatment and, if possible, give the date, place and approximate time it happened. You should bear in mind that in question 4 of this questionnaire you will be asking the respondent whether he/she agrees with what you say here.

2. consider that you may have discriminated against me contrary to the Sex Discrimination Act 1975.

In 3 you are telling the respondent that you think the treatment you have described in 2 may have been unlawful discrimination by them against you. It will help to identify whether there are any legal issues between you and the respondent if you explain why you think the treatment may have been unlawful discrimination.

- *You do not have to complete 3. If you do not wish or are unable to do so, you should delete the word 'because'. If you wish to complete 3, but feel you need more information about the Sex Discrimination Act before doing so, see the appendix attached.*

- *If you do decide to complete 3, you may find it useful to indicate what kind of discrimination you think the treatment may have been ie. whether it was:*
  - *direct sex discrimination;*
  - *indirect sex discrimination;*
  - *direct discrimination against a married person;*
  - *indirect discrimination against a married person; or*
  - *victimisation;*
  and which provision of the Act you think may make unlawful the kind of discrimination you think you may have suffered.

3. I consider that this treatment may have been unlawful because:

3

This is the first of your questions to the respondent. You are advised not to alter it.

4. Do you agree that the statement in 2 is an accurate description of what happened? If not, in what respect do you disagree or what is your version of what happened?

This is the second of your questions to the respondent. You are advised not to alter it.

The questions at 5 are especially important if you think you may have suffered direct sex discrimination, or direct discrimination against a married person, because they ask the respondent whether your sex or marital status had anything to do with your treatment. They do not ask specific questions relating to indirect sex discrimination, indirect discrimination against a married person or victimisation. Question 6 provides you with the opportunity to ask any other question you think may be of importance. For example, if you think you have been discriminated against by having been refused a job, you may want to know what the qualifications were of the person who did get the job and why that person got the job. If you think you have suffered indirect sex discrimination (or indirect discrimination against a married person) you may find it helpful to include the following questions:
· *'Was the reason for my treatment the fact that I could not comply with a condition or requirement which is applied equally to men and women (married and unmarried persons)?'*
If so,
· *What was the condition or requirement?*
· *Why was it applied?*
If you think you have been victimised you may find it helpful to include the following questions:
· *'Was the reason for my treatment the fact that I had done or intended to do, or that you suspected I had done or intended to do, any of the following:*
  · *brought proceedings under the Sex Discrimination Act 1975 or the Equal Pay Act 1970;*
  · *gave evidence or information in connection with proceedings under either Act;*
  · *did something else under or by reference to either Act; or*
  · *made an allegation that someone acted unlawfully under either Act?'*

5. Do you accept that your treatment of me was unlawful discrimination by you against me?
   If not:
   a) why not?
   b) for what reason did I receive the treatment accorded to me?
   c) how far did my sex or marital status affect your treatment of me?

   Other questions *(if appropriate)*:

6.

7. My address for any reply you may wish to give to the questions I have raised is:

   on page 3, at question 1 ☐ *below* ☐ *(please tick appropriate box)*

The questionnaire must be signed and dated. If it is to be signed on behalf of (rather than by) the complainant the person signing should:
· *describe himself/herself e.g. 'solicitor acting for (name of complainant)'; and*
· *give business address (or home address, if appropriate).*

Signed

Date

Address *(if appropriate)*

How to serve the papers
· We strongly advise that you retain and keep in a safe place, a copy of the completed questionnaire.
· Send the person to be questioned the **whole** of this document either to their usual last known residence or place of business or if you know they are acting through a solicitor, to that address. If your questions *(ie the introduction, the questionnaire as completed by you and the reply form)* are directed at a limited company or other corporate body or a trade union or employer's association, you should send the papers to the registered or principal office. You should be able to find out where this is by enquiring at your public library. However, if you are unable to do so you will have to send the papers to the place where you think it is most likely they will reach the secretary or clerk. It is your responsibility to see that they receive them.
· You can deliver the papers in person or send them by post.
· If you send them by post, we advise you to use the recorded delivery service *(this will provide you with evidence of delivery)*.
By virtue of section 74 of the Act, this questionnaire and any reply are (subject to the provisions of the section) admissible in proceedings under the Act and a court or tribunal may draw any such inference as is just and equitable from a failure without reasonable excuse to reply within a reasonable period, or from an evasive or equivocal reply, including an inference that the person questioned has discriminated unlawfully.

Index